"To find our way to world peace and a truly creative society, we have to deal with our negative past, especially our colonialism. Kira Celeste offers an all-important depth psychological perspective on it, with many precious insights. I found her words inspiring, deepening my conscience about the terrible history that underlies my comfortable world."

Thomas Moore, *Author of New York Times #1 Best Seller Care of the Soul and Soul Therapy*

"*The Colonial Shadow: A Jungian Investigation of Settler Psychology*, offers the reader a deeply explored perspective and heart opening narrative on Canadian white settler racialized culture and the intergenerational trauma it has inflicted on Indigenous people. The brilliance of this book by Dr. Kira Celeste lies mainly in its powerful determination to keep the lens of her words moving in a revealing fashion that continuously engages the reader with knowledge of the psychology of white settler racism. The author successfully investigates mythology and alchemy using both, especially the latter, to take us on a journey of better understanding unconscious psychological states of attention. This investigation by Dr. Celeste offers us not only views of the alchemical poison of racism but also the potential remedy. There is no other book, from a Jungian depth psychological perspective, that so clearly articulates the historical psychological origins and traumas of colonization where the author contemplates her own ethnic lineage. In addition, the author recognizes the need to give voice responsibly, owning through the claiming of this voice, and the use of a culturally white alchemical lens, that for settlers, moving towards integrity and accountability is not only possible, but a responsibility. The Colonial Shadow is a brilliant book that brings us to the edge of the racialized abyss, inviting us to look down and see what is below. Dr. Celeste's powerful and meditative narrative can also give us the opportunity to gaze upwards to the stars and find the light there that is held by the darkness. This is a book of hope and courage, opening us to seeing new ways of healing centuries-long suffering of unconsciousness racism."

Fanny Brewster, PhD, MFA, LP, *Author of The Racial Complex: A Jungian Perspective on Culture and Race*

"A thought-provoking analysis of how the myths and stories of 'new lands' and 'white superiority' that explorers and white settlers carried from Europe forged a deeply ingrained colonial consciousness that perpetuates oppression and injustice today. Celeste encourages readers to dig more deeply into the roots of their own colonial consciousness in ways that are potentially healing, decolonizing, and transformative."

Paulette Regan, *Author of Unsettling the Settler Within: Indian Residential Schools, Truth Telling, and Reconciliation in Canada*

"Kira Celeste's study of European colonial consciousness and alchemy brings to light the hidden mythos that has been at work for hundreds of years in the settlers of North America. Through a series of compelling insights, she shows how alchemy also provides a way forward as a model for healing the generations deep settler colonial consciousness so desperately needed in our world today. In so doing, Celeste underscores the valuable contribution that depth psychological perspectives bring to issues of colonialism and race. What she offers is a way for people of colonial European descent to reflect and engage with collective shadow material through mythopoetic material so to engender healing and ultimately greater understanding of our shared human condition."

Dr. Safron Rossi, *Author of The Kore Goddess: A Mythology & Psychology*

"In this very timely and valuable book, "Colonial Shadow," Dr. Celeste uses concepts drawn from the works of C.G. Jung to explore how reconciliation and reparation can occur. She believes that settlers must face and be accountable for their own personal and cultural shadow. Celeste argues for the importance of settlers engaging in this work with humility, a willingness to sit with discomfort, and with an openness to letting ideas about themselves they have held dear, fall away. "Colonial Shadow" poignantly addresses the needs of our times."

John Allan, PhD, *Professor Emeritus, Counselling Psychology, University of B.C., Vancouver, Canada*

The Colonial Shadow

The Colonial Shadow examines the colonial psychology that has shaped what is now known as Canada. This psychology has perpetrated devastating harm over the last half a millennium and continues to oppress Indigenous people and degrade the environment. This book is inspired by the tenet of depth psychology that stories and myths from one's own ancestry can bring about transformation and deep changes in perspective. As such, it investigates how an alchemical way of imagining into white settler-colonial consciousness might contribute to its accountability and psychological healing today.

The Colonial Shadow will be an invaluable resource for professionals, academics, and students of Jungian and post-Jungian ideas, settler-colonial and First Nations studies, sociology, anthropology, and cultural studies as well as for anyone interested in addressing the colonial complex.

Kira Celeste, PhD is passionate about supporting individuals in their journeys towards integrity with self and others. As a white settler, she gratefully acknowledges that the land on which she lives and works as a depth psychologist and writer is the Unceded Traditional Territories of the K'ómoks and Qualicum First Nations. Her Doctorate is in Depth Psychology from Pacifica Graduate Institute. Fifty percent of the author's proceeds from this book will be contributed to First Nations organizations.

The Colonial Shadow

A Jungian Investigation of Settler Psychology

Kira Celeste

LONDON AND NEW YORK

Designed Cover image: Getty

First published 2023
by Routledge
4 Park Square, Milton Park, Abingdon, Oxon OX14 4RN

and by Routledge
605 Third Avenue, New York, NY 10158

Routledge is an imprint of the Taylor & Francis Group, an informa business

© 2023 Kira Celeste

The right of Kira Celeste to be identified as author of this work has been asserted in accordance with sections 77 and 78 of the Copyright, Designs and Patents Act 1988.

All rights reserved. No part of this book may be reprinted or reproduced or utilised in any form or by any electronic, mechanical, or other means, now known or hereafter invented, including photocopying and recording, or in any information storage or retrieval system, without permission in writing from the publishers.

Trademark notice: Product or corporate names may be trademarks or registered trademarks, and are used only for identification and explanation without intent to infringe.

British Library Cataloguing-in-Publication Data
A catalogue record for this book is available from the British Library

ISBN: 978-1-032-28376-0 (hbk)
ISBN: 978-1-032-28374-6 (pbk)
ISBN: 978-1-003-29654-6 (ebk)

DOI: 10.4324/9781003296546

Typeset in Times New Roman
by MPS Limited, Dehradun

With deep gratitude to Esk'etemc for welcoming this séme7 into your community. It has been the greatest honour working for you and with your children. The work in this book was inspired by your daily strength, wisdom, and laughter. With all my heart, Kukstsétsemc. Thank you to my family and my beloved partner for your support in getting me here, the first woman in our lines to get her doctorate. May the next generations be equally as able to pursue their passions, and may they walk more softly on this earth than we.

If you have come here to help me, you are wasting your time. But if you have come here because your liberation is bound up with mine, then let us work together. —Lila Watson

This work is dedicated to all the Esk'etemc, Secwépemc, Tsilhqot'in, Innu, Dene, and Kwakwa̲ka̲'wakw children and young women I have had the honour of working with, and for, over the years. May you walk on this land in any role you are called to, with all the freedom, love, connection, and empowerment that is your birthright here, which my people have tried so desperately to interrupt. This work is for you, and it will not be the last. Our liberation is bound, and it is my greatest privilege working together toward it. Kukstsétsemc, sechanalyagh, tshinashkumitin, mahsi-cho, gilakas'la, thank you.

Over the past four decades, the People of the White Earth (Esk'etemc) have been working on healing from past trauma. The work continues today on intergenerational trauma, mental wellness, and the impacts of Indian Residential Schools (IRS) in BC. Today, Esk'etemc continues to improve the understanding of the impacts of 'IRS' loss of ideals, culture, spirituality, and identity that have long been on the minds of leadership. Esk'et continues to be a leader in finding and seeking ways to recover, for the past seven generations, and the next seven generations.

While we focus as a community on healing from the impacts of colonization, it is important that white settlers also focus on their own processes of healing and accountability and on understanding their personal responsibility for the historic and ongoing harms of colonization. A meaningful transformation of white settlers and white settler society is necessary for true accountability and repair. Kira Celeste's book, "The Colonial Shadow," will hopefully be an important contribution to this imperative work.

Fred Robbins, *Kukpi7 (Chief) of Esk'etemc First Nation*

Contents

Acknowledgement   xiv

1 Introduction   1

  But Why Alchemy? 6
  Alchemy and Race 10
  Terms 11
  Statement of Positionality 11

2 Foundational Literature   15

  Colonialism and the Field of Psychology 15
  A Soul Illness 16
  Jung and Racism 18
  The Violence of Cultural Stealing and Appropriation 18
  Decolonisation 19
  Racism and Colonialism in Canada 20
  Settlers' Roles in Decolonisation/Unsettling Processes 20
  Issues with Reconciliation 21
  Decolonisation as a Settler Move to Innocence 22
  History of the Field 24
  Critical Race Theory 25

3 The Colonial Complex   27

  What Is a Cultural Complex? 27
  Colonial Complex 28
  Christianity and Colonialism 29
     Colonial Aversion to Dark and Veneration of the Light 31
     Air: Ascension and Transcendence 34

Water: Disconnection from Body/Sexuality 35
Earth: Disconnection from Land 37
Fire: Disconnection from Passion and Soul 39
Summary of the Colonial Complex 42

4 Historical Manifestations of the Colonial Complex in So-Called Canada 44

Timeline 46
Conclusion Without Closure 58

5 Alchemy and the Transformation of the Settler-Colonial Psyche 61

What Is Alchemy? 62
Alchemy and Christianity 64
The Prima Materia *of the White Settler Psyche 65*
Alchemy as Metaphor 66
The Alchemy of Settler Colonisation and Decolonisation 67
  Séme7 70
Concurrent Events 76

Introduction to Chapters 6–9 79

Helms's Stages of White Racial Identity Development 80

6 Air 81

Helms's First Stage of White Racial Identity Development: Contact 81
Introduction to Sublimatio *81*
  Air 82
  Cook's Journal 83
Sublimatio's Relationship to the Psyche: Positive and Negative Potentials 84
How the Colonial Complex Enacted the Negative Potential of Sublimatio *85*
  Transcendence 87
  Colour blindness and White Silence 89
  Colonial Suffocation 90
  Tuberculosis 91

*How the Colonial Complex Can Now Enact the
  Positive Potential of* Sublimatio *92*
Sublimatio/*Air Concrete Actions and Reflection Questions 94*

7 Water   97

*Helms's Second Stage of White Racial Identity Development:
  Disintegration 97*
Introduction to Solutio *98*
  Water 98
  Cook's Journals 99
Solutio's *Relationship to Psyche: Positive and Negative
  Potentials 100*
How the Colonial Complex Enacted the Negative Potentials of
  Solutio *102*
  White Body Trauma 103
  *Colonial Ideas about Cleanliness, Hygiene, and
    Disease 104*
  Colonial Violence toward Indigenous Bodies 105
  European Sexual Repression 108
  Colonial Fear and Hatred of Female Sexuality 109
  *The Impacts of Settler-Repressed Sexuality on
    People of Colour 111*
  Abuse in Residential Schools 112
  Oppression of Two-Spirit People 114
  Current Colonial Relationship to Water 114
  Venus and Cook: The Killing of a King 116
*How the Colonial Complex Can Now Enact the
  Positive Potential of* Solutio *118*
  *Embodiment: Landing in and Caring for
    Our Bodies as Home 118*
  Positive Potential of Solutio 119
Solutio/*Water Concrete Actions and Reflection Questions 120*

8 Earth   123

*Helms's Third Stage of White Racial Identity Development:
  Reintegration 124*
Introduction to Coagulatio *124*
  Earth 125
  Cook's Journal 125

Coagulatio's *Relationship to the Psyche: Positive and Negative Potentials* 126
How the Colonial Complex Enacted the Negative Potential of Coagulatio? 126
  Stealing of Indigenous Land 126
  Smallpox and Bodies: The Spread of Disease 128
  Degradation of Nature 129
  Ungroundedness 131
  Capitalism and Consumerism 132
  White Environmentalism 133
How the Colonial Complex Can Now Enact the Positive Potential of Coagulatio? 137
  Becoming Soil Soaked 138
  Healing Our Relationship to Nature Heals Us 138
  Caring for the World Around Us Is Good for Us 139
  Healing Colonial Disconnect from Land: Unearthing Trauma, Cultivating Care 140
Coagulatio/Earth Concrete Actions and Reflection Questions 140

9 Fire 142

Helms's Fourth Stage of White Racial Identity Development: Pseudo-Independence 143
Introduction to Calcinatio 144
  The Sacred 144
  Fire 145
  Cook's Journals 146
Calcinatio's *Relationship to the Psyche: Positive and Negative Potentials* 146
How the Colonial Complex Enacted the Negative Potential of Calcinatio 148
  Blood, Colonialism, and Fire 148
  The Danger of Being Scared of Fire 149
How the Colonial Complex Can Enact the Positive Potential of Calcinatio 150
  The Positive Potential of Calcinatio 150
  The Fiery Passion Needed to Combat Racism 151
  Activation of the Nervous System in Antiracism Work 152
  Activated Nervous Systems and Activists 152
  Healing the Nervous System from Christian Trauma 154

  Pendulation and Titration 155
  Creative Expression and Antiracism 156
 Calcinatio/*Fire Concrete Actions and Reflection*
  Questions 156

10 Conclusion   159

 Part I. Albedo (and a Little Citrinitas*) 159*
  Helms's Fifth Stage of White Racial Identity
   Development: Immersion/Emersion 159
  Peace, Reconciliation, and Assimilation: Navigating
   the Perils and Potentials of the Albedo 160
   Albedo and the Politics of Reconciliation 161
    Current Canadian and Indigenous Discussions
     Surrounding Reconciliation 163
  The Politics of the Albedo 167
  Albedo Conclusion 169
  Citrinitas, a Yellowing Transition 169
  Concrete Action 170
 Part II. Rubedo *170*
  Helms's Sixth Stage of White Racial Identity
   Development: Autonomy 170
 Rubedo *171*
  Racial Rubedo: Where We Go from Here 172
  Rubedo Concrete Actions and Reflection Questions 175
  Soeur Mystica 176
  Gold 177
  Kweèt'įį: Rock Diggers 179
  Captain Cook and George Vancouver 179
  Conclusion 181

References   183
Index   195

Acknowledgement

Thank you, Leanne Betasamosake Simpson, for sending me on this path all those years ago. Thank you, Lee Maracle, for reading my proposal for this work, and sharing your insights and your hard-earned approval. You and your words of wisdom have been a constant well of inspiration and call to action for me. I am forever grateful, rest in power.

Chapter 1

Introduction

At subsequent infamous moments over the last half a millennium, Columbus, Cook, and Vancouver rowed from their respective ships to the shores of the diverse landscape of what is now known as North America. The reverberations of those first sea-legged steps onto pebbled and sandy beaches continue to echo throughout these lands and waters today. The condemnatory lens through which the conquerors and their misbegotten inheritors perceived the hosts who helped pull their rowboats into the lush coastal ecosystems led to the death of tens of millions of Indigenous people, the largest genocide the world has ever seen (Stannard, 1993, Locations 57 and 91).

Settlers in these lands no longer die of scurvy, and for the most part, Google Maps has replaced celestial navigation for everyday travel directions. Much has changed for the descendants of these European voyagers over the last 500 years. And yet, since the first landing of European sailors in what is now called British Columbia, the lens through which Vancouver and Cook met the Nuu-chah-nulth people in 1778 continues to filter the gaze of modern settlers. This is the colonial lens that named the Nuu-chah-nulth people *savages* as they guided the newcomers to anchor their ships in the safety of *Yuquot*, which the sailors renamed Friendly Sound for the welcome and protection from the winds they received there. Not long after that first welcome, more than 90% of the region's original inhabitants would be dead (Arima, 2018, § 5). *Yuquot* is on an island off of a much larger island claimed in Vancouver's name. Vancouver Island is where I was raised and live today. Vancouver Island is a part of so-called British Columbia. Almost none, if any, of this land has ever been ceded by First Nations, and yet, 94% percent of the province is still legally "Crown Land"—that is, in name owned by the Queen of England (Province of British Columbia, 2020, § 1). Though the lack of vitamin C no longer ails settlers, the ailments of the soul that the early colonial explorers brought with them have not been cured by time nor by modernisation. This book aims to explore how the early voyagers' racism, sense of racial superiority, and exploitative worldviews tinted everything from their star-charting telescopes to our trendy hipster glasses

DOI: 10.4324/9781003296546-1

today. This book will explore how colonial consciousness lives on in the white settlers of what is now known as Canada and, through the reclamation of long forgotten navigational tools, will look for potential remedies for this continentally devastating disease.

What follows is my attempt to scramble for some way forward toward accountability and integrity today. My engagement with this topic began in 2014, in a lifechanging ethnobotany course with Leigh Joseph (Styawat), an ethnobotanist, teacher, and researcher from the Skwxwú7mesh (Squamish) First Nation. That was one of my first experiences of learning about colonialism and its far-reaching and continuing impacts beyond my short and insufficient grade school lessons on the topic. That class and Leigh's inspiring teachings changed the course of my studies to a focus on the colonial history of the land. A few months later, I enroled at Dechinta Centre for Research and Learning in what is now known as the Northwest Territories, a school for decolonisation and Indigenous resurgence.

Learning on the land, camping in −20°C weather, I became aware of my ingrained colonialism. Between my embarrassing displays of whiteness, I also learned from elders, my classmates, and professors Richard Van Camp, Glen Coulthard, and Leanne Betasamosake Simpson. During our time there, Leanne set me on a course that has deeply impacted my life and has led to this book. Leanne told me that the most important way that I as a white settler can be of service to Indigenous resurgence today is by addressing the cultural dysfunction and woundedness of settler-colonialism—of my own people.

She directed me to seek the healing of this illness within my own ancestral lineage:

> At one time, your people were connected too. Go find those stories that can lead your people back to your own connectedness to nature, to body and wholeness, so that they stop projecting their woundedness and disconnect onto the world and harming all those around them. (Leanne Betasamosake Simpson, Personal Communication, 2014)

I tried to smarten up and do just that, and during my doctoral research in depth psychology I turned to the study of the mythology of western culture for its unsettling and healing potentials. Rather than appropriating mythology from other cultures, especially those settler-colonialism has already stolen so much from, notably, First Nation's cultures, I looked instead to reconnect with settler-colonialism's own ancient heritage for healing to understand the psychology of where we went wrong and how we can now recover.

I hope that I am now a bit less cringey than I was while learning the history of colonialism out in the bush at Dechinta. However, I am a white settler woman and, therefore, intrinsically have racist beliefs ingrained within me and the culture I was raised in. Unlearning these will be a lifelong process. This adds complexity and complication to my relationship with this topic, what my role is in relation to it, and where my voice contributes, amplifies, and positively adds to the conversations, or when it is taking up space when it should be Black, Indigenous, or People of Colour (BIPOC) speaking on these topics instead. This enquiry was something I reckoned with throughout this entire research process.

This book examines colonial psychology and its history to identify insights into the transformation of settler consciousness. My work is not in and of itself antiracism work, rather it aims to be a racial accountability process, antiracism work should be being led by and directed by BIPOC. This work is instead a process of racial accountability taking for the colonial psychology found within me, my culture, and the history of this land and the horrors perpetuated on it for the last 500 plus years.

Part of this accountability taking is looking to find alternatives to appropriative spiritual practices for settlers, something I am very familiar with. Just a few months before attending Dechinta, my meditation teacher and mentor Michelle St. Pierre, who had been navigating through cancer for seven years, asked if I would take over her meditation retreat centre after she passed, I accepted. And so, at 21, I inherited and become responsible for a meditation retreat centre on Hornby Island. The process of leading that retreat centre continually made me reckon with my values, beliefs, and positionality. My constant question was what did it mean for me, a white settler to be running this retreat centre that had a 10-ft silk Hornby-made Kuan Yin hanging in a yurt. This yurt is where silent retreats loosely based on Zen Buddhist philosophy would occur, retreats I was now being asked to lead. And all of this took place on unceded K'ómoks and Pentlatch territory, on the island which those Nations had used for ceremony and summer whaling but which has now been taken over by back to the landers, hippies, and a thriving summer tourism industry. Throughout the years of leading the retreat centre, I continually realised we need to do better as white people and find more culturally appropriate meaning-making practices. This book grew from that time and as I left the retreat centre in my attempts to find more appropriate avenues for settler-colonial healing, accountability taking, and meaning making.

Toni Morrison said that we write the book that we need to read. This is very much true for me. When I speak about problematic white women in this book, I am not exempt, I will always reckon with—and be unlearning— my problematic whiteness. During the last decade, I have been seeking ways to reckon with my colonialism, my whiteness and my ingrained racism. I couldn't find a meaning-making practice that resonated with me that was not rooted in colonialism (such as Christianity) or appropriated spiritual practices. And so, I went on the search for something more appropriate for me as a white settler, which also supported and nurtured soulful connection and care. And so, this book was birthed, with lots of grief about the state of the world and questioning what one white woman can, or should, contribute to any of it, in between.

> "Settlers ought to look at their history, then look in the mirror."
> —Maracle (2017, p. 109)

In Maracle's (2017) *Conversations with Canadians,* she wrote from her perspective on the colonial consciousness of white settlers. Maracle addressed how the decolonising of settlers is vital in the pursuit of reconciliation and healing between Indigenous and settler nations today. Maracle explained that white settlers often ask Indigenous people: "What can we do to help?" (p. 49). She criticised that white settlers like to assume the role of White Saviour, offering to help the "needy" and be the hero. However, it is colonial culture that has created—and continues to create—the conditions for Indigenous oppression, and it is white settlers who benefit profoundly from the disenfranchisement of Indigenous people by occupying a land not their own.

Maracle wrote that instead of continuing to disempower Indigenous people by assuming that they need the coloniser's help to recover from generations of colonial harm, settlers need to work toward addressing the root of the problem itself: working toward decolonising so-called Canada (p. 49). This is a much more difficult feat for white settlers today; as Maracle explained, it is far easier to play the hero by believing they are helping the "needy" than to accept that they are part of the villainous system that has created the suffering and then working to change their role and the system of which they are a part (cue white woman tears). Maracle wrote that it is white Canadians, not Indigenous people, who are responsible for this process of changing Canadian society and its inherent patriarchal colonialism and racism (p. 50). She wrote that although the process is uncomfortable for Canadians, their participation in the decolonising of their society is ultimately morally in their best interest: "If you participate in dismantling the master's house and ending all forms of oppression, you are helping yourself" (p. 49).

Maracle's (2017) insights lay the foundation for my research and offer guidance for settlers exploring the decolonisation of the white psyche. This process is necessary so that individuals can stop perpetuating colonial values and, from there, truly work on the dismantlement of colonial society. Maracle directed settlers to no longer continue the patronising dialogue that Indigenous peoples need the coloniser's help to heal. Maracle's insights guide this work in focusing, instead, on being of service to Indigenous peoples and the reconciliatory process by addressing the root causes of the issues at hand—the colonial mindsets that live on in Canadians today and which continue the colonial oppression of

Indigenous people and the land which we occupy. Maracle did not provide guidance for what this decolonisation looks like for settlers and makes clear that it is our responsibility to find this healing for ourselves; it is not up to the colonised to heal the coloniser. This book posits that the healing must, in fact, come from the lineages of the settlers themselves, and that it must be settlers that find where their ancestral dysfunction began and discover within their own lineages where it can be healed. Listening to Maracle's and Simpson's directives that dismantling the master's house is settlers' responsibility, this research aims to explore guides for—and expressions of—this dismantlement. Based on Maracle's and Simpson's wisdom, this work speculates that this process must first happen psychologically within white settlers so that their activism does not continue to be fuelled by their colonial values and subvert itself into colonial roles such as the White Saviour. By looking for guidance from alchemy as one of the ancestral lineages of white European consciousness, this study will attempt to respond to Maracle's and Simpson's call for white settlers to work on their own healing and decolonisation.

My ideas on colonial psychology and history build on the work of scholars such as Maracle and Simpson as well as scholars such as Ruth King and Resmaa Menakem who look at the trauma of white supremacy that lives in white bodies and is perpetuated from those bodies onto the world around them. These authors call for white people to tend the intergenerational trauma that lives in their bodies and psyches, and which continues to actively project that trauma onto others. For my work on answering this call, I use alchemy as a metaphor for understanding the psychology of colonialism and its potential transformation today. But why the use of story and myth for understanding and transforming colonial consciousness?

Neuroscience studies show that stories are easier to integrate than facts and figures (Morris et al., 2019, p. 20). Neuroscience researchers Morris et al. refer to humans as *homo narrans*: "storytelling animals who are persuaded to make decisions based on the coherence and fidelity of stories" (p. 21). Stories are how we have communicated and made sense of our world as long as we have been human. Our brains have evolved with these stories (Bransford et al. 2000; Pinker 2003). We know now from diverse fields that stories and story structure match human neural maps and deeply effect our understanding of the world from birth (Donald 1991; Nelson 2003; Pinker 2003; Plotkin 1982). Our brains understand stories, and are deeply changed by them, in many ways, we are our stories.

Studies have also shown that people introduced to a narrative have an increased predictability of pro-social behaviour; they exhibited "story-consistent beliefs" and displayed higher levels of empathy, autonomic activation, and emotional arousal (p. 22). All of this means that exposure to a story engaged individuals and their brains in a way that changed their behaviour, emotions, and beliefs in a way that facts alone did not.

We are less defensive when hearing a story; it allows our guards to drop a little. And we know that the story of colonisation and the delusion of white supremacy is one that can get our hackles up. Therefore, to appease our brains, and maybe let some of these realities sink in and let us be changed, we will turn to mythic stories that may help us navigate through these topics. Engaging our emotional brain regions and hopefully laying the limbic stress system to rest allows us the chance to process and integrate the information coming in. Other cultures have long known what we settlers need peer-reviewed statistical data to prove to ourselves: stories teach, stories heal, stories are how we learn, how we grow into ourselves, our communities, and our humanity (McNett, 2016, p. 184). Facts and figures do not affect our brain, body, or being in the same way as a narrative always has, and hopefully, always will. And so, throughout this book, we engage the story of alchemy and read the story of colonisation through an alchemical narrative lens.

The intention of this approach is not to coddle settler colonials in this discussion or to say that they do not also need to face and deal with a lot of discomfort in this process of unlearning racist beliefs and behaviour because they do. In fact, reckoning with their deeply uncomfortable pasts is an essential first step in this process. Using this approach is about trying to make the process as accessible as possible so perhaps some people who would not normally be willing to engage in these conversations are a little more open to them through a different medium. The intention is also that engaging with these topics in this way can inspire deeper and more sustainable transformation and change.

But Why Alchemy?

A mostly forgotten practice from medieval times seems an odd story to go to when talking about colonialism. However, my educational background is depth psychological and Jungian, and a tenet of this approach is that stories and myths from one's own ancestry can bring about deep change of perspective, healing, and meaning making (which echoes Leanne's guiding insights as well). Alchemy also held more of a place in society when colonialism of so-called North America began, though it would not have been considered mainstream, it was more apart of the zeitgeist of the time. As such, learning more about it, I hope we can learn more about the psychology of that era, and how it continues to live on in us today.

Europe regained interest in alchemy in the twelfth century (it had been previously popular in the Roman Empire). However, the height of alchemy in Europe was in the sixteenth and seventeenth centuries (Jung, 1951/1968, § 274). Christopher Columbus landed in what would later be named North America in 1492, and so the next 200 years of colonisation overlap with the peak years of alchemical thought and interest in Europe.

Jung wrote that alchemy is the basis and inspiration of his psychological theories which in turn has deeply affected our understandings of psychology and depth psychology today. Many of the founding thinkers of the Western worldview were also captivated by alchemical ways of seeing and being in the world. This includes Newton, Paracelsus, Roger Bacon, Jakob Böhme, Shakespeare, Chaucer, and John Dee. Fun fact, Newton actually wrote much more about alchemy than mathematics or physics (Cambray, 2012, p. 38).

Newton and his scientific discoveries are foundational to so many ways in which we understand our world, think—gravity. That the thinkers that envisioned how we understand the world today were also influenced so greatly by alchemy means that it is woven even more deeply into our settler history and ways of understanding the world than we perhaps ever imagined. And yet we rarely, if ever, think about it, and if we do, we are surely not thinking about how much it impacts our lives. Alchemy's history being buried away and mostly forgotten is in part because over the centuries, the church has seen alchemy as such a threat. And so, this work hopes to bring this part of European ancestry, which has long been tucked away into the recesses of settler psyches and history, and take it out of the shadows, bring it back to life as a tool and resource for emotional healing. Alchemy is a way to navigate through life and meaning making, different from our colonial ways of finding meaning, but still belonging to us ancestrally, as something that has influenced our psyches and history. Moreover, it is not appropriated from other cultures (although other cultures did practice it in parallel as well). It is in great part because the church was threatened by alchemical ways of thinking (valuing nature, the feminine, body, sex, etc.) that it was purged from our society and history books and is still for the most part forgotten. This book hopes to be a part of reclaiming some of these alchemical stories and perspectives today.

When we think of alchemy, we are probably thinking of magicians with pointy hats trying to create potions to live forever or spells to create endless bounties of gold. Though these may be the images that are passed down to us, alchemy was far more complex and nuanced than these cartoonlike images. It seems much more likely that instead of trying to create physical gold, these alchemists were trying to create inner gold, and that their practices were actually far more concerned with inner transformation than external, elemental transformation or riches.

This book will use the mythology of alchemy to look into the cultural imagination of the settler colonial and as a metaphor in the understanding of the origins of colonial consciousness and its possible transformation today. Many scholars such as Jungian psychologist Marie-Louise von Franz valued alchemy as she saw it as fundamentally balancing and complementary to the one-sided, and yet foundational, Western paradigm of

Christianity. Von Franz claimed alchemy to be the completion of the Christian myth as she saw within it that balances the one-sidedness of the Christian ethos: "I think alchemy is the complete myth. If our Western civilization has a possibility of survival, it would be by accepting the alchemical myth, which is a richer completion and continuation of the Christian myth" (Papadopoulos, 2006, p. 274). As alchemy is seen as balancing to the Christian myth and Christianity is foundational to colonial consciousness, the research in this book posits that alchemy can offer balancing potentials for colonial consciousness.

Building off of von Franz's view that alchemy was the completion of the Christian myth, this book will explore how alchemy honoured the importance of the dark where Christianity deifies the light; it honoured the feminine, body, and sexuality, where Christianity can denigrate them; it honoured the earth, where Christianity can objectify it; and supported individuals in journeys toward embodiment and living the fullest most vibrant life on earth whereas Christianity at times focuses more on the afterlife. We will look at how colonial consciousness has been birthed from those places of degrading the dark, the feminine, body, sexuality, the earth, and focused on ascension and the afterlife, and how these values shaped the trajectory of colonial action, destruction, and genocide that we have seen across what is now known as North America and in many other places around the world.

For decades, settler-colonials have been searching for a meaning-making model to replace Christianity, which no longer holds the same role in many people's lives as in once did. Often white settlers have turned to appropriating meaning-making models from cultures that the West has already stolen so much from and oppressed, such as Eastern spiritualities, and teachings from Indigenous cultures that have been taken without permission, without the depth of cultural teachings or an understanding of their histories of oppression.

Part of what inspired my research was looking for a meaning-making model within settler colonial history that would be a more appropriate avenue for settlers to engage in rather than continuing their appropriative meaning-making practices. I also looked at how alchemical metaphors could not only lead to meaning making in settlers' lives but also serve as an avenue for being confronted with the parts of ourselves, our culture and history that has caused such global suffering, genocide, and cultural erasure. I found alchemy offered a useful framework to lead to this accountability as well as also being a more appropriate meaning-making practice than other stolen appropriated practices. (I'm looking at you multi-billion-dollar yoga pants industry and mala-wearing white women—full disclosure, I have definitely been that problematic mala-wearing, namaste-ing white women and did most of the problematic white woman things that we will address in this book at one point or another.)

One of the foundational thinkers in depth psychology James Hillman (1997) explicitly envisioned the colonisation of North America as an alchemical metaphor: "The imagination that invented the New World together with the secret oppression in its heart is quite clearly the same imagination of alchemy, which, within enclosed introverted laboratories and hermetically sealed language, sought above all else, Gold" (p. 9). This book takes up Hillman's imagining of the colonisation of North America as an aborted alchemical journey, the externalisation of that needed to be internally undertaken. Settlers came to the "New World" looking for hope and instead stole that hope from Indigenous peoples. The so-called North American landscapes still bear the scars of the colonial externalisation of this gold-seeking pursuit. By using alchemy as a metaphorical lens for the inner transformation that must occur in settlers today, this book hopes to investigate the inner gold-making journey that the early colonialists thwarted in their physical gold-rush frenzies. The hope is that instead of devastating the ecosystems and people of this land, as the colonial external focus on gold has entailed, this internal process can help in the racial accountability, reparations, and solidarity work required for settlers today.

There is an idea in alchemy that the soul is always in one way or another engaged in alchemical pursuits and that the soul is always striving toward union within and embarking on the gold-making journey, and that when not undertaken consciously, this path can be perilous (Hillman, 1997, p. 9). For the alchemists of old, a misstep in their laboratories could result in lead or mercury poisoning, exploding alembics and raging fires. Metaphorically, these dangerous missteps might involve misplacing our longings for psychological change on the external world and trying to seek there what we are internally craving.

Hillman likens the discovery of the "New World" to an attempt at an alchemical journey. He equates the early explorers to alchemists in their search for gold, ones that misread the map and instead of looking inward, travelled across the seas to look for their inner gold in vain (p. 9). This book imagines into the colonial impulse as a misdirected alchemical one. This research is not suggesting that this is the truth, in the Times-New-Roman-font-in-a-history-textbook kind of way, but rather as a mythic possibility, an ornate decorative initial at the beginning of a story, for sometimes stories allow us to peek into an unspeakable truth in the heart of a time, such as a time when a modern, new kind of Roman made his way across the sea 500 years ago, determined to discover and conquer lands—to him—as yet unknown.

We can imagine early explorers as alchemists in their search for gold, ones that misread the map and instead of looking inward, travelled across the seas in their futile extraverted search (p. 9). Perhaps this can be a useful model for some, an allegory for understanding some of the psychology of this history, a story to allow settlers to understand ourselves and history a bit better so we can work to change its impacts, and ourselves, today.

Alchemy and Race

The metaphor of alchemy being applied in racial contexts is not new, different authors in various fields have used alchemical language to describe race related and colonial topics. Matthew Jacobson (2005) conceptualised the founding of America as "racial alchemy" (Location 240). He saw the unification of European immigrants from diverse cultures into one racial group of "white" and "Caucasian" as an alchemical act not based in any racial reality (Location 240). He described this racial alchemy as "the process by which Celts, Hebrews, Slavs, and Mediterraneans became Caucasians" (Location 263). The consequence of this racial alchemy was the sudden grouping of white people versus everyone else, whereas previously there was not one distinct group called white, but rather a myriad of diverse cultures, histories, and origins (Location 2331). Jacobson called the process of racialized division in America the alchemy of imperialism (Location 4569). Haudenosaunee author Alicia Elliott has been described as a modern-day alchemist that the world needs more of as she "showcases her peculiar alchemy, lighting the darkest corners of racism, classism, sexism with her laser-focused intellect and kind-hearted soul-searching" (Elliott, 2019, p. 4).

Historian Richard Gwyn (2012) described the leadership of John A. Macdonald, the first and deeply problematic Prime Minister of Canada as "some strange alchemy" (p. 253). It was this strange alchemy which founded Canada as the colonial and racist country that we continue to see today. Manuel and Derrickson (2017) described the colonialism in Canada and the stealing of Indigenous land as an alchemical process as well. He wrote that only "the court understands how that alchemy happened, how bumping into became discovery and discovery became overlordship. It was made possible through the quicksilver of racism, that black magic of white supremacy" (p. 92). John Burrows (1999) condemned the "spell" cast by the Canadian belief in colonial sovereignty of a stolen land: "How can lands possessed by Aboriginal peoples for centuries be undermined by another nation's assertion of sovereignty? What alchemy transmutes the basis of Aboriginal possession into the golden bedrock of Crown title?" (p. 558).

This book takes up the use of alchemy as a metaphor in addressing the racial and colonial construction of North America, with the hope that in the same way alchemy can be used as a metaphor for how the chaos of colonialism ensued, it can also be used as a metaphor to aid in its deconstruction today.

Terms

Colonial consciousness in North America will be defined generally through this book as the European cultural consciousness that arrived to these lands to settle and colonise, which continues to exist today in white settlers, all of whom benefit from the oppression of Indigenous people and the land. Settler-colonials are white individuals of European descent who live in what is now known as North America.

The term Indigenous is used in this research to refer to First Nations, Métis and Inuit in so-called Canada, or at times the term may be used to refer to Indigenous peoples across all of what is now known as North America. This term is used while recognising that each First Nation, the Métis and Inuit are distinct and that each has its own history, identity, and relationship to settler colonialism.

The word *integrity* comes from the Latin root of *integritatem* (nominative *integritas*), which means "soundness, wholeness, completeness" (Harper, 2020). The aim of this work is restoring the settler colonial to integrity, which means righting with one's wrongs and past. Integrity means wholeness which requires integrating one's shadow and reconciling with all the different aspects of oneself. One cannot be in integrity by being in denial of one's personal or collective history, without taking responsibility for the violence one's whiteness and privilege continues to perpetuate—and the systematic powers of oppression one's whiteness is a part of—which continues to oppress and endanger BIPOC around the world.

This book addresses the problem of the colonial consciousness that continues to oppress Indigenous people and degrade the environment of so-called Canada. The intention of this work is to respond to the appeal from Indigenous people for settlers to tend the depths and wounds of colonial consciousness in service to accountability processes for settlers to Indigenous people and nations on what is known as Canada today (Maracle, 2017, p. 49). A foundational assumption of this book, then, is the need for colonial healing and accountability taking to occur. This book will be directed toward white individuals in so-called North America; therefore, the pronouns we/us will be used throughout in reference to white settler colonials in what is now known as North America.

Statement of Positionality

There are many more foundational texts written by Indigenous authors on the subject of colonialism of far more importance than this book. I want to re-acknowledge the primary role Indigenous and Black people and people of colour must have in antiracism work, and my positionality as a white voice talking about anti-racism. I do not have the experience of being a person of colour in this world and therefore will never be an expert on anti-racism and will always continue to take my lead from BIPOC.

Part of this taking direction has led to my research of becoming accountable to the responsibility of confronting colonial psychology, its history, and the devastation that it has created. I acknowledge that this process of navigating the places my voice and research is needed and where they take up space will forever be a learning process for me, and that there will be places in this work and in life that I get it wrong. I commit to always being willing to listen, learn, and amend my work and ideas in response to BIPOC experiences, writing, conversation, criticism, and feedback.

This book's focus is on potential changes of consciousness and ways of relating to the world around us. Our brains understand stories. The story of this book is not how to cure racism. The intention is rather to provide a potential entryway into these conversations; a model to look at why such destruction could have happened in the first place; and to frame some of the psychological work as well as direct concrete action that must happen in settler decolonisation, and racial accountability work today.

This book does not address the real and necessary policy changes that are central to antiracism and decolonisation. This is the work that needs to continue to happen now. I believe that consciousness change and policy change are inseparable. Policy change does not just happen without shifts in the culture that call for them: policy is a reflection of the people. We must change both to have a lasting, sustainable effect. Going forward, continued research and action must focus on systematic change of laws and policies. This necessitates concrete action leading to a more fair, just and equitable antiracist society for all.

At times I doubt the soft approach of this scholarship: looking at the settler soul through an alchemical lens and trying to understand the trauma at its core. I question if it is okay for me as a white settler to hold this topic tenderly instead of with the harshness it deserves after all the pain it has caused. That being said, I have felt the need to engage in this research in part, because for many settlers, their white settler fragility keeps them from engaging with this important field, its texts, authors, and advocates (Menakem, 2017, p. 13). We settlers need to work on our ability to stay in racialized discomfort, to build our resiliency to confront and be confronted by our complicity while still being in our windows of tolerance so that we do not dissociate or go into fight, flight or freeze reactions, leading to defensiveness or avoidance of the topic (p. 13).

Colonialism is inherently dysregulating and dysregulated, and a dysregulated settler nervous system will not aid decolonisation. We cannot heal the consciousness that created the problem with the consciousness that created the problem. As Einstein said, "The significant problems we face cannot be solved at the same level of thinking we were at when we created them" (Mitchell, 2018, p. 90). This is not an excuse to avoid working toward outer decolonisation until we are some idealised version of a saint (many of whom were colonially problematic anyway). Instead, I am suggesting that as we are working outwardly on our racial accountability efforts, we have an equal responsibility to be working on the decolonisation of our minds, bodies, and nervous systems so that we are not actively perpetuating more harm and acting from places of trauma and dysregulation while we are out in the world engaging with activism. If we do not take the time to address our own colonial natures and the trauma within them, then we will only continue to perpetuate more harm, despite our best intentions. That being said, I hope that this writing can be a bridge, an introduction, a starting point for individuals to enter into this work, build up their tolerances to racialized discomfort and strengthen their resiliency, humility and sanity, so that they may continue their settler decolonisation process in integrity. May this work support those individuals so that they can engage fully with the vast resources and brilliant thinkers of this field. May this work be only a beginning, a bridge to the real work being done by Indigenous and BIPOC authors, speakers, elders, and activists across what is now known as Canada, and across so-called North America.

Throughout this process, I often think of the value of Indigenous storytelling in Indigenous resurgence and decolonisation today. I believe that part of the colonial disease has been its separation from storytelling, which then led to its oppression of Indigenous stories and storytelling. My hope with this research, and with its approach, is that the storytelling in this scholarship be decolonial, and that the "softness" of the approach may subvert the violence of a colonial one.

I am a white settler woman. I have the luxury of spending my time reading the myths and tales of the ancient alchemists in their laboratories. Sometimes this pursuit includes learning the Latin words that permeate their manuscripts, words we have collectively kept close to our hearts for the last two millennia such as *coloni, conqueror,* and *impostor.* I was raised in the Canadian public school system, where racism is pervasively taught in the recounting of the discoverers' feats and adventures to gain us the land we now confidently call our own.

Societally, I benefit greatly from the continued colonialism in what is now known as North America. The awareness of the horrors of the past and present, which create my privilege, deteriorates my connection to my own morality and integrity. I believe that this is a condition in which many white settlers find themselves today, and it tends to require the consuming of many nightly hours of Netflix to numb out the reality of our complicity.

For four of the years I worked on this book, I also worked as a counsellor in a rehabilitation centre for young Indigenous women from across so-called Canada and then in an elementary school as a counsellor on a nearby reserve. There I have listened to the stories of the trauma of colonisation and how it has directly affected the lives of the young women and children

I work with, their families and communities. Part of what will be explored through this writing is the relationship between settler colonial disconnect from land, soul, body, and how this disconnect has allowed us to perpetuate such destruction, abuse, trauma, and horror.

In this pursuit, instead of using the colonially accepted tools of hyper focused rationality, I intend to work with tools colonialism has, up until this point, dismissed. I hope to discover this pathway back to integrity and morality, in part by looking at how to find cultural healing for colonial consciousness through old Medieval people who had vials full of faeces in their laboratories, thinking that they could turn it into gold. My hope is that it will become clear in this work that the study of alchemy as a tool for addressing colonial racism, instead of being only questionably absurd, can bring us to a place of recognising that in those old alchemists' vials lit by candlelight is the grime of our own history. The alchemists believed that in their darkened, smoke-filled laboratories, they could turn filth to gold; that the rawest, most base materials were needed for the transformative magic of gold-making to succeed. I hope, through the research in this book, to find that the same is true for ourselves: that facing the putrid and rotting parts of ourselves and our culture is exactly where we need to begin our own inner gold-making journey. That through care, diligence, and humility in facing our past, we can transmute this muck of ours and, thereby, reclaim our true riches of inner vitality, integrity, and antiracist direct action. In doing so, my hope is that we find that the settlers were enthraled with digging up and searching for when they first arrived in so-called North America, but this time we might find its golden radiance within the deep mines of our own being.

Chapter 2

Foundational Literature

Colonialism and the Field of Psychology

The field and practice of psychology has been entangled with colonial consciousness for millennia. The ancient Greeks developed a system of extensive ethical framework for psychological practice. However, the Hippocratic oath was relevant only for physicians treating those who were deemed citizens; enslaved people (most of the population) did not warrant the same ethical treatment (Miles, 2005, p. 147). These philosophers could not have developed their philosophical theories without the exploitation of enslaved people, and yet, enslaved people were not beneficiaries of these philosophical ideas in any way.

Psychology and medicine were used in the killing of millions in the Holocaust; in 1940, it was in the psychiatric hospitals that the first large-scale euthanasia testing was conducted for later use in concentration camps (Rubenfeld, 2011, p. 516). The field of psychology's dark history of colonial consciousness continued with the psychological experiment of attempting to "kill the Indian in the child" in Canadian residential schools (TRC, 2015). The psychological testing and the torture inflicted in those schools is a shameful period in the field of psychology's history (TRC, 2015). The continued ties between colonial consciousness and the field of psychology can also be found in the American Psychological Association's (APA) involvement in the psychological torture of prisoners and the APA working so closely with the Department of Defence in the United States, as well as the McGill and the CIA experiments in the 1960s and 1970s (LoCicero et al., 2016, p. 345). The psychological field has a history of dominance, superiority, and eradication or assimilation of the other, and contains within it a sinister history of psychological torture and experimentation often superficially glanced over in our "Psych 101" textbooks. These histories are sometimes included in the textbooks but are explained away or denuded of horror. In Psych 101 textbooks, there will sometimes be a research methods chapter with "unethical experiments" that go over cases many of us have heard of—Stanford prison experiment, Milgram's experiment,

DOI: 10.4324/9781003296546-2

Harry Harlow's monkey experiments, Robber's cave, etc.; all of these will be listed beside the horrifically racist Tuskegee syphilis study as though they were the same—and equivalently unethical.

The colonial history of psychology will be conceptualised in this work as part of the *prima materia* of the colonial psyche. The intention of this work is to be a part of the movement that is working to change the field of psychology's relationship to race, power, privilege, and oppression today.

A Soul Illness

In *Mythic Figures* (2007), Hillman wrote that the myths of one's lineage deeply influence one's psychic structures and tendencies and offer a roadmap of one's personal and collective psyche. In Hillman's (1975) *Re-Visioning Psychology*, he championed the use of myth to tend the modern Western psyche. He described the mythopoetic healing that can occur through connecting to the imaginal world for the overly rational Western soul. Hillman asserted that above all, the malaise of the Western psyche is a soul illness, a spiritual void (p. xv). As Hillman suggested that it is soul illness that needs to be addressed, it must be soul medicine that is offered. He believed that the soul is a world of "imagination, passion, fantasy, reflection" (p. 68). He suggested that the timelessness of myth re-enlivens the imaginal, the passionate, the fantastical, and the reflective, and that myth's essence is the revitalising of the soulful. Myth is based on the beautiful: the beauty of story, of human folly, potential and purpose, of disconnect and connectedness and the sacredness of human existence and its trials. Hillman advocated that it is beauty itself that can cure the psyche, and beauty that brings soul healing (p. 38). Hillman suggested that this beauty can be found in the mythology of our ancestral traditions.

Hillman (1975) insisted that the best way to understand the psyche is through recognising the processes within it as mythic (p. 146). Personal lives can be infused with meaningfulness and aliveness when we recognise our personal challenges, successes, longings, fears and aspirations within ancient mythic understandings of what it means to live, love, and suffer in our human lives. Hillman believed that the fantasy images that arise from the human psyche through myth, poetry, art, and dreams are what allow us the deepest insight and access to the human soul (p. xvii). He suggested that the care of the soul, through the beautiful, also necessitates the dedicated tending of the painful—the parts of the psyche that need our care (p. 56). This book aspires to address this need that Hillman identifies for caring for the colonial soul through the tending of psychopathology, with the aid of the beautiful and mythic. In this work, we will look at transforming colonial consciousness in so-called Canada through the mythological lens of alchemy and the caring and changing of its most broken, destructive parts.

As there is the tendency to divert attention away from our own neuroses, we have done the same in our mythologies. The settler-colonial has turned to every culture but our own looking for narratives to cling to for enlightenment and salvation. Hillman (2007) named some of these new-age psychologies and spiritualities: "pop-polytheisms and astro-mytho-typologies." He wrote that these new "isms" are delusional in their thinking that in taking from mythologies of other cultures while running from our own, we will transcend our ancient psychic structures, our millennia-old pathologies and the reality of our mythic pasts (Location 3610). Hillman wrote of these groups' desperation to no longer be Western and their desire to immerse themselves only in "Native American healing rites" and other forms of cultural appropriation (Location 3611). Instead, Hillman argued that the tending of the soul necessitates working through our dysfunctions through the mythologies of our lineage. These ideas of Hillman's amplify the justification of this work invoking alchemy to bring healing and integration to the white psyche.

There has been a tendency for settlers to appropriate healing modalities from other cultures, often cultures that we have already colonised and stolen from with devastating consequences. I believe that for settlers' actual healing and integration to occur, this healing must come from our own ancestral lineages and not continue the colonial practice of taking from cultures we have oppressed: white women wearing feather headdresses is just not going to cut it.

There are some practices from lineages outside of the West that are shared with consent with individuals or people of European descent. Learn the history of the practices you take part in, what teachers in these lineages say about appropriation, and listen and learn about appropriative practices and the harm they cause from BIPOC. For Jung, after years of studying Eastern philosophy and spirituality, alchemy and its myths from the Western lineage began to resonate more deeply with him as relevant to the Western psyche, and alchemy thus became a historical grounding for his Western psychological theories. In *Memories, Dreams, Reflections* (1963), he described how within alchemy he found deep resonances with his approaches to psyche, healing and wholeness (Location 3336). Jung observed that people have a very deep fear around facing ourselves and our unconscious, but he saw this descent as the only way to know oneself. In alchemists' texts, he found that same sentiment echoed from their laboratories of the past (Location 3134). Jung understood alchemy to be the ancestral cord that connected Western traditions of the past, such as Gnosticism, with modern psychologies of the unconscious, all of which shared a similar groundwork in how they related to human potential, the importance and vitality of the unconscious, and the sacredness of the psyche (Location 3346). It was through his study of alchemy that Jung arrived at the concept of individuation. His study of the ancient alchemical work directly informed his theories and concepts of psyche, wholeness, and the sacred (Location 3471). Jung believed alchemy to be intrinsically woven into the Western psyche as it addresses the depth of the one-sidedness of Christianity and offers a counterbalancing narrative for the Western soul. As Jung found that alchemy was such an integral part of the development of the Western psyche and a key link in the lineage of depth psychology through the ages, its ancestral wisdom will infuse this study. This book hopes to reach back to this link of the past and unravel it into the needs of today and tomorrow.

Jung and Racism

Jung's work quite rightly continues to face criticism for his treatment of "the other," the "primitive," and races other than his own. Like the multiplicity Jung studied within the psyche, Jung too contained much complexity, variance, and contradiction. He is still being justifiably criticised for his racism and sexism. Post-Jungians are today redeeming the revolutionary ideas of other aspects of Jung's philosophies by translating them into contemporary understandings toward race, gender, power, and privilege. This research will attempt to be a part of that movement, transmuting Jungian concepts into politically conscious and responsible catalysts for antiracist and anticolonial transformation today.

The Violence of Cultural Stealing and Appropriation

Appropriation in Canada has a sinister history. In 1884, an amendment was made to the Indian Act that outlawed First Nation's ceremonial regalia, and traditional clothing, First Nations ceremonies were also banned by law (Collison, Bee, & Neel, 2019, p. 7). "Canada outlawed Aboriginal spiritual practices, jailed Aboriginal spiritual leaders, and confiscated sacred objects" (TRC, 2015b, p. 2). The ceremonial ban also applied to Potlatch ceremonies that were a central component to "the social, economic and legal systems of Indigenous Peoples in BC" (Collison, Bee, & Neel, 2019, p. 7).

During this time, First Nations people were arrested for wearing regalia or taking part in ceremonies, and ceremonial regalia and sacred items were seized and taken by the RCMP (Lebeuf, 2011, p. 38; Wilson, 2018, p. 66). These sacred items and ancestral remains were sold to museums or individuals for their private collections. While First Nations people were being jailed for participating in ceremony and their cultural items were stolen by police, settlers everywhere got to admire and fetishise them in museums or buy them for their own personal collections. There was a lot of money to be made in the stealing of these cultural items and selling them to museums and individuals: "The Ancestors and belongings that were taken from Indigenous communities were traded around the world, most landing in museum and university collections, some others in private collections" (Collison, Bee, & Neel, 2019, p. 8).

If one thinks that appropriation today is "not that big a deal" or believes things like "it's just a Halloween costume, it's just for fun," we must remember the history of cultural stealing, and appropriation and the violence that came with it. First Nations ceremonies were outlawed by white people and today as First Nations communities reclaim them and heal they have white settlers replicating them without permission. The repatriation of the stolen ceremonial sacred items and ancestral remains back to their rightful caretakers and Nations continues today, it is a long and intensive process and inevitably not all will be able to be found and returned (Collison, Bee, & Neel, 2019, p. 9). This loss continues to be felt today throughout all the Nations whose ceremonial items and ancestral remains were stolen by the RCMP and government of Canada.

Decolonisation

Taiaiake Alfred and Jeff Corntassle (2005) understood decolonisation as an internal as well as external process. They explained that the outer process of decolonisation begins internally with the self (p. 611). For Alfred and Corntassle, decolonisation and resurgence are internal shifts and changes within thinking and behaviour as well as recommitments to self that can lead to broad-scale, societal shifts in thinking and action (p. 611). Maracle (2017) recognised that though the internal decolonisation process was important, it was not the totality of decolonisation and she made clear that decolonisation necessitates external structural and political changes such as return of land and Indigenous governance (p. 96).

Oluo (2018) acknowledged that conversations surrounding race and oppression can be difficult and uncomfortable but that this discomfort does not compare to how difficult it is facing racial oppression as a person of colour. She advocated: "our humanity is worth a little discomfort, it's actually worth a lot of discomfort. But if you live in this system of White Supremacy you are either fighting the system, or you are complicit" (p. 211). She challenged that if we believe in equality and justice that we must take action toward these values in our society, as initially uncomfortable as this may be. Oluo encouraged all white people to examine their relationship to race and privilege, that no matter how enlightened we think we are on these topics, we must keep investigating within ourselves for our "defensive impulses run deep" and need to continually be addressed (p. 216). This book starts from this understanding that there is always more work to be done in unravelling white racial identities and racism.

Racism and Colonialism in Canada

Glen Coulthard (2014) emphasised the importance of addressing the patriarchal underpinnings of settler colonialism. He advocated for the necessity of acknowledging the "entangled relationship among racism, state power, capitalism, and colonial dispossession" and that colonialism's foundation of patriarchal rule often gets overlooked (p. 29). Arthur Manuel & Derrickson (2017) insisted that racism is the foundation of colonialism and colonial practices and that if we do not understand the workings of racism, we will not understand Canada, or Canadian colonialism (p. 81). Manuel condemned Canada's historic use of racism and described it both as a colonial weapon and colonial illness that he argued is white Canadians' responsibility to cure (p. 81). He contended that racism is a "debilitating mental illness that you must cure yourself from if you hope to see the world as it is and begin to make the healthy choices that you must make for your own, as well as our, survival" (p. 81). He claimed racism as the core of colonialism and that together, they are "the evil heart of Canada" and its history (p. 81). He asserted that the only way forward for Canada, its health, and hope is facing and combatting this racism and colonialism still embedded in Canadian lives and hearts (p. 81). Manuel's assertion that colonialism continues to beat as the "evil heart" of Canada necessitates the investigation into Canada's heart centre, and the suffering, malice, and trauma at its core.

Settlers' Roles in Decolonisation/Unsettling Processes

Howard Adams (1997) stressed the importance of a more in-depth understanding of white settler colonialism to inform work toward repairing its legacy today (p. 30). This book's aim is to respond to this call by investigating white settler colonialism so that white settlers can better understand this history and work toward altering its course today and in years to come.

Jeannette Armstrong (1990) advocated that settlers must stop trying to fix the Indian problem and direct their gaze toward themselves when she wrote:

> Imagine how you as writers from the dominant society might turn over some of the rocks in your own garden for examination. Imagine ... courageously questioning and examining the values that allow the de-humanizing of peoples through domination ... Imagine writing in honesty, free from the romantic bias about the courageous 'pioneering spirit' of colonialist practice and imperialist process. Imagine interpreting for us your own people's thinking towards us, instead of interpreting for us, our thinking, our lives, our stories. (p. 242)

This book aims to turn over the rocks of colonial consciousness in the "garden" of the colonial psyche and start the necessary weeding that Armstrong calls for within colonial consciousness. I also commit in this work to steer away from romanticisation of the "pioneering spirit" and instead look critically at it and the harm it has caused.

In the preface to *Unsettling the Settler Within* (2010), Taiaiake Alfred wrote about the importance of settlers engaging in the kind of critical investigation into settler colonialism that Paulette Regan undertook in the book's writing. Alfred wrote that many non-Native scholars fall into the trap of "telling Native people how we must live" and that instead Regan appropriately directs her work toward what settlers must do to fix "the settler problem" (p. x). Alfred believed that Regan responsibly directed settlers to "confront their own colonial mentality, moral indifference, and historical ignorance" (p. x). Alfred agreed with Regan's approach of "exposing the mindset that perpetuates 'benevolent' colonialism" and her urging settlers to "take responsibility for decolonising themselves and their country" (p. x). Alfred emphasised that this change must include more than just words of apology and must involve action being taken throughout all of Canadian society (p. x).

Issues with Reconciliation

Corntassel and Chaw-win-is (2009) explained that the origin of the name Canada comes from a Kanien'kehaka word, *Kanatiens,* meaning "they sit in our village." They explained that a modern translation of the word can be understood as "squatter" (p. 139). Corntassel and Chaw-win-is addressed how a whole nation named squatters and the descendants of these squatters on Indigenous land will find inherent difficulty in reconciling with the Indigenous people of this land (p. 139). Alfred and Corntassel (2005) argued that reconciling and dismantling the entanglement that is colonialism in Canada will always be uncomfortable and messy, and regardless of this fact, it must still be undertaken (p. 145).

Leanne Betasamosake Simpson (2011) emphasised that Indigenous people have been oppressed throughout Canadian history and continue to be oppressed even in the current politics surrounding reconciliation (p. 19). She questioned the validity of the reconciliation process if this process itself has colonial underpinnings. She advocated for citizens as well as governments to be involved in true reconciliation and for constant reminders that treaties are for individuals as well as governments (p. 19). She pressed that Canadians must embody their part of the relationship required by treaties to truly embody reconciliation (p. 19). Coulthard (2014) contended that the term reconciliation is defined as that which is brought into "agreement, concord, or harmony; the fact of being made consistent or compatible," and that this idea of reconciliation leads to continued practices of assimilation of Indigenous people into settler-colonial norms or society and can be an erasure of Indigenous sovereignty instead of a just peacemaking process (p. 204). This research acknowledges the complexity of the concept of reconciliation, the colonising potential that reconciliation itself can have, the move toward innocence that attempts at reconciliation can be for settlers, as well as the flaws of the term due to the connotation that both parties have amends to make and that the harm caused is a shared responsibility, instead of the blame lying solely with the settlers. Critiques from Indigenous academics such as Corntassle, Alfred, Simpson, and Coulthard will provide the foundation from which this book will build and take direction from in its analysis of colonial consciousness. As a settler researcher, it will be of vital importance for me to scrutinise my unchecked colonial bias and perspective and to be leaning on the writings of Indigenous authors, the writings of people of colour, and the writings of other white settlers investigating colonial consciousness to keep this research in integrity, decolonial in nature, and not causing more harm. This book will not directly explore possibilities of what a reconciliatory process may look like on what is now called Canada. However, the researcher's hope is that the psychological analysis of the dismantlement of colonial consciousness within this book contributes to paving the way for a just peacemaking and true reconciliatory restorative justice process to come.

Decolonisation as a Settler Move to Innocence

There are some scholars who criticise using the word decolonisation to mean anything other than the return of Indigenous land to Indigenous nations and people. Tuck and Yang (2012) condemned the use of the word decolonisation as an act of settlers "dressing up in the language of decolonisation," which while not as offensive as appropriating Indigenous regalia or wearing "Navajo print underwear sold at a clothing chain store," is nonetheless deeply problematic (p. 3). For Tuck and Yang, "decolonisation is not a metaphor. When metaphor invades decolonisation, it kills the very possibility of decolonisation; it recenters whiteness, it resettles theory, it extends innocence to the settler, it entertains a settler future" (p. 3). The authors argued that decolonisation is distinct from other critical social justice, anti-racist frameworks, and cannot be applied to any idea claiming to improve society (p. 3). The authors asserted that the use of the term decolonisation for anything other than the return of Indigenous land is a form of settler appropriation (p. 3). Part of Tuck and Yang's intention was to emphasise that which is inherently unsettling about decolonising and highlight the reality that the decolonising process should not make settlers feel comfortable or soothe their feelings of guilt (p. 3). They argued that if truly faced, decolonising will always remain unsettling for settlers (p. 3).

Tuck and Yang did advocate for the analysis of settler colonialism and for research into its dismantlement and wrote that they want others to join in those critiques and efforts (p. 3). However, they qualified that this solidarity work should always remain uncomfortable for settlers: "Solidarity is an uneasy, reserved, and unsettled matter that neither reconciles present grievances nor forecloses future conflict" (p. 3). They emphasised that for those wanting to engage in the critique of settler-colonialism, that process should always remain discomforting, and all attempts should be made to avoid engaging in the process as a move to innocence, which prematurely relieves feelings of guilt. Moves to innocence are found in "a settler desire to be made innocent, to find some mercy or relief in face of the relentlessness of settler guilt and haunting" (p. 17).

Tuck and Yang (2012) argued that the appropriation of the term decolonisation allows settlers to feel a part of the solution and therefore no longer complicit with the accused—that is, themselves as coloniser. Tuck and Yang acknowledged the discomfort and angst of settlers' experience being beneficiaries of a culture that has benefited from the oppression, assimilation, and erasure of Indigenous peoples (p. 9). They explained that this "misery of guilt makes one hurry toward any reprieve" (p. 9). For Tuck and Yang, claiming to be decolonising is a move to alleviate this guilt and is a hurried and premature movement toward reprieve from settler discomfort. While this work is committed to the importance of processing the discomfort of settler colonialism, it also acknowledges that use of the term decolonisation can serve to alleviate guilt, shed identification with the accused, and present oneself as the hero engaged in the "good" work. It also acknowledges that using the term decolonisation metaphorically may distract from the work of repatriation of Indigenous lands. And as I am focusing on the history of the psychology of colonialism, the process of working to heal, transform, and be accountable for that history, the act of de-colonising does seem to be the most accurate terminology. Thus, as much as possible, the term unsettling or "settler decolonisation" will be used in this book to describe the psychological, emotional, spiritual, cultural, and political process of shedding internal colonial influences for settlers so that they may come into integrity with themselves and devote themselves to true restoration of justice, equality, healing, solidarity, and allyship with Indigenous people and the land. This must come with the acknowledgement that we settlers will never be decolonised, we will always be settler-colonials and the work to mitigate harm and be accountability for it will be a lifelong process. I hope that the qualification of the term settler decolonisation allows for this distinction to be made between it and land back decolonisation processes. There will be times in this work that for ease of language, decolonisation, decolonial, or decolonising will be used, with the understanding that it is referring to this definition of settler decolonisation practices. Even with the use of the term settler decolonisation, I acknowledge the potentiality for it to be a move to innocence as well and am dedicated to continually checking in to mitigate premature attempts to move away from feelings of discomfort while engaged in this work.

The name of Tuck and Yang's article, "Decolonisation is not a metaphor," is unsettling for this work, as this book aims to address settler decolonisation through a metaphoric and mythopoetic lens. Tuck and Yang present a brilliant and challenging approach to the subject that pushes me to be continually aware of how my work may be engaging in moves to innocence. I acknowledge that this book does not directly lead to return of land to Indigenous people; it is solely conscientization, critical consciousness raising, and at best, perhaps a settler harm reduction model. All of these approaches Tuck and Yang identify as possible settler moves to innocence. I am dedicated to continuing to investigate how much of this project is a move to innocence. I encourage you, reader, to also investigate how much of your engagement with the work is an attempted move to innocence as well. This book intends to work toward true justice and integrity. However, I do not see settler integrity as synonymous with settler innocence. Integrity means wholeness and manifests as accountability for all of oneself, including the guilty places within. Integrity also means being responsible and accountable instead of trying to thwart racial discomfort with too quick movements that attempt to shed complicity or relieve oneself of accountability. Perhaps a way to carefully find commensurability between this book's intention and Tuck and Yang's critiques lies in the difference between moves to innocence and moves to integrity. This book's intention is to help move settlers toward integrity, and toward the internal regulation of that integrity while not having them too quickly move away from their feelings of discomfort around the subject of colonialism. The intention of this work is for moves toward integrity and not innocence. This being said, there are fundamental places of incommensurability between Tuck and Yang's article and this work. The discomfort of this incommensurability will continue to be felt, acknowledged, and processed. It can be ventured that Tuck and Yang would agree that wrestling with this incommensurability is itself a necessary part of this process.

History of the Field

Fanon began the process of looking at how colonisation has affected the psyches and unconscious of the colonised. Fanon (1961) wrote, "Imperialism, which today is waging war against a genuine struggle for human liberation, sows seeds of decay here and there that must be mercilessly rooted out from our land and from our minds" (Location 3369). His work brought to light the psychic poison of colonisation and the knowing that to find healing, the colonised must shed the deep burden of colonial psychic chains (Location 271). This book builds on the foundational assumption that it is the moral obligation of white settlers to address the injustices of settler colonialism and work toward both internal and external decolonisation practices today.

West African scholar and healer Malidoma Some (1994) shared that from his perspective, that Westerners are "a people who are ashamed of their ancestors because they were killers and marauders masquerading as artisans of progress" (p. 9). He saw this shame as the explanation for the sick culture of the Westerners. The Dagara, he wrote, believe that it is "the duty of the living to heal their ancestors. If these ancestors are not healed, their sick energy will want the souls and psyches of those who are responsible for helping them" (p. 9). Barbara Esgalhado (2003) also wrote on this theme and advocated that individuals must heal the trauma of their ancestors to bring changes and healing to their culture, and also so that they do not continue to perpetuate the trauma of their ancestors. (p. 483).

Some Indigenous nations share a concept for the settler-colonial disorder: world cannibalism. *Wétiko*, a Cree word that was used for the illness witnessed in European culture, also came to be used by other Indigenous peoples across what is currently known as North America. Other names for this illness include the Ojibway term *Windigo* and the Powhatan term *Wintiko* (Forbes, 2008, p. 37). *Wétiko* translates loosely as cannibal, or "an evil person or spirit who terrorises other creatures by means of terrible evil acts, including cannibalism" (p. 37). Powhatan professor Jack Forbes wrote, "I have come to the conclusion that imperialism and exploitation are forms of Cannibalism" (p. 37). *Wétiko* is thought to be a contagious disconnect from life and the aliveness of the world and causes greed, violence, and an empty hunger and longing for fulfilment (p. 22). Forbes (2008) denounced *Wétiko* as a kind of psychosis that his ancestors recognised in Columbus and his crew and that Forbes recognised in the current North American white settlers (p. 21). He believed *Wétiko* to be a sign of a cultural mental illness because it breeds disconnection and disrespect for other people and other life forms (p. 22). Forbes specified that this kind of cultural disconnect was foreign to his ancestors on Turtle Island before the settlers arrived.

Critical Race Theory

The field of Critical Race Theory and the study of power, privilege, marginalisation, oppression, and race was started by BIPOC and continues today because of them. Critical Race Theory emerged in the mid-1970s to "critically engage the intersection of race and the law and to advocate for fresh, more radical approaches to the pursuit of racial justice" (Schaefer, 2008, p. 344). Later, Critical White Studies (which this research could be considered a part of) evolved from the grounding of Critical Race Theory (p. 345). Hooks (2013) described how when she first started using the term "imperialist white supremacist capitalist patriarchy" to describe the dominant culture we live in, her lecture halls would erupt with laughter (p. 36). She saw this laughter not just as the audience's discomfort with the topic but also "as a way to deflect attention away from the seriousness of this naming" (p. 36). Many BIPOC researching and advocating for these issues were met with this same kind of ridicule hooks faced, and at times, it was far worse than laughter. Many individuals such as Dr. Martin Luther King Jr. died advocating for racial equality. This book is possible because of these thinkers and advocates and their work, the work that they were often persecuted for as they brought it out into the world.

Chapter 3

The Colonial Complex

Figure 3.1 Miss Europe.
Source: Kent Monkman, 2016. Acrylic on canvas, 84" × 132". Image courtesy of the artist.

What Is a Cultural Complex?

Jung (1948/1969) conceptualised complexes as parts of the psyche that were cut off from the greater whole; were unconscious, incompatible with the greater personality; and could be repressed for a short time, but not forever as they carry so much emotional energy and charge (§ 201). He appreciated complexes as the parts of oneself that when tended led oneself back to one's wholeness and the vitality of the unconscious. He called them the "living units" and the royal road to the unconscious (§ 210). All of this meaning that Jung thought that facing the uncomfortable parts of oneself and one's history is what leads to healing (it is the same theory underlying counselling

DOI: 10.4324/9781003296546-3

practices of today). The idea of cultural complexes was developed after Jung and understands cultures as having their own complexes. These cultural complexes are the parts of the collective cultural psyche that are cut-off, repressed, unspoken, and haunt the collective in some way (Singer, 2006, p. 197; Kimbles, 2000, p. 160).

This work understands the colonial complex as a part of the white settler psyche's collective shadow. When parts of the psyche are split off, living untended and unconscious within the shadow, they can wreak havoc on the personality and through the individual or collective. This book hypothesises that this is what happened to the colonial complex within the Western psyche's shadow. We can conceptualise the main aspects of the colonial psyche as the following dysfunctions: (1) its aversion to the dark and veneration of the light; (2) its hyper focus on ascensionism and transcendence at the expense of the corporeal and earthly; (3) its subordination of the body and sexuality; (4) its disconnection and domination of the Earth; and (5) its interruption of one's own connection to passion and the soulful. Conversely, the royal roads this complex can lead us on, to healing, redemption, right action, and back into relationship with the wholeness of the Western psyche, mirror, and counterbalance these five dysfunctions. These include healing and honouring: (1) the potential and importance of the dark to the whole; (2) attaining a balance between the embodied and transcendent; (3) honouring the body and sensuality; (4) the living earth and land; and (5) the importance of one having one's own connection to passion and creativity.

Colonial Complex

In my research, I narrowed in on five traits of colonial consciousness that I came to see as its foundational aspects. These aspects are as follows: (1) a deification of the light and vilification of the dark; (2) a focus on ascension and transcendence at the expense and detriment of that which is embodied, immanent, and mortal; (3) the sublimation of the body and sexuality; (4) a perceived separation and superiority over nature; and (5) a disconnect from a personal experience of passion or the soulful.

In response to these aspects of the colonial complex, this book looks at where alchemy has counterbalancing potentials and where it values: (1) the potential and importance of the dark to the whole; (2) attaining a balance between the embodied and transcendent; (3) the sacredness of the body and sensuality; (4) honouring the living earth and land; (5) and the importance of tending one's own connection to passion and the soulful.

This book is not an attempt to convert people to alchemy. In fact, there would be nothing to convert people to, as alchemy is not a religion. Instead, the research in this book uses the metaphors of alchemy as invitations to think alchemically—that is psychologically and mythically—and imagine into the possibilities of shifts in colonial consciousness. This research will explore alchemy as a historical myth from the Western tradition that can offer a salve for this exposed complex. The hope is that within the storytelling tradition of alchemy, we may find healing for these aching places of colonial disconnect that have caused the world such pain.

Christianity and Colonialism

Christianity has dominated the mythology of the Western world for the last 1,500 years; its narratives, values, myths, and directives have infused and fabricated the composition of Western culture, lives, and deeds. In the *Encyclopaedia of Religion*, it is written that the history of Western Europe is inseparable from Christianity (Pelikan, 2005, p. 1688). While exploring the origins of colonial consciousness in the West, it is imperative to dig into the Christian soil in which it has grown. Hillman wrote that the Christian "denial of soul" affects all European descendants, whether we are Christian, or not (Hillman, 2005, p. 72). Whether we identify as Christian or not, as white European descendants, Christianity impacts the very core of who we are, our beliefs, actions, and histories and must be investigated as such.

I want to make it clear that I am not suggesting that one must turn away from the Christian faith to engage in anticolonial practices. Some of the most fundamental concepts of Christianity encourage generosity, compassion, love, kindness, doing unto others as we would have them do unto us and non-violence. Many of the greatest leaders and activists the world has seen belong to the Christian faith, including Martin Luther King Jr. and Desmond Tutu. There is no doubt of the beauty possible, and experienced by many, in the Christian faith. Christianity also remains the most prevalent religion worldwide, making up 31% of the world's population, which accounts for 2.3 billion Christians as of 2015 (Hackett & McClendon, 2017).

There are many Christian mystics that have honoured the body, the sensual, the connectedness to nature and personal mystical connections to the divine in their lives and teachings. However, for the most part, the dominant Christian paradigm has not honoured these aspects of humanity. Jeremiah Camara said in a speech about his documentary *Holy Hierarchy: The Religious Roots of Racism in America*: "You can't talk about racism without talking about white supremacy. You can't talk about white supremacy without talking about Christianity. They're tied. They're interwoven. And it's the root of racism" (Camara, 2020, § 8). Nonetheless, I do believe that settler decolonisation within the Christian faith is possible, and I think that Christians' participation in this work has the potential to be powerfully reconciliatory and redemptive.

The Bible rarely offers a single narrative. Included within it, and its colonial teachings, there are also the more peaceful teachings that contradict its position on conquering in the name of God. This includes Jesus's Sermon on the Mount (The Beatitudes) in which he requires people to turn swords into ploughshares and adopt a more peaceful approach to their lives. There is also scholarship that views Revelation as being written as a response to Empire, where the one who was victorious was a slain lamb, so victory came out of supposed defeat (Koester, 2009, p. 5): "Worthy is the Lamb that was slaughtered to receive power and wealth and wisdom and might and honour and glory and blessing!" (Revelation 5:12, NSRV). Some argue Revelation is saying that those who were conquered by the Roman Empire were the ones to actually rise victorious in the end (Koester, 2009). This narrative adds a layer of nuance to the idea of Christianity as a main proponent of conquering in the name of God. This research notes that the different translations from Hebrew to Greek to English also vastly affect and filter our understandings of these Christian positions.

All this being acknowledged, it feels necessary to examine how aspects of the colonial complex are rooted in Christianity and how it continues to shape white settlers today. Though at times there are contradictory stances on it, the Bible does not attempt to hide its emphasis on conquering in the name of God as a righteous act. The following are some examples from scripture that are the early seedlings of the conquering aspects of the colonial complex, the growth from which has overtaken the historical narratives of the last millennium and a half and has sowed the seeds of global colonial exploits in the name of the Christian God:

- And should we not be the ones to possess everything that the LORD our God has conquered for our benefit? (Judges 11:23, NSRV)
- You shall conquer every fortified city and every choice city; every good tree you shall fell, all springs of water you shall stop up, and every good piece of land you shall ruin with stones. (2 Kings 3:19, NSRV)
- Whatever is born of God conquers the world. And this is the victory that conquers the world, our faith. Who is it that conquers the world but the one who believes that Jesus is the Son of God? (1 John 5:1, NSRV)
- To everyone who conquers and continues to do my works to the end, I will give authority over the nations; to rule them with an iron rod, as when clay pots are shattered—even as I also received authority from my father. To the one who conquers I will also give the morning star. (Revelation 2:26, NSRV)
- I will keep you from the hour of trial that is coming on the whole world to test the inhabitants of the Earth. I am coming soon; hold fast to what you have, so that no one may seize your crown. If you conquer, I will make you a pillar in the temple of my God; you will never go out of it. I will write on you the name of my God. (Revelation 3:10, NSRV)

These excerpts are examples of the mythology that this research posits contributed to creating the conquering aspects of the colonial complex. They are expressions of an archetypal style of consciousness that Christianity gives to body through its myths and religious principles. The psychology of Christianity and the colonial complex are connected at the archetypal level, as seen through these foundational Biblical excerpts.

A final note before continuing the investigation into the relationship between the colonial complex and Christianity is that some scholars, such as Koester (2009), have argued that Christianity is not in itself inherently colonial but rather that it adopted colonial ideals when Christianity became the religion of the Empire in the fourth century (p. 5). Koester argued that it was at that point that the narrative changed from God aligning with the conquered and marginalised to God Almighty, aligning with the conquerors (p. 12). It is important to acknowledge that scholars such as Koester believed that the roots of Christianity were initially in opposition to Empire and that it was later co-opted by power (p. 14). These scholars argued that it was after the fourth century that the interpretations of passages changed to serve the colonial agenda. St. Augustine's *City of God* and *Confessions* illuminate this idea more clearly. Regardless of where the origins of the colonial ideas stemmed, Christianity has enforced these ideas throughout its longstanding reign and the colonialists who invaded so-called North America used Christianity as a central justification for their conquests. Therefore, the investigation into the colonial elements of the Bible will continue to be explored in this research.

In the following sections, the specifics of the colonial complex will be unravelled as well as the particulars of how Christianity relates to the different aspects of the colonial complex. Within this research, the colonial complex is understood as a destructive psychological ailment and attitude that is characterised by the following five psychological dysfunctions: (1) its aversion to the dark and veneration of the light; (2) its disconnection and domination of the Earth; (3) the subordination of the body and sexuality; (4) the interruption of one's own connection to soul; and (5) its hyper focus on ascensionism and transcendence at the expense of the corporeal and earthly. These last four aspects of the colonial consciousness detailed here mirror the four elements—Earth, Water, Fire, and Air—which will be explored later in this research and will provide the alchemical narrative arc throughout the rest of this study.

Colonial Aversion to Dark and Veneration of the Light

Hillman (2015) emphasised how an inherent part of the white supremacist complex is an aversion to, and fear of, the dark (Location 1741). He argued that this originates from a fear of one's internal darkness which is projected onto that which is—or those who are—dark (Location 1744). Hillman (1986) believed that this inherent aversion to the dark comes from Christian lore, which demonises the darkness as that which is separate from oneself and separate from God: Satan (p. 31). Hillman (2015) described his belief that Western racism may have begun with this moralisation of colour terms. Long before any English-speaking explorer touched the shores of West Africa, fifteenth-century meanings of "black" included: "deeply stained with dirt; soiled; foul; malignant, atrocious, horrible, wicked; disastrous, baneful, sinister" (Location 1626). He explained that when the first English sailors saw people in West Africa, the first word they used to described them was "black" and at once, those people had projected onto them the centuries of Western negative connotations with darkness (Location 1626). Many of these associations originated in the Bible and the Bible's association of dark and black with bad and evil. Hillman explained that before this, Europeans had not yet labelled ethnic groups by skin colour, and so, Europeans had not considered themselves white. It was only upon meeting people in West Africa in 1604 that Europeans began using the word white to describe themselves (Location 1626). Describing themselves as white also flattered themselves with all their own Christian connotations of white as holy, pure, and filled with moral Christian values of goodness.

The first sentences of the Bible highlight this profound moral opposition that was created between light and dark that was seeded in the Bible and has since spread globally its dichotimization throughout the millennia:

> In the beginning when God created the heavens and the Earth, the Earth was a formless void and darkness covered the face of the deep, while a wind from God swept over the face of the waters. Then God said, "Let there be light"; and there was light. And God saw that the light was good; and God separated the light from the darkness. (Genesis 1:1, NRSV)

This dichotomisation of light as good and dark as evil continues throughout the Bible:

> This is the judgment, that the light has come into the world, and people loved darkness rather than light because their deeds were evil. For all who do evil hate the light and do not come to the light, so that their deeds may not be exposed. But those who do what is true come to the light, so that it may be clearly seen that their deeds have been done in God. (John 3:19, NRSV)

In the Christian narrative surrounding good versus evil, colours were quickly woven into its tapestry of extreme dichotomies. White became the symbolic representation of all that was pure, holy, Christian, good, "eternal, unblamed," whereas black became the opposite of white in every way (Hillman, 1986, p. 44). Hillman (1986) elaborated on the consequences of coronating white and denigrating dark: it "promotes missions to benighted natives, the moral justification of slavery, and the identification of dark-hued peoples with brute and bestial nature, dumb, without intelligence (for which modern terms are still borrowed from this topos: 'bright,' 'brilliant' and 'quick')" (p. 45). This moralisation of black and white, dark and light, coloured and contributed to the false justifications of the subsequent generations of slavery and racial genocides (p. 75).

Part of the colonial tactics of assimilation in so-called Canada was converting the Indigenous people to believe in this colour hierarchy and to have them believe that white was good and holy, would get them into heaven and was what they needed to strive toward. Indigenous people of what is now called Canada were thus forcefully taught to move away from their families, communities, culture and all that which they were told would inevitably lead them to the devil and hell. This was preached continuously in residential schools. A quote from a residential school survivor reads: "I just absolutely hated my own parents. Not because I thought they abandoned me; I hated their brown faces" (TRC, 2015b, p. 115). Another residential school survivor from All Saints Residential School in Saskatchewan wrote, "I wanted to be white so bad, and the worst thing I ever did was I was ashamed of my mother, that honourable woman, because she couldn't speak English" (p. 161).

From 1947 to 1996, the Latter-Day Saints church ran the Home Placement Programme, which placed Indigenous children with Mormon families off reserve. Photos were taken during their time with the Mormons to "track the change in the children's skin colour, from dark to light. Indeed, The Book of Mormon specifically teaches that dark-skinned Lamanites (Indians), as they accept Mormon gospel, will turn 'white and delightsome'" (King, 2013, Location 915). At a 1960 church conference, the head of the church celebrated the success of the programme, proclaiming that "Indians were 'fast becoming a white and delightsome people,' and that Indian children in the church's Home Placement Program were 'often lighter than their brothers and sisters in the hogans on the reservation'" (King 2013, Location 915). Of course, there was no truth in these perverse claims, just the seeding and perpetuating of colonial violence.

The severe colonial moralisation of colour deeply influenced colonisation in so-called Canada. Repression of colonials' own connectedness to land/ sexuality/body/soul was already repressed in their unconscious and it too was called evil and dark. Thus, when settlers encountered people still connected to that which they repressed, cultural and physical genocide ensued. Nuns tried to scrub children's skin white in residential schools (TRC, 2015c, pp. 39–42). Children had their pictures taken in Mormon homes to show how the more Christian they became, the whiter and more "delightsome" they became too. Children were taught their families were "savages" and their only way to salvation was to leave their associations with their families and try to become as white as they could.

Instead of seeing the unknown and untended parts of oneself as one's unconscious to be integrated as integral parts of one's wholeness,

Christianity named those parts deep in the recesses of oneself "sin" and decreed that they come from an externalised demonic source. With such a fear of, and disconnection from, one's unconscious, this internalised repression and self-hatred was projected onto people of colour. When one is disconnected from a part of oneself, or disallowed from embracing a part of oneself, there is also an unconscious longing to reconnect and reintegrate with that part of oneself (Jung, 1997, p. 261). As such, I posit that white people may have also experienced an unconscious jealousy of people of colour living outside of the Christian tradition who were more often allowed to connect with nature, the sensual, the earthly in ways that white people were forbidden to. This jealousy may have translated into resentment that exacerbated the judgements of the people allowed to have Earth-based, body-positive spiritualities as "savage." White people were not allowed to have this kind of connection within themselves and had been taught to hate it and think of it as an evil within themselves that must be cleansed. This disconnect and aversion to the shadow profoundly affected white relationship to self, to body, to the Earth itself, and the millions of people of colour that the early colonials met and sought out to physically or spiritually destroy. Thus, I argue that this separation from—and subordination of—the darkness is an inherent part of the colonial complex.

Air: Ascension and Transcendence

In the Bible, the Earth is conceptualised as the waiting ground, the testing ground before the afterlife, where it is determined if one will go to heaven or hell. In this way, the focus of earthly life becomes ascension; it is about living one's life not for life itself but as a testing ground for the afterlife. This focus on the heavenly, the transcendent, the intellectual or rational is the culmination of all of the complexes we have spoken of so far. It allows for the neglect and desecration of the body, the sexual, the feminine, the land, and of embodied soul practices. It is the culmination of all these aspects of colonial complexes we have just reviewed.

This notion of earthly life as solely a precursor to heaven germinates Christian beliefs and is found throughout the Bible:

- Put to death, therefore, whatever in you is earthly: fornication, impurity, passion, evil desire, and greed (which is idolatry). On account of these, the wrath of God is coming on those who are disobedient. (Colossians 3:5, NRSV)
- Do not be afraid; God has come only to test you and to put the fear of him upon you so that you do not sin. (Exodus 20:20, NSRV)
- Let the evil of the wicked come to an end, but establish the righteous, you who test the minds and hearts, O righteous God. God is my shield,

who saves the upright in heart. God is a righteous judge, and a God who has indignation every day. (Psalm 7:9, NSRV)
- Search me, O God, and know my heart; test me and know my thoughts. See if there is any wicked way in me, and lead me in the way everlasting. (Psalm 139: 23, NSRV)
- I the LORD test the mind and search the heart, to give to all according to their ways, according to the fruit of their doings. (Jeremiah 17:23, NSRV)
- Get behind me, Satan! You are a stumbling block to me; for you are setting your mind not on divine things but on human things. (Matthew 16:23, NRSV)

Having our eyes focused upward with fear in our goal of reaching heaven, the West has spent the last millennium and a half forgoing the care of the Earth. With the colonial reading of the Bible directing our gaze skyward and seeing Earth as a place where we are tested by God to gain entry into heaven, we have become disconnected and neglectful of the human and more-than-human beings living on this earthly plane.

This gazing upward also leads to an overemphasis on transcendent preoccupations, hyper-rationalism disconnected from the earthly and pursuits that have been upheld in the West as being more righteous than one's connection to embodiment and tending of the earthly, such as the children, the home, the sickly, and the cooking. The tending of all of these have often been women's vocations while men get to be the upward "rationally" focused ones. Jung (1931/1970) emphasised how this over-inflation of pursuits related to the mind and the heavens has left us disconnected from ourselves, nature and soul: "Hemmed round by rationalistic walls, we are cut off from the eternity of nature. Analytical psychology seeks to break through these walls by digging up again the fantasy-images of the unconscious" (§ 739). This tendency toward ascension leaves the world behind us neglected, despised for holding us back to earthly attachments, and exploited. Hillman (1997) wrote of how this consciousness was embodied in the New World and the harm it caused: "A stain of blood streaks the documents of all America's history from Christian colonial times to the times of contemporary capitalism. The indigenous and environmental disasters, the extinction of languages, customs, songs, insects, birds, plants and animals, the rape" (p. 12). This aspect of colonial consciousness attempts to disassociate from or ignore the harm that colonialism has inflicted on other people, cultures, land and in our own bodies, sensual natures, and the aliveness of this Earth.

Water: Disconnection from Body/Sexuality

Just as it directs us to dominate and subdue the Earth, the Bible would also have us subdue the body. In much of the Bible, the body is seen as an untrustworthy temptation that can lead to the devil and sin. The body itself, as well as sex, was seen as sinful. Nonetheless, the Bible also contains counternarratives that honour the body, as seen in the Song of Solomon and in aspects of Jesus as an embodied spiritual figure working to commune with and heal those who suffer. Despite those glimpses of respect of the body, the overarching message is one of separation and condemnation of the body and sexuality, which this research posits has exacerbated the Western psyche experiencing the trauma of separation from our own soma and sensuality. We can see in the following small selection of biblical passages the aversion to the sexual, and sensual that has inundated the Western psyche:

- Passion makes the bones rot. (Proverbs 14:30, NRSV)
- The heart is devious above all else; it is perverse—who can understand it? (Jeremiah 17:9, NRSV)
- So flesh and blood devise evil. (Sirach 17:3, NRSV)
- For this is the will of God, your sanctification: that you abstain from fornication; that each one of you know how to control your own body in holiness and honour, not with lustful passion, like the Gentiles who do not know God. (Thessalonians 4:3, NRSV)
- So then, with my mind I am a slave to the law of God, but with my flesh I am a slave to the law of sin. (Romans 7:25, NRSV)
- For those who live according to the flesh set their minds on the things of the flesh, but those who live according to the Spirit set their minds on the things of the Spirit. To set the mind on the flesh is death, but to set the mind on the Spirit is life and peace. For this reason the mind that is set on the flesh is hostile to God; it does not submit to God's law—indeed it cannot, and those who are in the flesh cannot please God. (Romans 8:5, NRSV)

Jung wrote that we in the West "suffer very much from the fact that we consist of mind and have lost the body" (Jarrett & Jung, 1988, p. 251). The shaming of the body as sinful, evil, and the devil's domain has created a deep disconnect between Western individuals and their bodies. Sexuality that was not between monogamous, cis-gendered, heterosexual married individuals with the sole aim of procreation was seen as sinful. This has created a deep divide in the Western person's psyche-soma wholeness, their wellbeing, sense of groundedness, pleasure, and sense of being at home in their body, sensuality, sexuality, and consequently, the Earth.

Jung (1918/1970) elucidated some of the consequences of this Western separation from body and instincts. He wrote that if we healed the Christian disconnect from our corporeal, animal nature we would treat life in all forms much better. "If every individual had a better relation to the animal within him, he would also set a higher value on life" (§ 32). He continued that the effects of this shift on the external world would be profoundly positive:

"Life would be the absolute, the supreme moral principle, and he would react instinctively against any in situation or organisation that had the power to destroy life on a large scale" (§ 32). A significant consequence of this disconnect from our bodies, besides the psychological and spiritual harm that it causes, is the lack of advocacy that ensues from it for all living creatures. If we are connected to our own corporeal aliveness, and love and care for it, then we are more connected to the aliveness and animate nature of the world as a whole. Studies show that when we love and are connected to something, we are far more likely to protect and take care of it. Elisabeth Bragg (1996) found that the more connected one feels to nature, the greater is one's "sensitivity to information about the environment, feelings of connectedness or sympathy to environmental entities, and activities that promote the connection" (p. 354). Clayton (2008) explored the concept of the ecological self and how an ecological identity, feeling a part of and connected to the natural world, allows for an "analogy between oneself and other elements of the ecosystem, to the extent that a person might react to threats to nature as if they were threats to themselves. Environmental identity, for example, is associated with greater environmental concern" (Clayton, 2008, p. 354).

Jung wrote of the importance of going "back to the body" and he called for us to "go into the body, and then everything will be right, for there the greatest intelligence is hidden" (Jarrett & Jung, 1988, p. 370). This research posits that the disconnect and aversion to body and sexuality is another foundational aspect of the colonial complex that has had profound consequences. By fracturing even more deeply the Western psyche from its connections to body, sensuality, and this vital part of its soul, this disconnect has also deepened the perceived chasm between it and the aliveness and animacy of the world at large and the *anima mundi* (aliveness of the world) itself.

Earth: Disconnection from Land

Jung wrote frequently of the Western tendency toward disidentification with nature. He wrote in protest of this disconnect: "Do you think that somewhere we are not nature, that we are different from Nature? No, we are in nature and think exactly like nature" (Jarrett & Jung, 1988, p. 1276). In many of his writings, he emphasised the impossibility of humans being distinct from nature and the harm that is caused by the Western perception of nature as subordinate, inanimate and there for our exploitation. Many studies have examined the modern Christian relationship to the natural world. Laski (1961) found that among nonbelievers, nature was the most common trigger for experiences of ecstasy, and among Christians, nature was the third most common trigger. Other studies have shown that "measures of religiosity, such as regular churchgoing, are negatively associated with environmentalism in

America" (Gardner & Stern, 2002; Schultz et al., 2000). This was corroborated by many studies including by Truelove and Joireman (2009) who studied "strong Christian beliefs" and found that "orthodoxy was negatively related to all measures of pro-environmental behaviour."

This does not mean that all Christians inherently care less for nature. Quite to the contrary, some churches emphasise that "nature is God's creation and humans should respect God's work" and that this is an important reason "personally to care about protecting the environment" (Clayton & Myers, 2015, p. 292). As such, many churches and religious organisations are trying to shift Christian care for the environment today by organising projects such as the "National Religious Partnership for the Environment [and] the Evangelical Environmental Network's Declaration for the Care of Creation (signed by over 500 church leaders) and other initiatives" (p. 293).

However, given the Biblical directives and references to nature, the aforementioned studies yield unsurprising results. For the last 1,500 years, the Bible has led the Western relationship to nature in ways that promote a power-over relationship to it. Those who still actively participate in the Christian faith may be most affected by the Biblical attitudes toward nature. However, all those in the West have been shaped by these philosophies and prescribed relationships to land whether we currently identify as Christian or not.

The following are examples of the Bible directing people to have dominion over the Earth: to subdue it and its aliveness (Genesis 1:22, NRSV). This instruction for a power-over relationship of separation and domination with the Earth has left Western culture disconnected from knowing its place as a part of the natural world. The gap that this has left in the Western psyche has been profound and has opened the way for first the obsession with transcendence and now materialism to fill the void that disconnection with the Earth has created (von Franz, 2003, p. 26; Fromm, 1976, p. 34). This research argues that this disconnect from nature and the void that it has created is a foundational aspect of the colonial complex. We can see the seeds of this disconnect take root in Bible verses that instruct us to have dominion over the land and animals and subdue it and that views "earthly" as corrupt and violent:

- Be fruitful and multiply, and fill the Earth and subdue it; and have dominion over the fish of the sea and over the birds of the air and over every living thing that moves upon the Earth. (Genesis 1:22, NRSV)
- The Earth was corrupt in God's sight, and the Earth was filled with violence. And God saw that the Earth was corrupt; for all flesh had corrupted its ways upon the Earth. And God said to Noah, "I have determined to make an end of all flesh, for the Earth is filled with violence because of them; now I am going to destroy them along with the Earth." (Genesis 6:11, NRSV)

After the Milvian Bridge epiphany of Constantine, and the resulting Council of Nicea in 325, the Bible became a reflection of, and tool for, the powers of empire. Hillman (1985) described how these Western worldviews instilled by the Bible have impacted the Western psyche and led to an exploitation of the natural (sometimes referred to as the more-than-human) world: "according to prevailing Western (or Northern) consciousness, the world is merely matter, not alive, and without soul" (p. 4). Hillman wrote of how this Western consciousness is deadening for human psyches and has profoundly negative impacts for the more-than-human world. He argued that the West must now return to a worldview where we see the whole world as animate, alive, and soulful, he called it "returning the soul to the world" (p. 4). Hillman described how this disconnected aspect of Western colonial consciousness has allowed for an exploitation of the natural world. This disconnection from—and perceived superiority over—the natural world is a defining and impactful feature of colonial consciousness which has left its scars around the entirety of this living globe.

Jung (2012) also wrote of the Western disconnect from the Earth, urging us to remember our rootedness and connection to the natural world. These reflections came in part from his valuing of Indigenous cultures and what he understood as their psychological well-being that is based in their relationship to nature (p. 29). He wrote that though there has been a collective desire in the West to escape the Earth and ascend, to shed all earthly desires and attachments, that this idea is not only impossible but also deeply destructive (p. 29). Both Jung and Hillman fervently rejected the notion of humans' superiority over, and separation, from nature; criticise the West's relationship to nature and the global harm it has caused; and advocated for the unquestionable importance of healing the Western soul's relationship to the Earth for the welfare of all life on this planet. Within the Bible, the theme of domination of nature is a prevailing theme. However, there are other biblically supported narratives that foster respect of Earth as God's creation. This being said, studying the Biblical references to the Earth and the West's historical and contemporary relationship to nature, the disconnect from nature proves itself to be a fundamental aspect of the colonial complex that will continued to be addressed in this work.

Fire: Disconnection from Passion and Soul

So far, the colonial aspects that relate to disconnect from Earth, sensuality and the body have been discussed. But another aspect of this colonial disconnect is its disconnect from one's own experience of soul—by which is meant the sense of being filled with the vitality of stories, myth, dreams, the creation, and expression of images from the psyche, of creative soulful expression and one's own connection to a sense of sacred in life. It is the sense of being fully, truly alive through whatever medium resonates with us.

This can be a secular, spiritual, or religious experience. Jung (1952/1967) believed that this connection to one's own inner images, aliveness, and creative soul is one's birthright (§ 631; Jarrett & Jung, 1988, p. 667). However, in the Christian tradition, this inner vitality at times has been chastised and repressed as frivolous, sinful and fleshy. Within the Catholic tradition, confessing to God or being in relationship with God must be conducted through a priest, through the church itself, rather than through one's own inner connection to the sacred. Jung (1976) wrote that the church mitigates the full "primordial experience" of contact with the sacred because it claims that the experience is too "over-powering" and instead that connecting through the divine must be mediated between an individual and the clergy, which is mediated by the Holy Spirit, to Jesus, to God (p. 424). This separation between an individual and soulfulness is another layer of disconnect and woundedness within the colonial psyche that distances us from the sacred and experience of wholeness and vitality.

Of course, there are Christian sects and denominations, as well as certain saints and mystics, that have emphasised the importance of, and possibility of, a personal connectedness and mystical connection to Jesus and God. However, over the last 1,500 years, the dominant Christian paradigm seems to have generally encouraged this connection be facilitated and channelled through the Church and its clergy.

Hillman (2005) described this moving away from soul in the Christian tradition as "the turn away from sleep and dreams, away from nature and community, away from personal and ancestral history and polytheistic complexity" (p. 78). Hillman wrote that at the council of Nicaea what is now known as Turkey in 787 CE, images were "deprived of their inherent authenticity," and that it was at that moment in the West that "the soul lost its dominion" (p. 71). Hillman continued that it was then that "our anthropology, our idea of human nature, devolved from a tripartite cosmos of spirit, soul, and body (or matter), to a dualism of spirit (or mind) and body (or matter)" (p. 71). Hillman believed that this split between spirit and soul, and the West losing its relationship to soul, stems from the Christian faith, and since those early councils decided what would be included in the Christian mythos, we have been deprived of the "realm of images and the power of imagination—from which we were exiled by theological, spiritual men more than a thousand years ago" (p. 71). Hillman concluded that these early councils deluded the future of the Christian church and "are responsible for the malnourished root of our Western psychological culture and of the culture of each of our souls" (p. 72).

Throughout the Bible, we can find passages that stoked the flames of this separation between the individual and their personal and embodied relationship to the soulful and their connection to the sacred now having to be mediated between them and the church:

- You shall bring it to the priest, and the priest shall scoop up a handful of it as its memorial portion, and turn this into smoke on the altar, with the offerings by fire to the LORD; it is a sin offering. Thus the priest shall make atonement on your behalf. (Leviticus 5:12, NRSV)
- Jesus said to them again, "Peace be with you. As the Father has sent me, so I send you." When he had said this, he breathed on them and said to them, "Receive the Holy Spirit. If you forgive the sins of any, they are forgiven them; if you retain the sins of any, they are retained." (John 20:21, NSRV).

In the aforementioned quote, Jesus gave the apostles, those who would found the church and transmit their power to the church's clergy, the power to forgive sin and the power to refrain from giving forgiveness so that those individuals retain their sin. This idea became reinforced in the fourth century teachings and beyond. In the Reformation (1517–1648), this was one of the key points that Martin Luther advocated for: that no intermediary was needed between a person and God.

In the first century, Ignatius of Antioch wrote of the hierarchy in the church, who had the most access to God, and thus, who were the most pure and free of sin as a result of their associated closeness to God:

- Take care to do all things in harmony with God, with the bishop presiding in the place of God, and with the presbyters in the place of the council of the apostles, and with the deacons, who are most dear to me, entrusted with the business of Jesus Christ. (Jurgens, 1970, p. 19)
- He that is within the sanctuary is pure; but he that is outside the sanctuary is not pure. In other words, anyone who acts without the bishop and the presbytery and the deacons does not have a clear conscience. (p. 21)

Hillman (2005) wrote that all those in the West, whether they identify as Christian or not, have been affected by Christianity's denial of soul and personal disconnection from the sacred. Hillman believed that this denial of soul has deeply affected our collective Western psyche (p. 72). He wrote that there is "a latent Christianity, an antisoul spirituality, in our Western soul. This has led eventually to a psychological disorientation" (p. 72). Hillman emphasised Jung's important role in trying to restore the Western soul to the collective and individuals' relationship to it; he acknowledged "Jung's part in prying loose the dead fingers of those dignitaries in old Turkey (at the council of Nicaea), both by restoring the soul as a primary experience and field of work and by showing us ways—particularly through images—of realising that soul" (p. 72).

Jung (1955–56/1970) wrote of the deep dysfunction and psychic ails of those disconnected from their soulfulness: "So long as he knows that he is the carrier of life and that it is therefore important for him to live, then the mystery of his soul lives also" (§ 201). Jung continued that if someone does not see the meaning of their life or its fulfilment and "no longer believes in man's eternal right to this fulfilment, then he has betrayed and lost his soul, substituting for it a madness which leads to destruction, as our time demonstrates all too clearly" (§ 201). This estrangement from one's embodied soulfulness is a fundamental aspect of colonial consciousness and impacts greatly the Western psyche, its connection to the sacred and has a detrimental effect on psychological wellbeing. This connection to soulfulness for an individual may look like the joy of gardening, writing, dancing, making or listening to music, cooking, loving, or any number of activities that fill one with a sense of aliveness, meaningfulness, peace, or joy.

Summary of the Colonial Complex

Colonial Disconnect from:	Description	Psychic Effects	Global, Historical Effects
Darkness	Valuing light over dark, naming light: good; and dark: bad.	Disconnect from, and repression of, personal and collective unconscious or "shadow"	Colonial fear of others who settlers project their unconscious onto and direct oppression and violence toward. Settler dissatisfaction living a life cut-off from this aspect of themselves.
Air: Personal Embodied Spirituality	Seeing Earth as a testing ground before heaven or hell. Earth not as end goal. Not having a balanced embodied relationship between transcendence and embodiment.	Disconnect from a healthy relationship to spirit and instead either an escapist relationship to spirit that must be channelled through the church. Or a secular focus only on pursuits of the mind and a disembodied experience of the world.	The disrespect of the earthly, exploitation of land, people, and degradation of the environment.

Colonial Disconnect from:	Description	Psychic Effects	Global, Historical Effects
Water: Body/ Sensuality	Disconnect from an embodied, sensual experience of oneself and the world; disconnected from the joys and freedoms of body, identity, gender sexuality and sensuality. As well as disconnection from experiencing the world and existence through the senses and instead only through the mind.	Sense of rootlessness, psychic void created by alienation from body and sensuality, a rigidity, harshness, callousness to the world created by sensual alienation, dissatisfaction, and repression.	Oppression of one's own body, and the oppression of bodies of people around the world (oppression, genocides, and slavery). The condemnation and forbidding of other cultures' expression of sexuality.
Earth: Nature	Disconnect from land, dominating and subduing land and nature and the more-than-human world.	Material hunger to fill the void of the disconnection from matter and Earth, leading to a culture of consumerism.	Degradation of land, global pollution, exploitation of resources.
Fire: Passion	Disconnect from soul, passion, creativity, and love for the world.	Feeling of numbness, deadening, emptiness, lack of creativity, joy, creative engagement, and aliveness in the world.	Consumerism leading to destruction of the planet as a result of lack of true embodiment and caretaking of the planet.

Chapter 4

Historical Manifestations of the Colonial Complex in So-Called Canada

Figure 4.1 The Scream.

Source: Kent Monkman, 2017. Acrylic on canvas, 84" × 126". Collection of the Denver Art Museum. Image courtesy of the artist.

Scattered Shells: A timeline of how colonial Canada broke the agreement made in the Two Row Wampum Belt Treaty, and how colonial consciousness and actions have impacted the Indigenous people of what is now known as Canada over the last half a millennium.

Before looking further at the colonial complex and its relationship to alchemy, or what can be done about the colonial complex today, it feels necessary to provide a brief overview of the harm the colonial complex has perpetrated in so-called Canada. The following timeline shows how

DOI: 10.4324/9781003296546-4

colonial consciousness has manifested in what is now known as Canada in an attempt to ground the theory and show the real and devastating impacts colonialism has had on the lives of millions of Indigenous people in so-called Canada. It is impossible on these pages to convey the immense suffering that colonialism has inflicted on these lands, nor is this a complete account of the historical events that have defined this era. Rather, this outline traces just some of the defining moments that illustrate how colonial consciousness has impacted Indigenous people over the last 500 years. This is not an extensive list of the actions of colonial forces in so-called Canada, only a rough sketch, leaving barren the gaping holes of the millions of individual lives affected by colonialism in this time. See King's (2013) *The Inconvenient Indian* for an example of a more comprehensive account. I would be remiss if I did not acknowledge that tracing the map of this time in such a linear way is a very colonial way of conveying the horrors of this period, which carry on to this day. This is no way to make sense of it, and its effects are not linear or logical.

This is a deeply painful timeline; it also reflects what Canadian settlers must honestly confront if we have the slightest chance of participating positively and aiding as allies in the creation of a more just future for the Indigenous people of this land and those who were enslaved and brought to so-called North America against their will. We must face the facts outlined in this timeline before we can start to tend all the wounds that colonialism has inflicted on what is now known as North America, Indigenous people, and on the souls and morality of colonial settlers themselves.

For the most part, this timeline follows the events of colonial Canada over the last 500 years, although some historical dates in the rest of the so-called Americas are included as well to give context of parallel events.

Included in this timeline are details of individual lives that were affected by these colonial exploits. In no way do these few strands of stories encompass the extent of the personal and collective damage and harm inflicted during this time. There are millions more individual stories and lives that could be recounted and honoured here. Included here are just a few mentions of individuals' lives as reminders of the humanity affected here. These are not just numbers or statistics—they are lives, over and over again affected by the actions of the colonial psyche.

The following are some of the main points in the fraught story of colonialism in so-called Canada. These events are the pivot points, the experiences, and the history that have shaped and still haunt the Canadian psyche. These events have forged this nation and continue to live on through and within us. This history is the *prima materia*, primary material of the Canadian psyche. While reading the following timeline, one can look out for the historical manifestation of the five main components of the colonial psyche detailed in the previous chapter: (1) its aversion to the dark and veneration of the light, one of many examples included in the timeline being the taking and placing of Indigenous children with Mormon families in the hopes that the Indigenous children would be saved from their savage ways and that their skin would reflect this salvation by turning from dark to "white and delightsome" (King, 2013, Location 915); (2) the colonial psyche's disconnection and domination of the Earth, for example: the Dominion Lands Act of 1872, where Indigenous people were forced off of their lands and the lands were given for free in 40-acre parcels to settlers from Europe to clear and cultivate (LHF, 2014); (3) the subordination of the body and sexuality, an example being the rape and murder of Indigenous women and girls that continues today. Today, Indigenous women and girls are 12 times more likely to be murdered or missing than any other women in Canada (NIMMIWG, 2019, p. 7); (4) the interruption and distortion of the colonial psyche's connection to soul and morality, for example, a minimum of 37,951 cases of physical and sexual abuse that were inflicted on Indigenous children in the Christian-run Indian Residential Schools by their abusive priests and nuns (TRC, 2015c, p. 125); (5) finally, its hyper focus on ascensionism and transcendence at the expense of the corporeal and Earthly, one of many examples being the extensive medical experimentation that was inflicted on Indigenous children that involved them being malnourished, abused, and sometimes dying in the name of furthering colonial research and knowledge with complete disregard for human lives (Hardy v. Canada, 2018, p. 14). Throughout this narrative, we can see many other examples of how these dysfunctions were embodied in this history and the horror they wreaked in their societal manifestation. Also keep watch in this timeline for the distorted mythic longings that we can imagine propelling the destructive actions within it, looking for cities of gold, fountains of youth, "New Worlds" etc.

Timeline

1492–1493: Christopher Columbus attempts to sail to Asia, and instead comes upon land that would later be known as the Americas. At the time of his voyage, he believed that he had reached the East Indies (Kelly, 2019).

1493: Papal Bulls: The Papal Bulls of 1493 and 1494 are sometimes referred to as the "Bulls of Donation." They represent four bulls that Pope Alexander decreed, all concerning Spain's "claim to the Americas." The first bull, the Inter Caetera Divinae, gave Spain ownership of any lands they found that were not already governed by Christian powers, as long as the Spanish then converted the Indigenous people of the land to Christianity. The next three bulls supported Spain's claim and further defined details of Spain's land ownership of the Americas (TRC, 2015a, p. 16).

1493: Doctrine of Discovery: With the Papal Bulls came the Doctrine of Discovery, which stated that if there were not Christians occupying the land or "European-style agriculture" being conducted, then that land could be considered "no one's land," "Terra Nullius," and was free to be claimed by those who "discovered" it. According to this doctrine, Indigenous presence on the land did not "void a claim of terra nullius" as they were seen as only occupying rather than owning the land (TRC, 2015a, p. 17).

1513: Spanish conquistador Juan Ponce de León found and named Florida. Legend has it that he was trying to discover the Fountain of Youth (Kelly, 2019).

1513: Twenty-one years after Columbus first landed on an island that he had renamed Hispaniola in the Caribbean, the population of the island had been decimated. On Hispaniola, "nearly 8,000,000 people—those Columbus chose to call Indians—had been killed by violence, disease, and despair" (Stannard, 1993, p. 21).

1534–1536: Álvar Núñez Cabeza de Vaca, a Spanish explorer, was on a mission to find the "Seven Cities of Gold" and believed they were located in New Mexico (Kelly, 2019).

1613: Two-Row Wampum Treaty was made between the Haudenosaunee, the people of the land whose territory spreads throughout what is now called Ontario, Quebec and New York, and the Dutch. This treaty is represented by a Wampum belt, a belt made of tiny white shells with two purple bands running parallel along it. This treaty "is understood by the Haudenosaunee as the basis on which all subsequent treaties were made and as a model of relationships between peoples" (Mackey, 2016, p. 157). The following is the Haudenosaunee reply to the treaty proposal and their terms in the agreement:

> You say that you are our Father and I am your son. We say, We will not be like Father and Son, but like Brothers. This wampum belt confirms our words. These two rows will symbolize two paths or two vessels, traveling down the same river together. One, a birch bark canoe, will be for the Indian People, their laws, their customs and their ways. The other, a ship, will be for the white people and their laws, their customs and their ways. We shall each travel the river together, side by side, but in our boat. Neither of us will make compulsory laws nor interfere in the internal affairs of the other. Neither of us will try to steer the other's vessel. (Mackey, 2016, p. 157)

1620: Earliest missionary school: The first residential school for Indigenous children founded outside of Québec City (LHF, 2014).

1629–1834: Enslavement of Black and Indigenous people in Canada: Thousands of Indigenous and Black African people were enslaved in Canada. Enslaving people of colour continued until 1834 in Canada, when it became illegal throughout British North America and the British Empire (Glover & Cooper, 2020).

1688: Scalp Bounties: The governor of Canada offered ten beaver skins in exchange for any enemy Indian scalp (Nichols, 1986, p. 59).

1696: The British government in 1696 declared a six-pound reward for Christians who killed an Indian (Nichols, 1986, p. 59).

1704: Scalp bounty laws were changed to be graduated based on age and sex: "men or youths capable of bearing armes' were worth £100; women and children ten years and above, only £10; and no reward was given for killing children under ten years" (Nichols, 1986, p. 59).

1739: Harman Verelst, an advocate for the colonisation of North America, wrote that "this Right arising from the first discovery is the first and fundamental Right of all European Nations, as to their Claim of Lands in America" (TRC, 2015a, p. 17).

1749: Scalp Proclamation of 1749: In Nova Scotia, a scalp proclamation is released, with the intent to clear the land of all Mi'kmaq. Bounties were issued as rewards for Mi'kmaq scalps.

> His Majesty's Council do hereby authorize and command all Officers Civil and Military ... to annoy, distress, take or destroy the Savage commonly called Micmac wherever they are found ... (and) do promise a reward of 10 Guineas for every Indian taken or killed, to be paid upon producing such Savage taken or his scalp (as is the case of America) if killed, to the Officers commanding at Halifax, Annapolis Royal or Minas. (Boileau, 2016, p. 10)

1763: The Royal Proclamation: British government issued the royal proclamation. Its intention was to keep the commitment made by the British government and Aboriginal allies during the Seven Years' War to slow and control the "colonial expansion into Aboriginal land" (TRC, 2015a, p. 53). In the Royal Proclamation, the King recognised the harms and abuses that had been done to First Nations in the colonial land expansion: "Great Frauds and Abuses have been committed in purchasing Lands of the Indians, to the great Prejudice of our Interests and to the great Dissatisfaction of the said Indians" (p. 53). The proclamation declared that colonial settlement was banned from Indigenous lands that had not already been sold or ceded to the British Crown. The proclamation was meant to protect First Nations land from the trend of being continually taken over by colonial forces at an expanding rate. The proclamation declared that from then on, exchange or transfer of First Nations land would require a formal treaty process. This proclamation recognised that the land belonged to First Nations people until they agreed to sell it to the British crown. In effect, the proclamation made void the claim of Terra Nullius as it recognised that the land belonged to the First Nations people until otherwise agreed upon (TRC, 2015a, p. 53).

1763: At Fort Pitt in Philadelphia, during the French and Indian War, a negotiation took place between local Native Americans and the British. After the parley, the Native Americans asked for provisions for their travel back home that night. "Out of our regard to them," wrote William Trent, "we gave them two Blankets and an Handkerchief out of the Small Pox Hospital. I hope it will have the desired effect" (Fenn, 2000, p. 1554). Commander in Chief of British forces Sir Jeffrey Amherst wrote to his subordinate Col. Henry Bouquet, who was stationed on the western front of the war: "Could it not be contrived to Send the Small Pox among those Disaffected Tribes of Indians. We must, on this occasion. Use Every Stratagem in our power to Reduce them" (p. 1556). Bouquet replied in his letter to Amherst: "I will try to inocculate the Indians by means of Blankets that may fall in their hands, taking care however not to get the disease myself" (p. 1556). Amherst replied approvingly in a letter to Col. Bouquet: "You will Do well to try to Innoculate the Indians by means of Blanketts, as well as to try Every other method that can serve to Extirpate this Execreble Race" (p. 1556).

1764: New Two Row Wampum Belt Treaty: Copies of the Royal Proclamation were distributed to First Nations and First Nations leaders were invited to a meeting in Niagara in the summer of 1764 (TRC, 2015a, p. 54). That meeting was attended by chiefs from 24 nations. At the meeting, Johnson presented gifts to the chiefs, read the Royal Proclamation, "then invited them to enter into a Treaty that would be symbolised by the presentation of a wampum belt, the traditional belt of shell beads used to commemorate Treaties and other significant events" (p. 54). The First Nations chiefs and their communities understood this ceremony along with the Royal Proclamation as constituting an agreement between First Nations people and the Canadian and British governments recognising the right of First Nations to self-govern (p. 54).

1778: Vancouver and Cook sailed into Yuquot, which they renamed Friendly Cove. This is the first time English sailors came on shore of what is now called British Columbia (Cook, 2003, p. 449).

1815–1912: In these 97 years, 2.5 million people emigrated from the British Isles (TRC, 2015, p. 13).

1830 to 1840: In the ten years between 1830 and 1840, immigration from Europe to North America rose by 40% (TRC, 2015, p. 13).

1833: Slavery was abolished throughout the British Empire (Henry, 2015, §2).

1834: Slavery was abolished throughout British North America (Glover & Cooper, 2020).

1845: Manifest Destiny was declared, which proclaimed that it was America's right and destiny to expand over and claim all of North America (Robinson, 2019, §1). The concept of Manifest Destiny also became a part of Canadian philosophy and encouraged Canadian expansion westward and northward (Robinson, 2019, §7). With the belief in Manifest Destiny, the colonial "destiny" of expansionism superseded any Indigenous rights and helped colonial powers rationalise the harm being done to Indigenous people in the name of Manifest Destiny (Robinson, 2019, §7 and 8).

1850: The Haida Gwaii gold rush in what is now called British Columbia began (TRC, 2015a, p. 98).

1857: The Gradual Civilisation Act was passed, which called for policies to gradually assimilate Indigenous people to colonial society. The act required that all Indigenous males over 21 who could read and write in English or French renounce their treaty rights and Indian Status and assimilate into colonial society (LHF, 2014).

1858: The Fraser River gold rush brought thousands of colonial settlers over from Europe to British Columbia in their search for gold. "The miners and prospectors had little respect for Aboriginal people or their rights and sought to separate them from their land" (TRC, 2015a, p. 98).

1864: During the Chilcotin war in central British Columbia, five Tsilhqot'in chiefs were invited by colonial officials to meet for peace talks and upon arrival were hanged. The following year, a sixth Tsilhqot'in chief was executed (Smart, 2018).

1865: Slavery was abolished in the United States

1867: Canada came into being through the Constitution Act (LHF, 2014). The federal government now claimed "responsibility" for all "Indians and lands reserved for Indians" (Wilson, 2018, p. 66).

1872: The Dominion Lands Act invited Europeans to settle in Canada and promised 160 acres of land to any settler who would cultivate at least 40 of their gifted acres of land and build a homestead for themselves (LHF, 2014).

1876: The Indian Act is enacted throughout Canada. It established who the Canadian government deemed Indian, what lands were Indian lands, and what legal rights Indians had (LHF, 2014). "The Indian Act became law, and Indigenous governance systems were replaced with elected or appointed Band Councils. Women were not allowed to participate" (Wilson, 2018, p. 66). The act became a tool through which reserves were "drastically reduced in size or relocated" (TRC, 2015a, p. 110). The relocation of reserve land has been an incredibly harmful act of colonialism, separating Nations, communities and people from their ancestral and traditional land and limiting opportunities for self-reliance and livelihoods, being separated from ways of being on the land that sustained them physically (rivers for fishing, gathering places, territory near caribou or moose) and spiritually (Kimmerer, 2015).

1876: Custer's Last Stand or The Battle of the Little Bighorn: George Armstrong Custer led the Seventh Cavalry against Crazy Horse, Sitting Bull and Gall, who led the Lakota and Northern Cheyenne. "Five companies under Custer's command—258 soldiers—were wiped out, along with 7 civilians and 3 Arikara scouts. There were never any figures on Northern Cheyenne and Lakota casualties" (King, 2013, Location 262).

1879: The Davin Report is released in Canada recommending "the creation of a system of industrial schools where children are intentionally separated from their parents to reduce the influence of the 'wigwam'" (LHF, 2014). Residential schools become mandatory for Indigenous children and they were forcibly removed from their homes and communities. Those who tried to hide or keep children from attendance of the schools could be jailed (Wilson, 2018, p. 66).

1883: "When the school is on the reserve, the child lives with its parents, who are savages, and through he may learn to read and write, his habits and training mode of thought are Indian. He is simply a savage who can read and write"—John A. Macdonald, Canada's first prime minister, is still the face on the Canadian 10-dollar bill (Pilling, 2020, §1).

1884–1951: Ceremonies banned: An amendment to the Indian Act was made which prohibited by law potlatches and other traditional First Nations ceremonies (Collison, Bee, & Neel, 2019, p. 7). People were arrested for taking part in ceremonies and ceremonial sacred items and regalia were seized and taken by the police (Wilson, 2018, p. 66). Many of these items were then sold and can now be found in collections around the world.

1885: North-West Rebellion: First Nations and Métis rebel and fight for land and treaty rights in Saskatchewan against the oppression of colonial forces. Louis Riel is hung, Poundmaker, Big Bear and others are imprisoned (LHF, 2014).

1886: After tuberculosis was introduced to the Qu'Appelle Reserve around 1880, it devastated the population and led to "one of the highest tuberculosis death rates ever recorded" in the world (TRC, 2015a, p. 384). In 1886, the death rate for tuberculosis on Qu'Appelle Reserve was "9,000 deaths per 100,000 people" (p. 384).

1889: First official allegations of physical and sexual abuse at a residential school were made. As of 1889, The Canadian government had been officially aware of the abuse taking place in residential schools. Regardless, the schools continued for another 107 years (LHF, 2014).

1892: Canadian government and Christian churches make a formal agreement for churches to operate the Indian Residential Schools (LHF, 2014).

1892: Lieutenant Richard Pratt in Florida wrote in response to the sentiment of the time "the only good Indian is a dead one," which "I agree with the sentiment, but only in this: that all the Indian there is in the race should be dead. Kill the Indian in him, and save the man" (TRC, 2015a, p. 137).

1900: Through the colonial mass immigration to North America, by 1900 only one third of the English-speaking people of the world remained in Europe (TRC, 2015a, p. 13).

1903: A letter was sent to the Presbyterian Church by missionary W.S. Moore, who had visited the Regina industrial school in Saskatchewan and been disturbed by what he had seen. He wrote of a young child there who after "having been shut in a room for running away, had tried to hang herself. Her teacher was able to save her; however, he then gave her a revolver and told her to shoot herself. She pulled the trigger, only to discover it was not loaded" (TRC, 2015a, p. 527).

1906: An amendment is made to the Indian Act that limits the growth of reserves. Now, "Aboriginal peoples can be removed from reserves located near or within towns of more than 8,000 inhabitants" (LHF, 2014).

1908: Over a period of three months, 31 children in a residential school in Chapleau, Ontario die (TRC, 2015a, p. 400).

1911: "For a period of one year and after the date hereof the landing in Canada shall be and the same is prohibited of any immigrants belonging to the Negro race, which race is deemed unsuitable to the climate and requirements of Canada"—Wilfred Laurier, Canada's seventh prime minister, who continues to be the face of the Canadian five-dollar bill today (Pilling, 2020, §2).

1912: A study shows that 30% of the students in United States Indian boarding schools had trachoma, a disease which when left untreated often led to blindness. In Oklahoma, 70% of the children in the Indian boarding schools had trachoma. An inspector of the schools in 1912, William J. McConnell, noted, "of the seventy-three students sent to boarding schools from the Wind River Reservation in Wyoming between 1881 and 1894, only twenty-six were still alive in 1899. The rest, almost two-thirds, had died in school or shortly after being discharged." McConnell wrote a letter shortly after his inspection to the Department of the Interior in which he wrote: "The word 'murder' is a terrible word, but we are little less than murderers if we follow the course we are now following after the attention of those in charge has been called to its fatal results" (TRC, 2015a, p. 140).

1914: Deputy superintendent of the Department of Indian Affairs Duncan Campbell Scott, who advocated for compulsory attendance of Residential Schools, wrote: "fifty per cent of the children who passed through these schools did not live to benefit from the education which they had received therein" (TRC, 2015a, p. 375).

1918–1951: Between 1918 and 1951, reserve lands were taken from First Nations by the Canadian government without their consent (Wilson, 2018, p. 66).

1920: Residential School Made Mandatory: Duncan Campbell Scott created the national policy that attendance of Indian Residential School was mandatory for all First Nation children between 7 and 15 years old (LHF, 2014). Scott said of this policy: "our object is to continue until there is not a single Indian in Canada that has not been absorbed into the body politic" (TRC, 2015a, p. 4). Scott also said: "the goal of the Indian Residential School is to 'kill the Indian in the child'" (Cull et al., 2018, p. 42).

1922: A National Crime: Chief Medical Officer for Indian Affairs Doctor Peter Bryce published an article titled "A National Crime," concerning the abhorrent treatment of Indigenous people on reserves and in residential schools (LHF, 2014). He detailed the health conditions he had observed and included the letters he had sent appealing to various Canadian government officials to institute changes, as well as their denial of these changes that eventually led them to forcibly retire him. One of the statistics he gave in this report was that in a study of residential school students, 93% of those tested had tuberculosis (Bryce, 1922, p. 14). Dr. Bryce believed that the conditions in these schools were criminal. He reported that of the students who attended the Residential School on the File Hill Reserve, "75 per cent [of children] were dead at the end of the 16 years since the school opened" (Bryce, 1922, p. 4).

1927–1951: Prohibitions added to Indian Act: First Nations people cannot hire legal assistance or solicit funds for legal claims without permission from the Canadian government: "Status Indians barred from seeking legal advice, fundraising, or meeting in groups" (Wilson, 2018, p. 67).

1927: Nineteen boys died at the Beauval Residential School in Saskatchewan because they were trapped in the school during a fire (TRC, 2015c, p. 3).

1930: In Cross Lake Manitoba, 12 children died as the residential school burned down. There were inadequate fire escapes, and the children were not able to escape the burning building (TRC, 2015c, p. 3).

1939: "We must keep this part of the Continent free from unrest and from too great an intermixture of foreign strains of blood, as much the same thing as lies at the basis of the Oriental problem. I fear we would have riots if we agreed to a policy that admitted numbers of Jews."—W.L. Mackenzie King, Canada's tenth Prime Minister. In 1939, Canada refused entry to the passenger ship MS St. Louis that held 900 Jewish refugees. Canada sent them away, as did Cuba and the United States. The ship was forced to return to Europe and many of its passengers were killed in concentration camps (Pilling, 2020, §3).

1941: Four students ran away from the residential school in Fort Albany, Ontario. They never made it home, and their bodies were never recovered (TRC, 2015c, p. 3).

1942–1952: Nutrition research and human biomedical experimentation were conducted in residential schools and Indigenous communities across Canada. These experiments were in cooperation with the federal government and did not have consent from the participants or their parents (Mosby, 2013, p. 145).

1942: Medical experimentation relating to malnourishment and vitamins: Research was conducted after scientists discovered astonishing rates of malnutrition in northern Indigenous communities. The scientists wanted to study the effects of malnutrition on the body and whether vitamins alone could improve the conditions of malnourishment. They used a group of 300 malnourished Indigenous test subjects in Cross Lake over a two-year period, and 125 of them were given vitamins. Over the two years, no emergency care or additional food was provided to any of the test subjects who were in extreme states of malnourishment (Mosby, 2013, p. 151).

1945–1981: Medical experimentation on Indigenous children in Indian hospitals across Canada was occurring which included; failure to give antibiotics to Indigenous children for tuberculosis while antibiotics were being used for non-Indigenous people; medically unnecessary restraints were being used for Indigenous children in hospitals, which included at times tying children to their bed or unnecessarily keeping them in full body casts at times for months, at other times years; and there was sexual, physical, and emotional abuse of children in those Indian hospitals (Hardy v. Canada, 2018, p. 14).

1947–1996: Many Indigenous children from what is now called North America were taken and placed with Mormon families off reserve in a programme called The Home Placement Programme. Photos were taken of these children to track what the Mormons hoped would be the changing skin colour of the children from dark to light as their sins were erased living a Christian life. They believed the children would soon become "white and delightsome" (King, 2013, Location 915).

1948: Medical research and experimentation conducted by Pett on the effects of malnutrition on 1,000 students in residential schools across Canada (Mosby, 2013, p. 161). Students were intentionally fed diets known to be deficient in calories and nutrients for a period of five years to study the effects of malnutrition (p. 161).

1952: Research published named: "Development of Anemia on Newfoundland Enriched Flour," a five-year study done at a residential school studying the effects of "vitamin—and mineral-fortified flour" fed to children (Mosby, 2013, p. 164). Tests on the children who were fed the experimental flour show "their blood haemoglobin levels decline" compared to the control school where the experimental flour was not being fed to the children (p. 164). This study was able to be conducted because of Pett's access to a test population in the residential schools that were "chronically malnourished and vulnerable children who, as wards of the state, had little say in whether or not they participated in the study" (p. 164). This experiment required that the students both in the experimental residential school and the control residential school were "fed, for anywhere between two and five years, diets known to be nutritionally inadequate or, for that matter, that they were being actively denied certain types of dental care for the duration of the study" (p. 164).

1940s and 1950s: Residential schools were implemented in Northern Canada for Inuit children (LHF, 2014).

1951: Revisions to the Indian Act were made which included the removal of prohibitions on First Nations clothing, regalia and ceremony. First

Nations people could now organise politically and culturally and seek legal counsel. Women were only now permitted to participate in band democracy (LHF, 2014; Wilson, 2018, p. 67).

1951–1980: Sixties Scoop: Amendments to the Indian act gave provinces jurisdiction over child welfare acts, provinces were allowed to take Indigenous children and infants without informing parents or communities and, without their consent, placed the children in non-Indigenous homes. Current research estimates 20,000 Indigenous children were taken from their homes and placed in non-Indigenous families, some in Canada and some adopted out to other countries, between 1960 and 1990. This was a continuation of assimilationist policy as residential schools were beginning to be phased out. However, the taking of Indigenous children from their families and communities without consent and raising them in white culture mirrored the trauma of residential schools (Gallant, 2019).

1956: At the residential school in Sioux Lookout, two boys tried to run away to return home. "The principal waited a month before reporting that they were missing. They were never found" (TRC, 2015c, p. 3).

1958: Indian Affairs regional inspectors recommended the federal closure and abolition of Indian Residential Schools in Canada (LHF, 2014).

1960: There were still 60 residential schools in operation across Canada (LHF, 2014).

1961: Indigenous people across Canada enfranchised. For the first time, Indigenous people could vote without having to give up their Indian status (LHF, 2014).

1969: The White Paper: a paper comprising of assimilationist policy that moved toward terminating Indian Status and assimilating Indigenous people into Canadian political status, by gradually removing Indian status, land treaties and rights (TRC, 2015a, p. 4).

1969: The federal government took over operation of residential schools from the churches (LHF, 2014).

1990: A resistance formed amongst the Mohawk Nation against the Canadian government, its police and military, in Oka, Quebec. The Oka Crisis lasted six months (LHF, 2014). The Mohawk Nation was protesting the expansion of a golf course and condominiums on unceded Mohawk land that included a Mohawk burial ground. After the Canadian military was called in, the protest was violently dispersed. During the violent dispersal, Waneek Horn-Miller, a 14-year-old Mohawk girl, was stabbed in the chest by a Canadian soldier's bayonet while carrying her four-year-old sister out of the camp to safety. Waneek survived the stabbing, the bayonet narrowly missing her heart, and is now an Olympian and an impassioned advocate for Indigenous rights (Conn, 2018).

1995: Former supervisor of the Alberni Indian residential school was incarcerated and sentenced to 11 years in prison. He pled guilty to 16 counts of indecent assault against students (LHF, 2014).

1996: The last federally run Indian Residential School in Canada, the Gordon Indian Residential School in Saskatchewan, was closed down (LHF, 2014).

1999: Nova Scotia and Canadian governments were pressured by concerned citizens to rescind the Nova Scotia Scalping Law of 1749. There was debate about whether it remained a provincial legal bounty as it had never formally been rescinded (CBC, 2000). There were questions raised about whether citizens could still receive bounties for delivering Indigenous scalps to the Nova Scotian government.

2006: The Indian Residential Schools Settlement Agreement (IRASSA) is reached following the largest class action lawsuit in Canadian history. The class action suit was against the Canadian government for harm inflicted by residential schools, with financial settlements being awarded to survivors. Some individuals found the idea of payouts for the trauma inflicted on them and their families and communities problematic (LHF, 2014).

2007: The United Nations passed the Declaration on the Rights of Indigenous Peoples (UNDRIP; King, 2013, Location 2587).

2008: Prime Minister Stephen Harper apologised on behalf of Canada to the survivors and families of the Indian residential school system (LHF, 2014).

2009: Harper says at the G8 summit that Canada does not have a history of colonisation: Canadians have "no history of colonialism." Harper continued, "we have all of the things that many people admire about the great powers but none of the things that threaten or bother them" (Coulthard, 2014, Location 2235).

2008: The Truth and Reconciliation Commission (TRC) is launched in Canada to investigate the Indian Residential Schools' legacy and history in Canada (LHF, 2014).

2012: Idle No More: Prime Minister Stephen Harper attempted to pass omnibus Legislation, Bill C-45, which affected over 60 acts, including "the Indian Act, Navigable Waters Protection Act and Environmental Assessment Act" (Marshall, 2019, §1). Indigenous and allied activists came together under the name "Idle No More" to protest this omnibus legislation which would take away Indigenous rights and make it easier for the government to approve projects on Indigenous land without Indigenous permission or environmental assessment (Marshall, 2019, §1). Thousands of people participated in protests across Canada and the movement grew into a movement for Indigenous rights and sovereignty beyond just the omnibus legislation.

2014: Tina Fontaine is murdered: Tina Fontaine, a 15-year-old Indigenous girl, was raped and murdered in Winnipeg, Manitoba. The lack of action taken by authorities to protect her in the months leading up to her death and the acquittal of the man charged with her murder led to demands for a federal enquiry into missing and murdered Indigenous women and girls.

These demands eventually led to the formation of the National Enquiry into Missing and Murdered Indigenous Women and Girls (Conn, 2019, §12).

2015: The Canadian Truth and Reconciliation Commission (TRC) reports were released. The reports show a minimum of 150,000 First Nation children were taken from their homes and sent to residential schools (TRC, 2015a, p. 4). The number is in all probability much higher than this, but an exact number cannot be known due to poor record keeping. The report showed that the Canadian government had received "37,951 claims for injuries resulting from physical and sexual abuse at residential schools" (TRC, 2015b, p. 106). The TRC report states that a minimum of 3,200 children died at residential schools. The actual number is probably far higher but because of poorly kept or destroyed records, no exact number is known (TRC, 2015c, p. 125).

2018: The Canadian government exonerated all six Tsilhqot'in chiefs who were hanged in 1864–1865 and apologised for their murder by colonial officials (Smart, 2018).

2018: Colten Boushie, a 22-year-old Cree man, is shot and killed by Gerald Stanley. Stanley is acquitted of all guilt. $223,327 was raised in support of Gerald Stanley on GoFundMe. This was considerably more than was raised on the GoFundMe site for Colten Boushie's family and their legal costs (Roach, 2020). Métis author Chelsea Vowel tweeted in regard to Stanley's GoFundMe account: "The scalp bounty never ended, today it's collected through @gofundme" (Russell, 2018).

2019: The National Enquiry into the Missing and Murdered Indigenous Women and Girls report was released. The report shares the statistic that Indigenous women and girls are 12 times more likely to be murdered or missing than any other women in Canada (NIMMIWG, 2019, p. 7). The report also cited Statistics Canada, which showed that "between 2001 and 2015, homicide rates for Indigenous women were nearly six times higher than for non-Indigenous women" (p. 7).

2020: Over the course of the two weeks it took me to write this timeline, three Indigenous people were killed by the police in the city of Winnipeg in three separate incidents. "Winnipeg Police Killed Three Indigenous People in 10 Days. The Indigenous Bar Association is calling for an enquiry after the recent shooting deaths of two men and a 16-year-old girl" (Berman, 2020). Eishia Hudson was unarmed and shot by police on 8 April. She was 16 years old (Berman, 2020). On 9 April, Jason Collins, age 36, was killed by police (Gowriluk & Grabish, 2020). On 18 April, Stewart Kevin Andrews, loving father of three, was shot and killed by Winnipeg police (Berman, 2020). Many Indigenous people have been killed by police, but I want to honour these three who lost their lives as I was writing this timeline. May you rest in peace and a better world than the one we created for you. I am sorry that we did not do better for you.

2020–Unknown: Another plague spread throughout so-called North America, once again disproportionately affecting First Nations people. As a result of colonialism's impacts, First Nations people are at one of the highest risks of serious illness and death from COVID-19 in so-called Canada (Hawthorn, 2021; Mashford-Pringle et al., 2021, p. 2). One difference from the smallpox pandemic is that there is a vaccine to stop the spread of this plague, and yet one out of every 10 Canadians have refused the vaccine. White settlers from all political parties meet in their privilege and refuse to get vaccinated to stop the spread of a plague disproportionally affecting the most marginalised populations.

Mashford-Pringle, Skura, Stutz, & Yohathasan's (2021) study of how COVID-19 has impacted Indigenous populations in so-called Canada shows that the social and economic inequalities due to colonialism exacerbated the effects and risks of COVID-19 for Indigenous individuals and communities (p. 2). Some of these risk factors due to colonialism include, "health inequities such as a high burden of cardiovascular disease, food insecurity, lack of clean water, etc," lack of access to medical support, as well inadequate housing resources that lead to overcrowding and the inability to "physically distance or self-isolate as houses are overcrowded and there are insufficient community buildings to house those who are infected (like a makeshift hospital)" (p. 2). These factors as well as all the other inequalities that Indigenous communities face are amplified in a crisis, and contribute to the higher risks of infections as well as deaths due to COVID-19 for Indigenous people and communities. (p. 2)

2021: On 27 May, Tk'emlúps te Secwépemc, Kamloops Indian Band announced that 215 unmarked graves of children were found at the Kamloops Indian Residential School (Tk̓emlúps te Secwépemc, 2021). These children died while at the school and no records of their deaths, nor of their graves were previously recorded. This tragic finding prompted the investigation of other residential schools throughout so-called Canada, resulting in the discovery of hundreds of other unmarked graves of Indigenous children who attended residential schools throughout so-called Canada. Their deaths were not recorded, their graves not marked, their families often given no notice or explanation of their deaths.

Conclusion Without Closure

The events detailed above have moulded the Canadian psyche, how white settlers move on this land, interact with the society that was created for them at the expense of so many others, and how they continue to relate to their positionality within those systematic structures, the Indigenous people whose land they occupy and their own selves. This timeline is more than a historical delineating of events and instead can be viewed as part of the mapping of the twists and turns of the formation of the Canadian psyche itself. These events continue to live on in the Canadian psyche today, still actively directing its course. Festering, this history stays barely tended, acknowledged and unredeemed.

Some estimates of the number of Indigenous people who died in the colonisation of the Americas average 95% of the total population pre-contact, or around 95–100 million, making it the largest genocide the world has ever seen (Stannard, 1993, Location 57, 91, p. 268). After writing a timeline of horrors such as this, it is hard to think about now moving into discussing mythology, alchemy, everyday white people's sex lives, or how connected those individuals feel to nature. It all seems so superfluous and perhaps even disrespectful in the face of such historical horror. And yet, I maintain my belief that the only way people, or a group of people, can commit such horrors as are detailed in this timeline is if they as a culture are deeply disturbed. Only deeply dysfunctional people can inflict such trauma. And therefore, it feels a moral necessity to look more closely at the dysfunction of settler colonialism itself—to examine the dysfunctions and complexes within a group that could lead them to perpetuating such destruction. I think then that it is also a moral necessity to look at how we can address those dysfunctions in modern settlers today. As settlers, we carry within ourselves the same dysfunctions that have caused such horror, and without addressing and healing them, we will continue to perpetuate crimes against life, and Indigenous people in continued timelines of violence.

Though amassing the courage, strength, and dedication to undo our own damage may be the most difficult task imaginable, we must try. We have no other choice than to let life within and without continue to wither under our hands. Indeed, we cannot let this come to pass—we must try to undo the damage.

Scholars such as Menakem (2017) discussed the importance of seeing and acknowledging the pain that settler colonialism has caused. Menakem advocated that facing the horror has to be the first step in healing. "White supremacists created whiteness and then defined it as something childish, selfish, and closed-minded. But it doesn't have to be. Whiteness can mean taking responsibility. White activists can deliberately reclaim whiteness." Menakem continued, "They can first call it out as the sleight of hand and the swindle it has always been. Then they can publicly redefine it as something caring, open, and grown up" (p. 271). Though this work of redeeming the colonial psyche within a lineage that can construct such a timeline of horrors feels impossible, accountability is possible, and we must work toward it relentlessly.

Jung wrote about how in alchemy, the *prima materia* and the *lapis* were the same: "'*lapis*' is meant both as the initial material, the *prima materia*, and the end-product of the *opus*, the *lapis* in its strict sense" (Jung, 1955–56/1970, §36). The above timeline is the *prima materia* of the colonial psyche, its perversions leaving a wake of destruction and violence behind it, as Cook's Resolution and Discovery left in theirs. "The world's greatest demographic disaster was initiated by Columbus and Cook and the other marinheiros, and Europe's overseas colonies were, in the first stage of their modern development, charnel houses" (Crosby, 2015, Location 3258).

Cook constantly said in his travels, *"nemo me impune lacessit."* No one provokes me with impunity. "It was a constant refrain throughout the three voyages that natives should never be allowed to think that they had defeated him, outwitted him, or got the better of him in any way" (Cook, 2003, p. 629). This is the legacy that Cook and so many other colonial voyagers brought over that we settlers have continued to perpetuate, perhaps unaware that we carried the same fundamental complexes within our way of viewing the world as those who initially wreaked so much destruction upon their arrival. If so much of this timeline is not even acknowledged in our taught history, how can we have any hopes of reconciling and healing the dysfunctions within our culture that caused these events and actions in the first place? It is not possible. So, as this timeline is the *prima materia* in the colonial psyche, it is the lead and the *lapis*: the dung and the gold. It represents what needs to be addressed for healing and redemption to occur. Without the tending of this history, reparations, reconciliation, healing, wholeness have no chance of coming to pass. Today, we must face it, we cannot look away.

In timelines that extend on from here, may this madness stop. May settlers each work to pick up the scattered shells of the two row wampum belt and through diligent patience, humility, and unwavering accountability, work to stitch each shell back on, so that we may have the chance to honour an agreement that we never allowed to pass. May there be a future where the two-row wampum can come to be: different sovereign nations living in parallel, respectfully with one another.

Chapter 5

Alchemy and the Transformation of the Settler-Colonial Psyche

Figure 5.1 Emblem XLII: "Nature, the Guide and Light of the Alchemist".

Source: Michael Maïer, *Atalanta Fugiens*, 1618. Etching from an alchemical text depicting Nature as a feminine deity, guiding the alchemist through the night.

DOI: 10.4324/9781003296546-5

For the last two millennia, Christianity has been the dominant paradigm in the Western psyche. Its mythologies and morals have seeped into and helped shape every aspect of our Western worldview and lives. Thus, even if as individuals we do not personally identify as Christian, as Europeans and their descendants, Christianity has fundamentally shaped how we interact with the world. As such, our psyches are deeply Christianised.

Western consciousness has been infused with Christian mythology for the last 2,000 years. However, throughout this time, there have been modes of thought which have attempted to diffuse or dismantle the Christian philosophical monopoly and perspectives and have endeavoured to free the Western psyche from the dominant Christian paradigm. Some of these equalising forces survived from the pre-Christian era, such as what the Christians labelled paganism. Others, like Gnosticism, were birthed alongside Christianity but were repressed from the start. Others still, such as alchemy, were formed as a synthesis of many of the counterculture strands outside of—and within—the Christian paradigm. In this chapter, I will explore how this "countercultural" practice of alchemy has a balancing potential for the Christian narrative. Specifically, I will be looking at the potential of alchemy in the healing of whiteness manifest in settler-colonialism in North America. I will explore how the conquest of the Americas can be understood alchemically and how using the metaphor of alchemy in individuals' journeys toward individuation can be seen as redemptive of the failed alchemical attempts of the early colonialists. I begin by providing a brief overview of alchemy, the history and relationship between alchemy and Western consciousness, and the decolonising potential of alchemical processes for the settler-colonial today.

What is Alchemy?

Alchemy is an ancient framework for understanding psychological and spiritual development and its origins are situated in the Western European lineage. In "Aion: Research into the Phenomenology of the Self," Jung (1951/1969) argued that one cannot just resolve and then discard any of the archetypes within. He said that rather than thinking that one can understand and then leave any of one's complexes surrounding these archetypes in the past, one should, instead, enliven the myths anew that give them meaning and make them relevant for today (§ 271). What Jung argued here demonstrated that instead of thinking that one can dispose of the psychic structures of our past, rather, one should work toward reanimating myth by making it accessible and significant for the time, while understanding myths as capable of communicating the deepest values and needs that we have. He argued that the structure of our psychology is grounded in our past, and that we must come to terms with this personal and historic past instead of thinking that we can run from it. He wrote that one must "dream the myth onwards" (§ 271). This serves as a premise for the work of re-enlivening alchemical understandings of the psyche and remembering the archetypal structures it enlivens within by investigating alchemical models for psychological insight for modern colonial consciousness.

Alchemy in the Western tradition was a prescientific philosophy, art, and spiritual practice which re-emerged in Europe in the twelfth and thirteenth centuries but was at its height in the West in the sixteenth and seventeenth centuries (Jung, 1951/1968, § 274). Different forms of alchemy also has roots in various cultures throughout time, including Greek, Chinese, Arabic, and Egyptian traditions (von Franz, 1980, p. 43). In this sense, these processes are deeply archetypal and resonances of them can be found throughout different cultures across time. Thus, alchemy belongs to a transcultural imagination throughout the world.

Much has been written about the motives and goals of the alchemists, which in reality were probably as varied as there were practitioners of the art. Put simply, the goals of alchemy were generally seen to be the transmutation of base metals into noble metals (for example, turning lead to gold); the creation of panaceas to cure ills; and the creation of a philosopher's stone, *lapis philosophorum*, which would bestow immortality on those it touched. Some believed that the intentions of the alchemists were as simple and delusional as these basic fantasies. Today, most people who have heard of alchemy consider it a naïve and foolish attempt at prescientific inquiry in the pursuit of magical, mythical prizes and wealth (Schwartz-Salant & Jung, 1996, p. 1). Some see it as an endearing, and somewhat embarrassing, beginning to the forming of our scientific mind, laboratory experimentation and rationalism (p. 1). However, for those who have studied alchemy carefully, it is clear that many alchemists had ambitions far greater than the creation of physical gold (Eliade, 1979, p. 13). Mircea Eliade (1979), philosopher and religions scholar, wrote that although the alchemists did contribute to the natural sciences, their experiments were more profound than purely the transformation of physical substances (p. 13). Instead, many alchemists had a loftier goal: they sought the transmutation of oneself, of one's "own mode of being" (p. 183). It could be that for some alchemists, the sole aim was to create gold from lead and acquire riches. However, it seems more likely that most of them were involved in something much deeper and richer.

Jung (1943/1968) saw alchemy as the ancient parallel to the modern individuation journey of coming to psychological wholeness. He recognised in the work of the alchemists the pursuit of psychological transformation. Perhaps to stay in the patronage of the kings who were funding them, the alchemists wanted to appear as though they were working toward the creation of purely physical gold. However, what many were truly attempting to create in their laboratories and cookstoves was spiritual gold and the transmutation of the heavy leadenness inside themselves into the riches of aliveness and vitality.

Alchemy is a practice of embodiment, of honouring the earthly, the chthonic, the natural and corporeal as sacred to our humanness and necessary to our soul and our individuating journeys. In this way, alchemy is the counterbalance to Christianity, which values ascension and the upward-focused spirituality of transcending earth toward God. Alchemy honours the animism of the elemental and sacredness of the physical and earthly and strives to marry the transcendent and immanent: spirit and soul.

There is a tradition of contemplation woven throughout Western history, from Plato to the Gnostics, to the alchemists, to counselling psychology today. Alchemy is a vital thread in this Western tapestry of contemplative traditions that was for a long time almost forgotten until Jung revived its study. Remembering the alchemical metaphors and stories today has the potential to offer valuable insight into the development of the Western psyche and its current state.

Alchemy and Christianity

European alchemy arises within a Christian worldview. Alchemy does not oppose Christianity, but rather offers a counterbalance to the Christian mythos. Christian mythology has negated the dark and evil from its god images in the separation of the devil into a distinct entity from God, whereas alchemy aims to recover this separation and move toward a wholeness of being, of embracing "light" and "dark." Due to its basis in the physical, natural, corporeal world, it was seen as a pagan threat by many Christians in the medieval period. Jung (1977) wrote that "alchemy, aims precisely at the synthesis of opposites, the simulation of the blackness, the integration of the devil. For the 'awakened' Christian this is a very serious psychic experience, for it is a confrontation with his own 'shadow'" (p. 228). It has already been mentioned how taken von Franz was with the idea of alchemy as the counterbalancing antidote to the Christian psyche, in great part because she believed alchemy "balanced the prevailing Christian myth by including the shadow, the body, and the feminine, areas of life denied and relegated to the margins by the orthodox religious view" (Goodchild, 2006, p. 64). Alchemy holds the tension of opposites, and its goal is the union of god, transcendent, good, spirit, reason, with the immanent, chthonic, soulful, evil, and instinctual.

Alchemy holds these opposites together and its theory can help individuals and collectives reconcile systems of consciousness that generally separate and divide these perceived polarities. One of alchemy's goals is the synthesis of opposites. von Franz (2003) believed that in the medieval period, there was an opportunity for alchemy to be an equaliser to Christianity, the possibility of it becoming the balance of the Christian mythos (Location 2890). However, the Christian disconnect from the multiplicity and darkness in the human experience was too great for a union between the two to arise at that time (Location 2839).

Hillman promoted alchemy's nondual and expansive relationship with colour as the answer to transmuting our Western relationship to white and black and thereby ending our adherence to the delusion of white supremacy. Hillman corroborates that the opus of alchemy works to resolve the "problem of opposites" (p. 50) and therefore he saw in such works the potential to resolve one aspect of the delusion of white supremacy, describing their connection: "If inherent to white supremacy and if supremacy maintains itself by denying shadow, then it is 'only natural' to white consciousness to think and feel in opposites ... Give up the opposites, and you can move beyond white supremacy" (p. 50). Giving up these opposites is where alchemy can lead. Hillman supported Jung's return to alchemy as "a return to a colored soul and a colored world" (p. 49). Hillman thus saw alchemy as a way toward healing the delusion of white supremacy and as having the potential to archetypally explain, transmute, and heal white consciousness (p. 49).

The *Prima Materia* of the White Settler Psyche

Alchemy is part of the Western European ancestral lineage of transformation. Jung wrote: "alchemy is rooted in and has sprung from the Western psyche" (Jung, 1943/1968, p. 5). This odd and forgotten aspect of Western history can be used to better understand the collective complex of the Western psyche.

Alchemists thought that for transformation of a material to occur, it first must be reduced to its "original, undifferentiated state" or its *prima materia* (Edinger, 1991, p. 10). After a material was reduced to its prime matter, then it was thought to need to go through a "process of differentiation whereby it was separated into the four elements, earth, air, fire, and water" (p. 10).

In depth psychology, *prima materia* is understood to be that which is annoying, distressing, and disturbing within ourselves, it is our psychological sore spots and our shadow material (Edinger, 1991, p. 12). *Prima materia* is that which has been excluded, rejected, deemed of little worth and avoided (p. 12). Alchemists advocated that when worked with and healed, this *prima materia*, the most uncomfortable emotional material of individuals' lives, can be transformed into libido: life energy. Often *prima materia* is perceived as a disruptive symptom that keeps individuals from living their lives, but alchemy shows that instead it is the answer, the key to life, the gold in the lead. Individuals often want to be free of a symptom, and rightly so want to be free of its discomfort. But alchemy, like Jungian psychology, tells us that one cannot be free of the symptom until one processes and integrates its energy; one has to work with the despised *prima materia* to get to the gold (§ 207). In alchemy, the *prima materia* is the gold, it is the demon that is not being tended, but when tended to is the vitality of life (§ 207). *Prima materia* is what is rejected, despised, hated, discarded within, but when healed, ends up being the building stones for the psyche (Jung, 1942/1967, § 209). *Prima materia* is often referred to as the "raw materia of the opus" or lead of the psyche; that which is heaviest within, and the material that is to be transformed into gold (§ 209).

Western cultural *prima materia* is the parts of the psyche that have been labelled as evil, such as sexuality, instinctual natures, pagan connectedness to nature and nature spirits, all of which the church cast out of heaven, damned to hell and called "the devil." When these parts of psyche were conceptualised as separate and evil, they then became repressed, and perhaps it was only then that they become dangerous. This "evil" part of the Western psyche is the *prima materia,* the material necessary for its transformation and healing.

A foundational aspect of the *prima materia,* the lead of the Western psyche, is its racism and colonial violence. Michael Dyson wrote: "It is not enough to be a rhetorician and a semiotician to deconstruct and demythologise whiteness. One must be a magician of the political and the social, an alchemist of the spiritual and psychological too" (DiAngelo, 2018, p. ix). An alchemical understanding of the Western psyche's development is that it became so fearful of the unknown within itself that it projected its own fear of darkness out onto the world. This fear of its own rejected shadow material led to the Western psyche's dissociation from its own unconscious, thought of as shadow, which it then projected onto the rest of the world, not allowing black or dark anywhere, except in the cloth of the clergy—it tried to whiten the world.

Alchemy as Metaphor

Alchemists often talked about how deadly alchemy could be due to the danger of their physical metallurgical experiments working with toxins. However, Jung (1943/1968) also talked about the dangers of alchemy psychologically; there are many places for it to go wrong without guidance or when the depths of ourselves are not tended and handled with the care that they require (§ 564). For what we are imagining as the alchemical process of the Western Christian psyche, the effects of its complexes projected on the world have been deadly and, in fact, genocidal. The killing of the Indigenous people of North America in the colonial invasion was the largest genocide this world has ever seen (Stannard, 1993, p. 146).

Hillman (2007) wrote of the importance of not reading alchemy literally, that by doing so we cement it into "either primitive chemistry or spiritual magic," neither of which is the intention of reading alchemy psychologically and metaphorically (p. 157). He said instead it is the "alchemical mode of imagining," the "restoration of imagination" that is meant by the return to alchemy (Hillman, 2015, Location 210).

This approach of using an alchemical lens in this book can also be thought of as engaging in the story of alchemy. If we follow the alchemical metaphor, perhaps we can see Christian crusaders as seeking their own "gold," but they were misguided and looking for it externally, without turning inward and first facing their own depths. Tarnas (2013) wrote of

Western consciousness's restlessness and ceaseless striving for more, bigger and higher on an endless pursuit of development, freedom, and success and of its focus upward toward heaven, while negating and destroying the earthly (p. 4). Western consciousness sought gold without first realising its own depths and unconscious material. It split the "dark" from within itself and banished it, calling it the devil. Disconnected from the "dark" and repressing it within, the colonisers sought only the "light."

Jung (1943/1968) spoke of how the image of Christ failed to lead Western individuals to wholeness as it was so one-sided (§ 7). Viewed alchemically, these crusaders, with their one-sided object of veneration, went into the world with a lopsided glorification of goodness, disconnected from the depths of horror they carried within them. They carried inflated ideas of their own godliness and pureness, wanting to spread the light and purify the world and "savages" of their pagan dark ways, not realising that they were trying to run away from their own darkness and avoid the inevitable reclamation and redemption of their own dark natures (Schenk, 2012, p. 21). The early settlers saw themselves as displaced people "arrived from a rejected past, breaking into a glorious future, on the move, fearless himself, feared by others, a killer but cleansing the world of things which need killing" (p. 21). They missed that perhaps the void they were needing to fill was turning back toward and healing the unconscious material. Hillman wrote that we both fear and long for "the soul's desire to descend into darkness, like Persephone unto Hades. We fear what we most desire and desire what we most fear" (Hillman, 2015, Location 1747).

Alchemically, we can understand the purification that this Christian consciousness was looking to impose on the world as an internal process needing to happen, less so about a whitening of the world and more about a tending of its own consciousness, a return to wholeness. Thus, using the alchemical metaphor, we see that consciously engaging in the alchemical process is the antidote to the "whiteness" of Christianity and its puritanical whitening of the world. Consciously engaging in the process of facing the shadow, reconciling with that which has long been oppressed, allows for the necessary reconciling with "darkness."

The Alchemy of Settler Colonisation and Decolonisation

Today, using alchemical imagery, facing the internal shadow from which settler-colonials continue to run may be a way to engage with a redeeming process for the unfinished collective alchemical course of their ancestry. Our responsibility then becomes to heal ourselves of their fear of the dark and unknown within ourselves, the world and the other. Tarnas (2013) wrote that "attending carefully and critically to this tradition [of Western consciousness] fulfills a certain responsibility to the past, to our ancestors, just as attempting to understand its deeper implications fulfills a responsibility to the future, to our children" (p. 2). We settler-colonials would then need to look at the heavy, the leaden within that has been repressed for the last millennia. This colonial repression of this darkness has been preaching whiteness and poisoning the world for thousands of years.

Many believe that it was the longing for a different, better life that spurred settlers to leave everything they knew behind in Europe and seek out something new (Veracini, 2010, p. 96). However, using an alchemical lens, we could understand the longing for a New World as also being birthed from the desire for a fresh start and new world within. Jung believed that individuation, the move toward wholeness, is instinctual. But when one is culturally directed away from that wholeness, to a one-sided desperation reaching toward lightness, these attempts toward wholeness can be thwarted by the inner repressed chaos and untended shadow material. Each of alchemy's processes has productive and destructive potentials, aspects that lead toward the gold or away from it. The rest of this book will explore viewing colonisation of so-called North America as a misguided and destructive alchemical process. It will look at this process as an attempt at collective individuation gone terribly wrong. It will also look at the potential of following the alchemical metaphors today, to allow settlers to engage in the redeeming potential of these processes.

An alchemical understanding of the Western Christian psyche is that it has been in its process of development and an attempted path toward individuation; however, it has attempted to individuate by cutting off half of itself, its shadow, and damning it to "hell." It attempted to bypass the *nigredo* process of alchemy, whereby one faces the unconscious within oneself, and tends to its wounding. Through this lens, it could be understood that the colonial psyche tried to move straight to the *albedo*, stage of work, and tried to not only whiten itself but also the rest of the world. What resulted from that misguided attempt was that the repressed aspects within the Western psyche took over and perpetuated the largest genocide this world has ever seen, all in the name of purity, light and greed. It is the worst-case scenario that can happen with repression and an alchemical *sublimatio,* a spiritual bypassing (also common within spiritual communities today) gone horrifically wrong.

Instead of colonials finding their inner gold, they were sent even deeper into their lead, and the depths of their inner repression continue to be revealed. No matter how much they have attempted to avoid their own unconscious, they cannot. An alchemical understanding would postulate that the impulse to individuate had driven colonials toward these alchemical processes but that they were undertaken in maimed, destructive ways. Engaging consciously with these processes now is a potential redemptive opportunity. Today, to consciously engage with the alchemical journey, settler-colonials must face and go through their process of being burned by the fires of transformation, having all the known and comfortable parts of themselves and their privilege and power dissolved, having something form again from the ashes and puddle they have melted into, and be able to rise above all the places they have been unable to let go.

Alchemy is an essential part of the Western lineage of the elemental, earthly, grounded, soulwork, as there was a time in the history of the West when the elements and aspects of nature were seen as vital in the transformation of self and one's place in the world. That alchemy has been so rejected by the dominant culture is perhaps another sign of the West fleeing from its own depths and darkness within its psyche and history. We see it also in New Age healing circles today, the impetus is to reach for models of transformation from other cultures instead of turning back into oneself and facing the heaviness of the material of the content and resources of one's own past and shadow found within Western lineages, such as alchemy (cue more white people with mala beads, smudging sage and love and lighting).

Alchemy can offer psychological, soulful guidance which originates within the Western lineage. For generations, the West has had a deep longing for spiritual teachings outside of Christianity, and many have turned to the appropriation of Indigenous spirituality, including First Nation culture and ceremony without permission as well as to the Eastern spiritual practices. Today there is also the rise of people who are dubbed "Pretendians," that is, white people pretending to be Indigenous, who falsely claim Indigenous ancestry. These individuals appropriate not only specific Indigenous practices but identities as a whole. They attempt to shed their complicity with whiteness and colonialism completely by "becoming" Indigenous. Perhaps all of these appropriating pursuits, are more appealing to many than facing their own settler complicity, or turning to traditions from their own lineages as they do not require an individual to face the problematic history and material of their own personal and cultural psyche. These practices have allowed individuals to bypass what they do not want to face within their own culture and jump into a practice of the oppressed. This has enabled them to identify with the oppressed, thinking that they can thereby shed the identification of the oppressor and the associated guilt. However, to engage with the alchemical philosophy, one cannot eschew one's cultural past. In fact, the very thing alchemy requires of an individual in order to achieve the psychological and spiritual fulfilment they so desire is the confrontation with their past: the facing of their *prima materia*. This is, in part, why I find alchemy a compelling practice for the settler-colonial called toward integrity today.

Alchemy contains the Gnosticism, the pagan, and the witchy of the Western, settler-colonial lineage. Reclaiming it is reclaiming the Western responsibility of working with nature and wonder that are available through mysticism instead of with hierarchical structures that have oppressed so much of the world. It is a thread and a route back to our Western decolonising potential. It is a pathway to a cultural soulfulness to which all people have a right and responsibility, and it is definitely not all love and light.

Engaging the alchemical metaphor would require that the Western psyche face the darkness within that it has been avoiding for 2,000 years. That murkiness has built up, and it is scary. Perhaps the most frightening aspect of it all is the thought of encountering within that which is unknown, which may contain the chthonic earthiness, and corporeal natures that the West has been running from. The West has terrorised the "dark" of the world, as it has been terrified of its own darkness and earthly aliveness within itself. Beneath all the other steps and alchemical processes lies the necessity for this one: the working of this deep *prima materia,* the primary material which is also the gold. The laboratory work now involves turning toward the depths of ourselves, working in the dark, candles lit, all of our vessels, potions, and hearths roaring. It is the work of the return to our soul and the soul of the world, our descent back to earth and its healing, through fire, water, earth, and air. It necessitates stripping away the colonial armour that has never served us and diving into the depths of our deepest, truest, most vulnerable selves: an alchemical rebirth, a redemptive, anticolonial healing.

Séme7

I have worked in the community of Esk'etemc for the last four years. It is one of 17 (out of 32) remaining communities that speak a dialect of *Secwepemctsín,* the Secwépemc language group. In *Secwepemctsín,* the name for white person is *séme7.* Before the arrival of the *séme7,* the *tkwilc* (shamans) of the Secwépemc communities had visions that "foretold the coming of White people, the advent of epidemics, the final extinction of the Indians, the introduction of whiskey, stoves, dishes, flour, sugar, etc." (Ignace & Ignace, 2017, p. 426). The root of the word *séme7* is thought to be *sem* for "to tell stories" (p. 426). It is thought that this name could have been chosen for the settlers as the *tkwilc* had already told stories about the ones who were to arrive and that they were thus those "storied beings" (p. 426). Perhaps another reason settlers were named *séme7* was that they were foretold as the ones who would change the story that would take place on these lands with their destruction (p. 426). Another term used for white people by the Secwépemc is *stsptékwle* which is "the term used for the ancient transformers" (p. 426). So again, we see the settlers being characterised as the ones who would change and transform ways of life, culture, communities, etc. Perhaps here we can see how the Secwépemc perceived the distorted story we settlers were playing out upon our arrival to these lands, as well as the role we settlers, *séme7, stsptékwle* the storied ones, would have in bringing great change, destruction and the altering of the story of so-called Canada and Secwépemc territory. So far, the story that has happened in what is now known as Canada since the *séme7* arrival has mostly (if not completely) been negative. Today, perhaps changing our relationship to our distorted story could bring about positive changes for all in how we *séme7* affect the story from here. Perhaps going forward, the story will no longer be dominated by our actions and will instead be collaboratively written with the Secwépemc and other nations in so-called Canada about where, together, we and our shared story go from here.

When I was at Dechinta bush school in 2014, I was told that when white people first arrived in Denedeh territory in what we now call the Northwest Territories, the Dene called the white people *n–>kweèt'ii̧*. In Dogrib, this word means "rock finders" or "rock seekers" (Gordie Liske, Wıı̀lıı̀deh Yellowknives Dene, Personal Communication, October 2014). The white people were given this name because to the Dene, they seemed to be interested in nothing except seeking rocks—that is, gold. They were *n–>kweèt'ii̧*, gold seekers. The beginnings of colonialism in what is now called North America was based on this pursuit of gold. The gold rush shaped the trajectory of colonial settling and development perhaps more than any other force. Perhaps beneath the obvious economic gains the gold entailed, there was another rush within it those early settlers, *n–>kweèt'ii̧*, were seeking. Another kind of riches they were craving. Though they were seeking this gold by tearing up the earth, an alchemical interpretation could posit that they would have had more luck finding what truly would have fulfilled them by seeking out the creation of the gold within. Rock seekers: perhaps this is the most accurate description of settler-colonials. It is what alchemists are, seeking the philosopher's stone: seeking gold. And it was foundational to what fuelled the colonising of what is now called North America. Tragically, those early settlers got the recipe for how to make and find the gold they sought terribly, terribly wrong.

Hillman (1997) saw the imagination that dreamed and sought the "New World" as an unfolding alchemical longing (p. 9). This longing sought gold, silver and jewels, empire building in the names of imperial kings and queens, and it met dark skinned kings and queens of unexplored territory. It sought the fountain of youth and seven cities of gold. It craved a "New World": a redemptive rebirth and freedom from the confines of their known worlds: "The project of the new world is an alchemical projection of renewal, an extraversion of European alchemy's introversion. The New World carries in its psychic substrate an alchemical desire for redemption by transformation of material nature" (p. 9). Voyaging to the "New World" can be seen as the manifestation of the Western European dream of freedom from its oppressive hold. Hillman proposed that really the Western psyche longed for this freedom internally, this adventure to find the newness, vitality, riches within, find the reintegration of the kings and queens, the dignified sovereigns within our own shadow, the places we too were once connected to land, body, sexuality, soul, and the earthly (p. 9).

However, though the Western psyche may have longed for this internal rebirth and gold seeking, the institutional oppression of that longing was too much. During this time, European authorities were frequently burning women at the pyre for being witches (Stannard, 1993, p. 136). This sentence was given to women for many reasons: if they were seen as sexual; if they had a strong knowledge of plant medicines; if they could help tend the village people; or even if they could aid successfully in the delivery of new babes into the world. The institutional world of British rule in the sixteenth century did not have much tolerance for a colourful renaissance of psychological vitality (though the Renaissance itself, an awakening from the Dark Ages, was happening at the time) and so instead, this seeking was externalised.

Hillman (1997) imagined the pursuit of the New World as an alchemical attempt gone wrong. He wrote that the pursuit of the "New World" was a "geographical alchemical retort, a labyrinthine laboratory" which continually attempted to "transform the leaden weight, the *massa confusa* and *materia prima* of physis into the gold of noble and sophisticated accomplishments" (p. 9), mining for metals, gems, any precious physical material it could: "With this extraversion of alchemy into a geographical project an inevitable concretisation occurred. Classic alchemy warned ever and again: 'Beware of the physical in the material'" (p. 9). Alchemy warns that it is dangerous when we misplace our psychological needs for physical ones, and when our longing for a richer inner experience gets mistakenly concretised as a longing for more physical riches. These early colonialists sought physical gold when the true longing was for the internal smelting of lead to gold, of the deep healing of our core complexes: "The Gold of alchemy was not the usual gold that is smelted, not metallic gold, monetary gold, but a noble and sophisticated elixir, a condition of soul" (p. 9). Hillman wrote that with the extraversion of this pursuit in the Americas, this "gold petrified, became that mineral madness obsessing the conquistadores into modern times, and appropriately named 'black' gold of the Maracaibo oil wells, a 'gold' still being sought in the wilds of Ecuador and the depths of the Mexican Gulf" (p. 9). Today, we continue to see this addiction to the black gold of oil persisting throughout the world, and closer to home, it continues to fuel Canada's economy through the black gold of Alberta's tar sands.

Hillman (1997) wrote that the only way to extract ourselves from this delusion of destruction created surrounding the "New World" and all it could offer would be to shed the cultural obsession with the "New": "America's dominant myth, Newness" (p. 10). It is true that this "New World" has brought the Western world unimaginable riches, the white, middle-class person now living like aristocracy of the "Old World," the rich now living beyond what any royalty before could have imagined. This obsession with newness has not stopped since settlers' arrival here. The extraversion of the internal desires still has modern settler-colonials believing that by externally acquiring they can fill their spiritual void—these voids which had their ancestors harness the winds to blow their souls toward that which they most longed for, but still have not managed to find: the inner New World.

Hillman (1997) wrote of how the American delirium of newness continues to be seen in the North American obsession with development: the development of land, economies, personalities, technologies, and anything else we can think of to profit off its growth (p. 11). Always seeking the new, we are "recapitulating the ocean-crossing, heroically each of us a captain of our fates, a pioneer, conquistador, converting whatever is unknown, strange, spontaneous or odd into the single category of newness, with our backs always turned against the old" (p. 11). He continued that this delirious pursuit keeps individuals "all the while secretly oppressed, not by the old, but by the designation of this Hemisphere as 'New'" (p. 11). He argued that this "manifest destiny of development" is what keeps settlers' freedom and hearts chained to dissatisfaction, which he described as that which is ceaselessly trying to find "ever more virginities to penetrate and own. The aging-terrified, limelight craving, throwaway civilisation begins in the fantasy of this, a 'New World'" (p. 11). Nothing in this chasing of the physical new can or will satisfy when what is longed for is truly for the internal and new space of freedom and connection within.

The tragic irony in this situation is that nothing about this "New World" was new, except to Europeans. Many nations and cultures that lived and thrived before Europeans invaded had been on these lands since time immemorial (Coulthard, 2014, p. 60). It is estimated that between 75 and 145 million people lived in North and South America pre-1492; estimates of other populations at the time include Europe with an estimated 60–70 million people, Russia with 10–18 million people, and Africa with 40–72 million people (Stannard, 1993, pp. 267–268). It is generally estimated that the death rate of the Indigenous population of North America was 90–98% post-contact (Location 53). The early settler-colonials, whose actions modern settler-colonials continue to benefit from, decimated whole nations and millions of individual lives who each held the preciousness of their peoples' unique ancient histories, languages, dances and sacred ceremonies. In *kweèt'įį* settlers' inability to reconcile with their longing for a deep rebirth of their internal experience of their connection to life, they killed. At times intentionally, other times unintentionally, millions of individuals were murdered.

Simpson (2011) shared that there is a word in Nishnaabemowin: *mino bimaadiziwin,* meaning "the art of living the good life" and a "continuous rebirth" (Location 337). There has never been one word to describe culture in Nishnaabemowin, as culture is so enmeshed in Nishnaabeg daily life, in the stories, songs, language, ceremonies. However, words that call forth the meaning of culture include: "*izhitwaa, nitaa, inaadizi, gaaminigoowisieng,* and *gaaenakowinid*" (Location 2310). The meaning that weaves these words together is their "overarching concern: the desire to produce more life" (Location 2310). In Nishnaabeg culture, the good life is about caretaking and tending Life itself. Simpson explained that this understanding of these words "resonated with everything I had been taught by Elders—that the goal is to promote life and to live it rather than just talk about" it (Location 2310). In colonial culture, there are not words such as these in the English language; we lack words that centre caring for life as that which constitutes a good life.

Penawahpskek author Sherri Mitchell (2018) wrote about the newcomers to her and her ancestors' lands, newcomers who believed "that it was manifest destiny that brought them to this land" (p. 16). Mitchell argued that these newcomers were mistaken in their idea that conquest was what brought them to these lands and instead she believed that "there was something much deeper calling them to these lands, an ancient impulse was guiding them back toward what they had lost" (p. 16). She related this to how when people are physically ill, they seek out the medicine that they need. She explained that her culture understands that the spirit does the same and will always move toward that which it needs to heal. Mitchell ventured that when the newcomers were drawn to this land, "they believed that they were here to conquer new lands. What they didn't realise is that they had been drawn here by spirit, to seek healing from the illusion of separation that they had been operating under" (p. 17).

Mitchell (2018) wrote that unfortunately the newcomers were so drastically disconnected from spirit that they were not open to receiving the wisdom that they needed when they arrived to so-called North America, that they arrived feeling "unquenchable longing inside them. This longing caused the newcomers to become increasingly more insatiable in their appetites. They travelled from place to place, consuming everything in their path, and yet the hunger in their hearts was never satisfied" (p. 17). Mitchell believed that the newcomers were unconsciously seeking a "healing from the illusion of separation" so they were led to a place where the knowledge of the interrelatedness of Life still existed, where the "umbilical cord with Mother Earth still throbbed with life. Though the Native peoples of this land also struggled with human conflicts, they had maintained their connection to the Earth and their awareness of the interrelatedness of all life" (p. 17). Mitchell explained how the Indigenous people of Turtle Island understood their connectedness with the living world around them and their place in the world in a way that the newcomers did not, that the newcomers had "lost their connection to the impulse of life and their understanding of the web that ties all life together" (p. 17).

Mitchell (2018) relayed that some of her ancestors felt that life itself was calling the newcomers to Turtle Island, "calling those who were lost back home. It was not calling them to a specific location but to a renewed connection to the lineage of life. They did not come here by accident" (p. 17). However, Mitchell believed that the newcomers "rebelled against the truth" when they met the Indigenous people of Turtle Island and witnessed the culture of interrelatedness there. When the newcomers saw an "expression of deep connectivity they became fearful and called that truth primitive and savage. Then, they dove deeper into the illusion, manufacturing histories to support it and creating laws to uphold it" (p. 18). The newcomers feared the connection that they were being offered, and as so often happens when great transformation or healing is offered to us, our minds can fear great change and push against it. "Many of the newcomers clung to their illusion with both hands, seeking to protect it at all costs, even if that meant destroying those who held that truth and burying it along with them" (p. 18). However, Mitchell does not believe that all hope is lost. She wrote that she believes that the call for the settlers to come back to Life is still there and that their reconnection to Life is still possible. She maintains that throughout this period of colonial horrors, "the truth remained—a steady beating rhythm, an unending call to the hearts and minds of mankind" (p. 18). A call that she believes settlers still have the opportunity to hear and heed.

I believe that one step on the road to integrity for *kweèt'ı̨ı̨*, rock seekers, today would be to undertake the journey that the colonial voyagers missed when they boarded their seafaring vessels 500 years ago. The voyage that they did not undertake, that could now be traversed, is one that perhaps evokes more fear than that of sailing the great landless expanses of the Atlantic and Pacific oceans. The journey they can undertake now is that of traversing the depths of their own fathomless psyches.

Undertaking this journey that was thwarted 500 years ago is perhaps how settlers can now return to the aliveness which they so desire. It is also how they may redeem the story of destruction that brought them to live on these lands and shores. This story is not over, it is only at the tragic climax, before the denouement in which the villains may recognise their wrongs and slowly start re-growing their hearts to work their ways toward redemption. Engaging in the alchemical journey of re-enlivening our hearts and souls, of reconnecting to our bodies, earth, sexuality, passion is not all that needs to happen in our decolonising efforts or all that will make us honest allies in integrity with what is now called North America and the Indigenous people and Nations of this land. But it could be at least a beginning, and the work of true reconciliation and settler decolonisation and accountability can begin from there. Instead of stocking up closets with Lululemon with the intention of becoming a peace-loving yogi or attending our friendly neighbourhood white-person-run, peyote or ayahuasca ceremony to connect to our spiritual selves, it might be a better move turning to alchemy.

Settlers can now pick up this story where it was left off 500 years ago and thereby undertake the re-enlivening journey subverted by those voyagers all those centuries ago. If we do not, we risk the chance of continuing the distorted externalised alchemical path that began 500 years ago and continuing in the frenzy for the newest trends, the conspicuous consumption of jewels and golds, the colonial insatiable hunger for them whether they come from the deepest mines or of the veins of the earth: black gold, oil to make plastic jewels we can self-coronate with from aisles 3–4 of Target or Wal-Mart. To halt this story of constant, hungry longing and consuming of food, jewels, fast fasion and riches which is destroying our planet, we *ain–>kweèt'ı̨ı̨*, rock seekers, must now throw ourselves back into the story, back to the fork in the path and this time choose the path evaded centuries ago. The chapters to follow will sketch a map of what that process may look like; the metaphors of alchemy will guide this work, as the metaphors of alchemy offer a compelling lens with which to understand what first called the voyagers across the sea. It is also of vital importance that alchemy comes from the Western lineage and is not appropriated from another culture. But alchemy itself is not what must be followed here. Use it as a metaphor if it is useful to you as well, but what must be followed now is that deep rhythm of longing leading not across the world but back into the pulsing heart of Life itself. Follow whatever map gives the clearest instructions for you (as long as it does not include you white person wearing a Pocahontas outfit for Halloween … please.).

Concurrent Events

While writing this last chapter, two more Indigenous people have been killed by the police in Canada, alongside other acts of police brutality toward Indigenous people. On June 1, 2020, a Royal Canadian Mounted Police (RCMP) was caught on camera purposely hitting a 22-year-old Inuk man with the door of his moving police truck in order to knock him to the ground before arresting him (Moran, 2020).

On 4 June, Chantel Moore, a 26-year-old mother originally from the Tla-o-qui-aht First Nation in BC, reached out for help to a former boyfriend who was out of town because she was being harassed and did not feel safe in her home. Her former boyfriend called the RCMP and asked them to do a wellness check to make sure Chantel was safe. RCMP ended up shooting Chantel in her own home during the wellness check (Ibrahim, 2020).

On 11 June, a week after Chantel was shot, Rodney Levi, a member of the Metepenagiag Mi'kmaq Nation, was shot and killed by police (Heidenreich & Boynton, 2020). Also, on 11 June, a dashcam video from the RCMP was released in an ongoing court case looking into the arrest of Chief Allan Adam after a RCMP officer noticed Chief Adam's license plate had expired. In the dash cam, we see after a verbal confrontation an "officer runs up and jump-tackles Adam to the ground. The second officer punches Adam in the head as he continues to struggle and a few seconds later places him in a chokehold. 'F--k you, don't resist arrest!'" the officer yells (Rusnell & Russell, 2020).

The RCMP was founded in Canada as a means to enforce the colonisation of Canada by British forces and continues to enforce the oppression of Indigenous people. RCMP are inexorably linked to the founding and continuation of colonialism in Canada and we continue to see their colonial foundations expressed in the violence and death they wreak disproportionately on the Indigenous people of Canada. As Canadian Senator Mary Jane McCallum wrote, "How can we have reconciliation with a police force that carries such negative and historical baggage?" (McCallum, 2020). Professor Jocelyn Thorpe explained that "the Mounties (RCMP) were created to assert sovereignty over Indigenous peoples and their lands" (McCallum, 2020). Steve Hewitt, a senior history lecturer at the University of Birmingham, said on the founding of the RCMP that the goal was that they "would control the

Indigenous people already living on the land." Hewitt continued, "The job of the Mounties effectively, was to clear the plains, the prairies, of Indigenous people. Ultimately, they were there to displace Indigenous people, to move them onto reserves whether they were willing to go or not" (McCallum, 2020).

Decolonisation cannot take place without a justice system which replaces the colonial systematic oppression that is the Royal Canadian Mounted Police, each of its officers having a mere six months of training, much of which is focused on fitness in bootcamp and firearm training (Government of Canada RCMP, 2019). In 1896, Prime Minister Sir Wilfred Laurier wanted to disband the Northwest Mounted Police, the precursor to the RCMP (Government of Canada RCMP, 2020). I believe that we need to revisit this disbandment today.

While writing this chapter, police violence also continued on in the United States. George Floyd, a black American, father to six-year-old daughter Gianna Floyd, was brutally murdered by the police, an officer kneeling on his neck for nine minutes until Floyd was killed. His murder was caught on camera (Fernandez & Burch, 2020). In just the few months, it took to write these last chapters, in the United States, the police killed George Floyd for allegedly using a counterfeit $20 bill. The police also shot and killed Breonna Taylor, a 26-year-old EMT and black woman who was shot eight times and killed by police while sleeping in her own home. The police responsible for her murder were searching for someone accused of a drug-related crime in the wrong apartment complex who had already been taken into police custody (Oppel & Taylor, 2020). What followed were Black Lives Matter protests and demonstrations across the United States and parts of Canada demanding human rights for black people, the end of police brutality of BIPOC, and the defunding of police departments.

In this particular moment in time, in comparison to the critically important and brave work being done in the world of activism, the work being undertaken in this book seems low on the priority list. As Ijeoma Oluo, the author of *So You Want To Talk About Race* (2018), said in a Facebook live video during the demonstrations: "We are trying to save lives. I am not trying to build a better, more enlightened white person, I don't care. I am trying to save lives. And I hope that that is what you are trying to do too" (Oluo, Facebook Live Video, June 2, 2020, 12:58 pm). Stopping the deaths of people of colour dying from white supremacist colonial systems always needs to be at the forefront and the reason why we engage in this work. That is, our goal should be the prevention of the continued loss of lives of BIPOC due to the delusion of white supremacy, complacency, and perpetuation of white supremacist systems of power.

Perhaps once Instagram hashtags for the movement no longer trend and white moderates return to their comfortable lives, forgetting about all the posts they shared and commitments to action they made, something of this particular scholarship in this book can seep into their lives. Maybe with the promise of self-growth engaging their interest, this work can help address the underlying places of stagnancy in white people's solidarity and allyship. We cannot wait until we get everything perfect to jump in; people are dying with every minute that action is not taken, with every chapter of this book I write. But after we start taking action, it is imperative that we continue to learn, work on ourselves, and work on our ability to no longer be active agents in the oppression of BIPOC. We must work toward true allyship and reparations.

BIPOC engage with social justice because for them, it is life or death. For white people, we can engage with social justice because it makes us feel better. There is tremendous privilege in that, and I acknowledge the deep injustice in that privilege. The main emphasis of this research is to show the violence that the colonial complex has perpetuated and argue that we need to heal those aspects of the colonial complex so that this violence will end. The sales pitch bonus to this work, that can be thought of perhaps as a hook to get people engaged with the subject who normally would not engage with social justice, is that undergoing this process is also what they need to do for their own wellness. I am not completely discounting the importance of this aspect of the work here, because I do believe that unwell people and culture have created the destruction the world has seen and that we do need to heal in order to stop this destruction. But I also acknowledge the privilege in this: that by engaging in social justice we will be healed and feel better. There is privilege here because our lives are not at stake whether we engage in these issues or not, just our wellbeing is at stake.

A basic tenet of most moral philosophies is that by looking out for others, we become better people ourselves. But I stress that this should not be the only goal in this work. We must also engage in this work because other peoples' lives depend on white people of North America doing so. However, if that is what it takes to get people on the track of doing this work, then I only hope that through the process they, and their intentions, are changed. We also have to be careful, as this work can easily feed the White Saviour complex. Lila Watson powerfully said: "If you have come here to help me, you are wasting your time. But if you have come here because your liberation is bound up with mine, then let us work together" (Haga, 2020). Watson's sentiment helps to strip out the binary of prioritising why we help and includes the interwoven liberation of our shared humanity. Haga (2020), in *Healing Resistance: A Radically Different Response to Harm,* contributed a similar sentiment to Watson: "White people shouldn't be working to defeat white supremacy in order to save people of colour. They should be doing it because white supremacy destroys the souls of white people" (Haga, 2020). As my approach and educational background is a psychological one, having part of the focus of this work be the self-development of settlers is an extreme privilege. I hope that acknowledging how decolonisation benefits all, including settlers, does not cause more harm, encourage engaging in the topic for the wrong reasons, or lead to further complacency.

Introduction to Chapters 6–9

Each of the following four chapters will examine a specific aspect of colonial consciousness which will be amplified through an elemental alchemical lens. Though between alchemists there could be great similarities in their methods and theories, there was also great diversity and variety in their beliefs, values, and approaches (Jung, 1937/1968, § 425). Some alchemists focused on the alchemy of colours. A simplified version of this might look like an initiate going through the experience of "the darkening," or *nigredo*; then the whiteness, *albedo*; the yellowing *citrinitas*; and then the reddening or *rubedo*.

These colours provide the main structure of this book. The first eight chapters of this book might be considered the *nigredo,* the period of time where alchemists are engaged in a reckoning with their shadow and work through the *prima materia* of their psyches. The *nigredo* is where the majority of alchemists spent their whole lives. It is safe to assume that most of us settlers *kweèt'įį,* rock seekers, involved in this work will also spend most of our lives in these depths and places of reckoning. The *nigredo* is thereby that which makes up the majority of this book. In Chapters 9 and 10, I will also look at the process of the whitening, yellowing, and reddening. In addition to, and sometimes instead of, working with colours, many alchemists worked very closely with the elements. The following four chapters will use the elements as a guide in investigating the colonial psyche. The elements will be held as roadmaps for the fundamental aspects of our humanity which mirror the main four aspects of this planet: earth, fire, water, and air. Reconnecting to these elemental processes within ourselves can be used as metaphors to aid in reconnecting to our own humanity and unsettling and rewilding our colonial, disconnected selves.

Alchemy points to fundamental needs and desires of the human psyche and the human experience which underlie everyday actions, thoughts, and behaviours. Hillman (2015) wrote, "Alchemy gives us a language of substance which cannot be taken substantively, concrete expressions which are not literal. This is its therapeutic effect: it forces metaphor upon us" (Location 181). Alchemists were trying to point toward the truths about human existence

DOI: 10.4324/9781003296546-6

underlying the everyday rhythms of life. Alchemy is found in the Western European tradition, but similar concepts were practiced around the world, including in Egypt, China, and the Middle East (von Franz, 1980, p. 43). Alchemy points to what may be archetypal human processes that connect us all, and it is expressed through the individuality and uniqueness of the diversity of cultures that birthed these ideas in different regions around the world.

Alchemy can at times feel like a very esoteric and abstract pursuit. However, at its core, I believe it is about reconnection to the Earth, life, and reembracing all aspects of existence, including the unconscious. In these next chapters, I will be focusing specifically on alchemy's relationship to the psyche through elemental metaphors. Across most cultures throughout time, the elements have been seen as the primary expressions of the Earth: they can be thought of as the quaternity, like the four directions that bring us into deep relationship with the workings, movements, and expressions of the planet. I believe true unsettling work calls us into this fundamental reconnection; it is about healing the colonial separation from the breath of this planet, its heat, soil, and flow. When we are in connection to these elements, we have more hope of feeling in connection to all living beings. And so, though I may at times delve into obscure references in alchemy, depth psychology, or historical texts, my hope is that at its core this work stays rooted in the elements and is devoted to reconnection with the life of this planet and all life that we share with it.

Helms's Stages of White Racial Identity Development

Another model that will be interwoven with the alchemical approach in the following chapters is Janet Helms's theory on the stages of white racial identity development (1993). Helms's model is a complementary model for this book's work on how white individuals reckon with their racial identity and how they move toward antiracist beliefs, actions and values. Helms's theory has six stages, which will be briefly explored throughout the remaining six chapters of this book. Helms's first stage, "contact," does not begin until a white individual has been confronted with race in some way. Before this encounter, white people live in ignorance of their own racial identity or the reality of racism for others. Helms contended that much of white America may still live in the pre-contact stage.

Chapter 6

Air

Helms's First Stage of White Racial Identity Development: Contact

Individuals in Helms' (1993) first stage of white racial identity development have had contact with the idea of race; however, their racial ideas are not grounded in their lived experience, and they have potentially had very little interaction with people with different life experiences, or who look different from themselves (p. 55). Individuals in the contact stage benefit greatly from systematic and institutionalised racism and are most likely oblivious to this privilege (p. 55). If they have any conceptualisation of how race should be addressed, it is probably through the idea of colour blindness. That is, they believe that if they do not see race, talk about race, or acknowledge race, then racism cannot be an issue.

In this stage, there is an airy lack of interracial contact or contact with concrete understandings of racism. There is a feeling of ephemeral fleeting racial awareness, but mostly wafting, complicit naivety. In this stage, something needs to happen to wake individuals from their ignorant racial stupor. Helms says that the stage of contact ends with an interruption to our naivety by a confrontation of some sort or another (p. 55). There must be a transition from airy contactlessness to actual contact: a condensation.

Introduction to *Sublimatio*

Earlier, this chapter on air was introduced as investigating the colonial psyche's focus on ascension: rationality, intellectualism, and transcendence at the expense and to the detriment of that which is embodied, immanent, and mortal. The Christian underpinnings of this disconnect were also explored, with its focus on ascension toward heaven being the ultimate goal and its associations with the earthly as being lowly and evil: "Earthly: fornication, impurity, passion, evil desire, and greed" (Colossians 3:5, NRSV). In this chapter, we will investigate how alchemy offers a counterbalancing antidote to this shadowy part of the colonial psyche by encouraging the attaining of balance between the embodied and transcendent.

DOI: 10.4324/9781003296546-7

Air is so ubiquitous in our lives that it seldom gets thought about or makes its way into our daily conversations or stories. And yet, the average person does not survive more than three minutes without it and today we know that taking a few conscious inhales and exhales can completely restart our brain's neurochemical reactions and subvert cataclysmic engagements of our limbic fight/flight/freeze systems. In the days of old, the alchemists recognised the vital importance of air to their alchemical work: how air, or the lack of it, changed reactions in their alembics, fuelled, or stifled fires and kept their own hearts warm and beating—or not.

This chapter will discuss how alchemists conceptualised air and its corresponding alchemical operation they called *sublimatio*. It will imagine into *sublimatio* as a metaphor for a part of what we are conceptualising as the distorted settler-colonial alchemical journey to the New World and explore how we can now consciously engage with this operation and element in our settler decolonisation journeys today.

Air

On May 27, 1768, Captain Cook ordered his crew to hoist up and open the sails of the Endeavour until they were at high mast and caught the wind; Cook set sail. Today a different kind of air travel is a significant source of the world's greenhouse gas emissions. In the last hundred years, our air pollution has increased by 33%, reaching 400 parts per million of carbon for the first time in more than 3 million years (National Geographic, 2019). Today, 50% of the Earth's landmasses are considered drylands, and 20% of these drylands are in the process of desertification due to climate change and changing weather and water patterns (United Nations, 2020).

Sublimatio is the alchemy operation related to air. Edinger (1991) wrote about Christianity that the "Christian spirit was the spirit of *sublimatio* … Christ arose upon earth as a ladder of many steps, and raised himself on high, so that all earthly beings might be exalted through Him" (p. 139). Edinger wrote that in alchemy, "all images that refer to upward movement-ladders, stairs, elevators, climbing, mountains, flying, and so forth-belong to *sublimatio* symbolism, as do all the psychological and value connotations associated with being high rather than low" (p. 138). Tarnas (2006) wrote about how when looking at Western bookshelves, one sees this obsession reflected in the libraries of books with titles such as "The Ascent of Man, The Discoverers, Man's Conquest of Space, or the like" (p. 12). Tarnas wrote about this Western obsession with ascension, and that in the West, colonial history is viewed as "onward and upward" (p. 12). Colonial perceived superiority, as well as the delusion of white supremacy, falls into this category of *sublimatio* that sees itself as higher, superior to all others; it is upward focused and is infatuated with success, knowledge, and progress.

On May 27, 2020, 252 years to the day that Cook first set sail across the seas, George Floyd said "I can't breathe" more than 20 times as he had the air forcibly removed from his body and he was murdered by police officer Derek Chauvin. Humans can only survive around three minutes without air—it is a most basic of human needs and rights. Today, it is BIPOC whose physical rights to air, breath, and life are most often threatened.

Whether we are speaking of the physical, human need for air or the imaginal power of the metaphor of air, humans need both. We can speak of the necessity of air both in sociocultural concreteness of injustice and lives taken and in the imaginal power of its metaphor. As humans, our survival depends on both our ability to breathe, and our ability to imagine better futures and stories that connect us all to our shared humanity. Air, composed of oxygen and nitrogen, is that which creates our atmosphere; the world as we know it can exist only because of these two little molecules. Hillman wrote that with its aspiration and inspiration and whirlwinds of thought, imagination itself can be thought of as a quality of air (Hillman, 1981, p. 274).

And yet, too much air can be dangerous too. An embolism is caused by a rapid change of pressure beneath the sea as we scuba dive: air bubbles fill the blood, leading to death. The same phenomenon will happen if we soar too high. In the late 1700s and the 1800s, many scientists died in hot air balloons, which were once called pneumatics (Glaisher, 1871, p. 111). On December 1, 1783, early aeronaut M. Charles wrote of one of his hot air balloon ascents: "My fingers were benumbed by the cold, so that I could not hold my pen ... when I left the earth, the sun had set on the valleys; he now rose for me alone" (p. 6). Wanting to reach higher and higher into the heavens, these aeronauts soared through the different levels of our Earth's atmosphere. Sometimes they undertook these ascents too quickly. Air bubbles filled their blood and they died, frozen above the clouds. High up in the sky, our heads too have become too full of air, bubbling our connection to body and earth out of our system. In our hot air balloons, we rose, too much air—we, white as snow-capped icy mountains, froze. Nervous system on overdrive. Always striving for higher success, knowledge, progress, like the scientists with embolisms in hot air balloons.

Air began our colonial exploits in our externalised search for the New World and it is not something we have as of yet reconciled with. Throwing our sails up, they caught, the wind pushed us across the sea, sometimes fair and cooperative, sometimes the squalls disastrous and deadly.

Cook's Journal

Fair winds:

> *1768: May 27th, Moderate and fair weather, at 11 am hoisted the Pendant and took charge of the Ship agreeable to my Commission of the 25th*

Instant, She lying in the Bason in Deptford Yard. From this day to the 21st of July we were constantly employed in fitting the Ship takeing on board stores and Provisions &c a when we saild from Deptford and anchor'd in Gallions reach where we remain'd until the 30th' (Cook, 2003, p. 11).

Squall winds:

1777: January, We continued our Course to the Eastward without meeting with any Sun. Nothing worthy of note till 4 oclock in the Morning of the 19th when in a sudden squal of wind the Fore Topmast went by the board and carried the Main Topg mast with it. (Cook, 2003, p. 495).

Sublimatio's Relationship to the Psyche: Positive and Negative Potentials

In alchemy, the process of *sublimatio* is related to the element of air. It refers to ascension and elevation. In the alchemist's laboratory, this looks like the sublimation of a solid directly into gas without it becoming a liquid in between (Edinger, 1991, p. 117). In *sublimatio*, earth is turned directly into air. In the colonial context, we can imagine this looking like the ascension-focused narratives of Christianity, where Earth is disregarded for higher, transcendent spiritual goals.

Other expressions of *sublimatio* states in the psyche are overintellectualism, hyperrationality and airheadedness, when they are disconnected from realities on Earth. "The Greeks called such folly hubris, and in their religion such inflation was regarded as a sin. Such fools were the puffers who exaggerated their claims and overworked the bellows" (Cavalli, p. 148). One modern word for this negative expression of *sublimatio* would be *spiritual bypassing*, whereby one bypasses the psychological work that needs to be done and jumps straight to thinking of themselves as spiritually elevated and superior. The missionaries, priests, and nuns who physically and/or sexually abused at least 37,951 children in residential schools in Canada (TRC, 2015b, p. 106) can be seen as examples of the extreme negative aspect of *sublimatio*. Perhaps these individuals also had severe psychological disturbances which led to them perpetuating the kind of abuse that they did, as not all those who have repressed sexuality express it with such violence and abuse. This being said, the *sublimatio* metaphor might be understood here in the deep cognitive dissonance and spiritual bypassing these abusive missionaries, priests, and nuns must have engaged in as they believed they were doing "spiritual work" teaching the importance of chastity, while, at the same time, they raped small children in residential schools perhaps in part because their own sexual issues were so deeply repressed and distorted.

Psychologically, the productive potential of *sublimatio* looks instead like rising above one's own arrogance or transcending the places one was stuck, elevating one's experience and perspective on life and evaporating the places where one was rigidly held in one's complexes (Edinger, 1991, p. 117). This could look like rising above one's need to be right, superior, powerful, or overcoming these complexes within and arriving at a place of openness and readiness for change and transformation. It might also look like a balance occurring between mind and matter: "We should return to the body in order to create spirit again" (Jarrett & Jung, 1988, p. 368). Imagining into the positive potentials of *sublimatio* for the colonial psyche, we can imagine a push toward a balance between body and mind, more of an emphasis on embodiment practices and showing up more fully on the earth and the realities that need our tending here on the ground.

How the Colonial Complex Enacted the Negative Potential of *Sublimatio*

Lebensraum is considered a primary motivation for World War II and is defined as the need for German people to have more living space, or specifically "breathing space" (Kruszewski, 1940, p. 966). *Lebensraum*, or breathing space, was conceptualised as "necessary for guaranteeing the life and development of the German people-physically, politically, and economically" (p. 964). Finding and developing more breathing space became an essential motivation for the Nazis: "The Nazis became increasingly convinced that nothing could save Germany except a genuine expansion of her Lebensraum and the unconditional return of her old colonies" (p. 964). This concept of *Lebensraum* has been applied to the English motivation for their earlier colonial exploits when "Britain's 'breathing space' became the British Empire, scattered over the globe, but connected by Britain's lines of communication-the lifelines of the empire. 'Life Line-Lebensraum" (p. 967). It is a chilling but poignant comparison to have the breathing space of the British Empire being equated to its lifeline in the same way that the Nazis equated their pursuits as in dedication to their lifeline, their breathing space.

Throughout the expansion of the British Empire, England itself became more and more overpopulated as birth rates rose. People were packed too tightly on a relatively small island. I believe that perhaps there was also a less conscious motivation fanning their desire for expansion, that what they were desiring was also more internal breathing room. A desire for more breathing room from the oppressive hierarchal class systems and freedom from the systems that kept peasants poor, dominated, and with no hopes of expanding their minds, potentials, passions, or joys. So they set out across the seas looking for the chance to breathe but took with them all the internalised suffocating hierarchies, biases, and beliefs and projected them all over the world that they found, making it far more like the old than anything truly new. In the distorted alchemical journey of seeking the internal gold and rebirth of a new world within, we can imagine the colonial psyche engaged with the pathological sides of the *sublimatio* operation by projecting its dysfunction onto the physical world around it, when perhaps what it was longing for was an internal fresh start, a deep big breath, and psychological breathing room.

This need for breath and breathing room can also be understood through women's physical inability to breathe during the colonial time period. Throughout the fifteenth to twentieth centuries, the women of England and then the settlers arriving in the New World were corseted. Corsets significantly reduce lung capacity, displace and atrophy organs, and permanently distort and misshape the entire musculoskeletal system (Klingerman, 2006, p. 14). Nineteenth-century Englishmen prized "the pale face, weak demeanour, and slight, waif-like figure" that came with tightly corseted women being unable to breathe and thereby think properly and were thus prone to frequent fainting spells (p. 19). "The delicate, refined woman was highly valued as a beauty, while the healthy or robust woman lacked femininity" (p. 19). During this time period, doctors would recommend young girls be corseted to correct and prevent "wild tendencies" from occurring and foster submissiveness and feminine docility sometimes even before the age of six years (p. 10).

> 52,432 corsets were sold in the year 1886. The average waist measurement was 23 inches, which gave a compression total (taking the number of corset wearers in England at 3,543,000, and their natural waist measurement at 27–28 inches) of 134 miles. The annual mortality rate resulting from this compression stood ... at 15,000. (Klingerman, 2006, p. 9)

These women needed to breathe. The oppression of the feminine occurring in this specific form of disallowing women from being able to breathe can be seen as another form of the imperial, patriarchal distorted relationship with the element of air, used to smother and suffocate instead of to fan the flames of life. These suffocating women then proceeded to inflict suffocating trauma on others, and instead of ally with the women of the "New World" took an active role in perpetuating harm on them starting the legacy that continues to this day of white feminism, white ladies looking after only themselves and not standing with or for women of colour. Menakem (2017) described this phenomenon of "blowing" one's own trauma through others to try to rid oneself of it, and instead this just spreading that trauma around even further in the world and simultaneously even deeper into ourselves (p. 37).

We can think of the colonial complex enacting the negative side of the *sublimatio* operation in various ways. The colonial complex has a focus on hyperrationality, and a lack of emotion in its one-sidedness. It privileges: the intellect over body; thought over emotion; law over common sense; and the ideal over the human actual. Colonial mindset privileges the word, enlightenment living in the mind. The one-sidedness of these properties has produced a psyche that is profoundly disembodied.

All of these attributes can be imagined and understood as imbalances of air, of this negative side of the *sublimatio* alchemical operation. The following sections focus on three main additional ways that colonial consciousness has manifested these dysfunctions: hyperrationality, colour blindness and white silence, and finally the physical spread of lung disease that leads to suffocation.

Transcendence

Like Jung's colonial bird of prey soaring high above the problems of the world, landing on top of the spire of the highest ivory tower, colonial consciousness has lived amidst the clouds of its lofty ideas, theories, racist policies, and ideals. This "fantasy of individualism" of colonialism revels in "the splendid isolation of the colonial administrator, the captain of industry and the continental academic in his ivory tower" (Hillman, 1994, p. 33). Colonial consciousness has been disconnected from, in denial of and unperturbed by the real-world harm these policies and ideas have inflicted on individuals, specifically Indigenous people and people of colour: "The higher we go the grander and more comprehensive is our perspective, but also the more remote we become from actual life" (Edinger, 1991, p. 118).

Some of these devastating lofty colonial policies and ideas in Canada include the idea of Canada's first Prime Minister John A. Macdonald in 1880 that the Canadian state was to deal with the "native problem" by "wean[ing] them by slow degrees, from their nomadic habits, which have almost become an instinct, and by slow degrees absorb them or settle them on the land" (Joseph, 2018, p. 15). Later in Canada's colonial history, one of the goals of Indian Residential Schools in Canada was to "kill the Indian in the child" (Niessen, 2017, p. 20). Duncan Campbell Scott said in 1920: "I want to get rid of the Indian problem ... Our objective is to continue until there is not a single Indian in Canada that has not been absorbed into the body politic and there is no Indian question and no Indian Department" (p. 35). These are some of the policies so inflated with superiority and an idea of what was right, so disconnected from the reality of people's lives, culture, empathy, and humanity that they reveal some of the root causes of the genocide which occurred on these lands.

The denial and denigration of non-Western ways of knowing has been part and parcel of European colonialism and a primary means by which the universality of Western knowledge was asserted and used as a justification for the dispossession, destitution, and genocide of populations who were perceived to be lacking knowledge of universal worth (but who occupied lands of strategic importance). (Ahenakew, 2016, p. 327)

I want to emphasise that the unbalance between logos and eros, logic and emotion is the issue being addressed here, not rationality itself. There is great beauty and importance in the upholding of reason, the pursuit of knowledge and logos. It is when the upholding of these values comes at the cost of dismissing the emotional and physical realms that the danger occurs, in the same way that there is great danger in relying too heavily on emotions without the support of reason and rationality. Tarnas (2006) wrote of "the profound metaphysical disorientation and groundlessness that pervades" the Western soul and its hyperfocus on rationality and logos (Location 129). He also emphasised the "deep sense of alienation" in the Western psyche that cuts itself off from its emotion and the aliveness and eros of the world around itself (Location 129). He refers not only to personal isolation here but also to the "spiritual estrangement of the modern psyche in a disenchanted universe, as well as, at the species level, the subjective schism separating the modern human being from the rest of nature" (Location 129). Reason has shaped the West to such a great degree and has given us the beauty of the great philosophers, and intellectual freedom and the Age of Enlightenment. It gave us the great scientific advances that have relieved so much suffering, saved so many lives, and helped curtail plagues from further decimating populations and lives. Reason is of the utmost importance and value in our world, and we cannot privilege reason at the expense of emotion and eros.

The idea of *enantiodromia* was first formulated by ancient philosopher Heraclitus and is the idea of a pendulum of ideas swinging from one extreme to the other (von Franz, 2014, Location 1645). Jung took up the term *enantiodromia* as a psychological law, and von Franz wrote of how Jung viewed *enantiodromia* as the idea that "all extreme psychological states tend to tip over into their opposite: goodness into evil, happiness into unhappiness, exaggerated spirituality into surrender to instincts, etc" (Location 1645). *Enantiodromia* is when, in response to one extreme position, there is a swing to its farthest polarity; it is "a conversion of something into its opposite" (Jung, 1952/1967, § 581).

Authors such as Tarnas (2006) and Cambray (2012) conceptualised the Age of Enlightenment as the *enantiodromia* to the Dark Ages, which was the age of being suffocated in the doctrines of the Church. The Enlightenment, or the Age of Reason, which focused on logic and rationality, came as a breath of fresh air after people were dominated for too long by dogma, blind faith, and the fear of God. So, the West started to swing from the Church into an age where we became dedicated to reason. This time period has shaped our society as we know it today and has been a rich period of intellectual creativity, growth, and innovation. Cambray (2012) argues that these developments also came at the expense of the totality of ourselves, including our creative and emotional selves and our connection to the natural world (p. 46).

The Enlightenment is also thought of as birthing much of the colonial legal, administrative, and economic policy of the British Empire (Scott, 2004, p. 178).

In the "work of Enlightenment thinkers like James Mill and Jeremy Bentham, the new utilitarian rationalism of the eighteenth century simply provided the clarifying justification for more deeply entrenched, more sweeping, and more efficient practices of subjectification, surveillance, regulation, and discipline" (p. 178). In the centuries since, we have seen the results of our focus on reason and theory to justify supremacist colonial policies. We have also seen what it has done to the white psyche when we focus solely on the pursuit of reason and do not concurrently tend, honour and nurture our creative and emotional selves, recognise the real world impact our theories or policies have, and honour the natural world of which we are a part.

This being said about the dangers of an unbalanced valuing of reason above all else, public universities have been consistently and dramatically losing state and federal funding in the United States for the last several decades (Morris, 2020, p. 8). I am hesitant to fan the flames of the dismissal of research and learning for the sake of furthering knowledge, which is something so beautiful and integral to society, the experience of being human and the joy of learning more about this strange universe in which we find ourselves. The pursuit of knowledge can be one of the most beautiful explorations of the human experience. It is one of the great joys of my life, shown in this book's fairly esoteric and heady pursuit of knowledge. And yet, this pursuit cannot come at the expense of valuing the other aspects of human existence. Reason untethered from emotion can be profoundly problematic. However, emotion untethered by reason can also be a terrifying force, as we see in the pattern of fascist uprisings throughout history. Through the COVID-19 pandemic we have seen anti-science and anti-reason rhetoric come from both the far right and far left communities alike (MAGA supporters, as well as neospiritual hippies, as well as from many people between) in their demonstrations against the life-saving scientific breakthroughs of COVID-19 vaccines.

Colour Blindness and White Silence

White silence is the complicit silence of white individuals when they do not speak up against racism (Saad, 2020, p. 54). Layla Saad described white silence as "a defending of the status quo of white supremacy—a manifestation of holding onto one's white privilege through inaction" (p. 54). White silence and colour blindness are related, as to say that you are colour blind is to ignore race and to stay silent in the face of it and the racism, injustice and oppression that comes with it. Dr. Martin Luther King Jr. said, "We will have to repent in this generation not merely for the hateful words and actions of the bad people but for the appalling silence of the good people" (Saad, 2020, p. 53).

White silence and colour blindness is the intentional not hearing, seeing and therefore the assumed not doing of racism. It is the intentional looking away, the hyperconcentration on the white which "blinds" out all the other colours. Hillman's (1986) concept that Jung's re-enlivening of alchemy was an effort toward the recoloration of the Western soul seems especially relevant in the dangerously whitening "light" of colour blindness (p. 49). Lama Rod Owens (2016) described colour blindness as an attitude of "There's no colour! There's no system there! There's nothing. We just don't see it anymore" (Williams, Owens, & Syedullah, 2016, p. 159). Colour blindness is a dangerous and pervasive attitude toward race, that is, in itself, inherently racist.

You cannot see air, like so many pretend they cannot see racism; it is the denial of the ephemeral space between every interaction. And yet, we can see through air, like we must see through the denial of racism into the reality of the everyday oppression, the targeted police violence, the racist policies, and the underfunded resources of racist society. White silence is a disappearing act from action, a wispy aversion to the commitment of antiracism. It needs a condensation, to take form in direct antiracist action and words.

Colonial Suffocation

Another way of exploring this alchemical colonial metaphor is through psychologising physical symptoms. Ziegler (2015) wrote about "archetypal medicine," which is the idea of finding healing by looking at events or physical symptoms through an archetypal lens. Zeigler attributed this approach to Jung's ideas surrounding the value of archetypal imagination (p. 11). Zeigler wrote about how viewing things archetypally allowed for understandings, not through hard fact or "statistical reasoning" but instead through opening our minds to different possibilities and playing with ideas of meaning and potential insight (p. 9). In this way, this approach is reminiscent of a poetic, storyteller, or narrative worldview. Instead of arguing the validity of an argument, this way of archetypal imagining is meant to invoke wonder and curiosity and open one's mind and heart to possibilities of change (p. 10).

Looking at physical realities and symptoms of colonialism through this lens may itself be a *sublimatio*, a rising above ordinary ways of looking at the world and directing our gaze instead to the story as a whole. It is the movement of looking at the story to potentially see deeper threads of connection woven throughout it all, in the aim of shifting the narratives to aid in bringing about shifts of understanding and action.

And so, the previous and following sections weave together seemingly disparate and far-fetched ideas of colonialism's relationship to air in all of its various forms. This is not an argument that a distorted alchemical relationship was at the heart of colonialism, but instead to wander into the imaginal realm, to use *sublimatio* to rise above everyday thinking and gaze through a narrative lens into pieces of the past. If nothing else, the hope is that this can help us tolerate the examination of these horrific events more than if they were lists of stand-alone facts.

As we are storytelling and story-listening creatures, the hope is that this alchemical lens helps weave a story that can enter our hearts and change us deeply, in a way that only stories truly can. And so, we shift here to look at the psychologising of physical symptoms and events in the story of a colonial imbalance of air. The following facts about tuberculosis in what is now called Canada are true, putting them in the context of a distorted alchemical relationship to air is where we enter into the narrative realm.

Tuberculosis

And so we begin imagining into a more physical embodiment of this distorted colonial relationship to the element of air by looking at the horrific effects of the spread of a highly contagious lung disease throughout what is now called Canada after its introduction by settlers. Tuberculosis results in shortness of breath, patients who die of tuberculosis suffocate by their lungs filling with liquid, which leads to a death by drowning and suffocation. Captain Cook brought tuberculosis on his ships all over the world, spreading its suffocating symptoms and death rate around the globe (Crosby, 2015, Location 3595). Later, settler-colonials brought over tuberculosis from Europe specifically to what is now called North America, and with government legislation forcing Indigenous people into inadequate, overcrowded housing, it quickly led to a devastating epidemic in Indigenous communities (TRC, 2015a, p. 384).

Tuberculosis was also rampant in Indian Residential Schools, and at times it was left purposely untreated, and it was spread as part of the solution to the "Indian problem" (Palmater, 2014, p. 32). The resulting deaths and infection rates exposed "the genocidal practices of government-sanctioned residential schools, where healthy Indigenous children were purposefully exposed to children infected with TB, spreading the disease through the school population" (p. 32). Some residential schools had tuberculosis infection rates of up to 93% (Bryce, 1922, p. 14). Few or no preventative measures were taken to halt its spread and inadequate to no appropriate medical treatment was provided (p. 14). In one school, it was found that "75 per cent [of children] were dead at the end of the 16 years since the school opened," and many of these deaths were related to tuberculosis (p. 4).

Another aspect of the colonial relationship with tuberculosis was the creation of Indian hospitals to prevent settlers from being exposed to the disease (Hardy v. Canada, 2018, p. 7). Experimental tuberculosis vaccine trials were permitted to be tested on Indigenous children at these hospitals without consent (p. 7). Of the doctors at the Indian hospitals, 47% of them had not passed the Canadian medical licensing examinations so were not licensed or qualified to be practicing medicine anywhere but in Indian hospitals (p. 14). Devastating levels of malpractice and abuse were perpetrated against Indigenous children in these hospitals. A 2018 court case, the first of its kind against the Canadian government for its running of Indian hospitals, detailed the following additional abuses that happened to children within the hospitals. Children were subjected to:

> Beating with rods and sticks; isolation in hospital rooms for prolonged periods of time; food and drink deprivation without any medical reason; physical restraint to hospital beds; and forced feeding and forcibly requiring class members to eat their own vomit. In addition to physical abuse suffered by patient class members, there was widespread and common sexual abuse carried out by hospital staff members. (Hardy v. Canada, 2018, p. 12)

Many of these children were restrained without medical justification; medical restraints were being used on Indigenous children long after they had stopped being used to treat tuberculosis in any other population group (Hardy v. Canada, 2018, p. 13). Sometimes this abuse involved the children being put into full body casts unnecessarily for months or years at a time, keeping them immobilised and unable to move (p. 13). When antibiotics were being used to treat non-Indigenous populations in the comfort of their homes, they were withheld from Indigenous children who had to remain in Indian Hospitals and who were not given antibiotics (p. 13). This settler disease introduced into Indigenous communities paired with the colonially oppressive conditions Indigenous people and children were subjected to led to a tuberculosis death rate 45 times higher than the peak numbers of infection among the settler population. These were the highest tuberculosis death rates ever recorded in global history (TRC, 2015a, p. 384).

How the Colonial Complex Can Now Enact the Positive Potential of *Sublimatio*

In thinking about the redirection of the distorted alchemical journey we are imagining was undertaken in the colonisation of North America, we can wonder what it might mean to rewrite our relationship with the alchemical *sublimatio* and the air element today. The positive side of *sublimatio* is overcoming places of stagnancy by rising above where we have become immovable. If we can undertake this path of rising above in a responsible way instead of the colonial *sublimatio* pathologies previously described, we can pursue the positive potential of this alchemical operation today (Edinger, 1991, p. 117).

We can imagine that colonial ungroundedness has taken us too far into the clouds, so far from the earth, the embodied reality that our abstract, colonial theories, ideas, constitutions have created and the oppression, marginalisation, and violence that they enact on Indigenous people, people of colour and the living world. Jung wrote, "wisdom begins only when one takes things as they are; otherwise we get nowhere, we simply become inflated balloons with no feet on the earth," he continued, "So it is a healing attitude when one can agree with the facts as they are; only then can we live in our body on this earth, only then can we thrive" (Jarrett & Jung, 1988, p. 545). To move forward from here, learn what we need to, unlearn and re-educate our racial conditioning, we might need a big gust of air from the bellows to flame the passion for justice that will sustain our commitment to the journey of antiracism and the learning and unlearning it requires. Edinger (1991) wrote that "the whole history of cultural evolution can be seen as a great *sublimatio* process in which human beings learn how to see themselves and their world objectively" (p. 125). In its positive potential, *sublimatio* allows us to rise above ourselves and our societal roles so that we can clearly see the bigger picture of our positionality and the workings of society so that we can better understand what needs to change for true justice, reparations, and equality to take place.

In this alchemical narrative today, we would need to redirect our mind from its disconnected lofty heights back downward into our communities, societies, people, and land. Rossi (2017) reflected on this positive potential of air: "air is the fuel on which fire depends, air is the element of the intellect, contemplation, objective reflection, imagining" (p. 45). Rossi continued, the

> puffers and bellows in the alchemical kitchen are those instruments with which the fire is fed with air. The opposition of fire and air is a primary complementarity that draws out and fuels the fuller image of both essences. Invisible, air rarifies and condenses the fiery things of psyche. (p. 45)

With enough air, inspiration can strike, the mind can engage, and ideas can form. Hillman (2015) wrote that the act of breathing is our "first participation in the cosmos," he continued "Fire lives on mind, and the sustaining heat of our warm-bloodedness depends on inspiration, on fantastic invention, breezy wit and windy rhetoric, on brain-storming, rarefied theories and cool ideas" (Location 482). Directing our focus toward fanning the flames of an embodied earthly passion for justice and the world is the potential way forward for the colonial mind to today engage with breath, air, inspiration, pneuma, spirit and the alchemical *sublimatio* of positive transformation today.

Hillman (2005) believed that we must come back to our history as a way to land from our lofty heights: "The soul involves us in history" (p. 81). He believed that we must come back to nurturing parts of the past, back to writers such as Jung, to old myths, history and the specificity of geography, getting to know the actual land around us to nurture our souls back (p. 81). Hillman believed that an accurate history where we in the West are not its heroes has become the "Great Repressed" in our psyches (p. 80). Hillman wrote that our "history rumbles below," and in the depths of our psyches, "our complexes are history at work in the soul" (p. 80). He believed that it is much easier to transcend our history, than acknowledge and be accountable for it, and that the West has done just that, either ignoring our cultural history or glorifying it (p. 80). He argued for the importance of facing this history and letting it work on us. He argued that transformation today "requires recognition of history, an archaeology of the soul, a digging in the ruins, a re-collecting. And—a planting in specific geographical and historical soil with its own smell and savour" (p. 81). For Hillman, a descent into history is a grounding balance to airy abstraction and its lofty dangers. As settlers, part of this process may be asking what does it mean to land and live here, on lands we occupy, stolen lands not our own.

As part of the balancing potential to the loftiness, part of the descent back into ourselves and the world there must be a descent back into our own histories, the darkness within them, the recognition of our dark and terrible colonial past and no longer escaping it with fantasies of its heroic discoveries. This requires a reckoning with the reality of the scars those histories carved into the world and the intergenerational trauma still resounding in so many family lines from this colonial past. It also necessitates a reckoning and commitment to no longer be in denial of this past and to descend from the lofty heights Hillman described. The pathway down from the mountain top is what is needed for us to truly breathe once more, to shake the old colonial systems that keep us suffocated and suffocating. We have shed the corsets that impacted our ability to breathe, but now we must shed the other colonial systems keeping us and others, physically as well as metaphorically, unable to breathe.

Sublimatio/Air Concrete Actions and Reflection Questions

The root of the word activism is *actus,* the latin word for "doing," or taking action. Activism cannot just be changing ourselves, it also necessitates direct concrete action. And so, keeping in line with alchemical modes of imagining, we can now begin our attempt at embodying the ideas explored in this chapter through concrete action. As settlers carrying out the work of unsettling processes, we must heal the trauma within ourselves that has perpetuated such devastation. However, it cannot stop there, this work must happen concurrently with our antiracism work. What follows are steps that fall into both of these categories of psychological unsettling as well as direct action. Neither of these categories of actions alone will repair the damage that the colonial psyche has inflicted on this land and the Indigenous people that have been here since time immemorial. Rather these can be seen as potential precursors or concurrent practices that prepare us as individuals and settler society more broadly for the more fundamental reparations and change that is required and that Indigenous people are calling for.

In this chapter, we examined the colonial complex's focus on ascension: rationality, intellectualism, progress, and transcendence at the expense and detriment of that which is embodied, immanent, and mortal. We also looked at alchemy's focus on attaining a balance between the embodied and transcendent. Through the following actions, both in the categories of personally unsettling and direct action, we can begin to shift that balance.

- Are there places you are silent in the face of racism, where you do not speak out and up when you witness it? In what situations does your white silence lead to you attempting to be invisible, airy in your commitment to justice and antiracism?
- Are there places in which you dismiss emotion, the arts, creative pursuits, or the importance of the natural world?
- Do you ever value efficiency, progress, or policy as the gold standard, not to be derailed by "softer" considerations?
- Do you know the history of the land on which you reside, and if not, why do you not know? Seek out decolonial sources to learn this history now, preferably from the perspectives of the Indigenous Nation whose territory you occupy.
- Seek out resources to learn about the current legislation at provincial or federal levels that continue to perpetuate racist and colonial policies. Study what people are saying about these policies, write your representatives in office, and join rallies in protest of them.
- Read *My Conversations with Canadians* (2017) and *The Inconvenient Indian* (2013) to learn more about the real-world impact of colonial Canada's policies on Indigenous people. Read *The Winter We Danced* (2014) to hear personal stories from Indigenous people in the Idle No More movement and how Canadian racist policy and culture have directly impacted their lives.
- See Layla Saad's (2020) chapter in *Me and White Supremacy* on white silence for more journal prompts and reflections on the subject of white silence and complicity (p. 59).
- Read Ijeoma Oluo's *So You Want To Talk About Race* (2018).
- Are there settler groups in your area? If so, join one, or start your own where you can work through any of the books above. Layla Saad (2020) gives instructions on forming a book study group at the end of *Me and White Supremacy*.
- Finally, begin or deepen a breathing practice that helps you learn to regulate your nervous system and connect with this powerful resource for circumventing panic/fear/anger/dissociation responses which can help nurture calm/connected/regulating responses instead.
- Do you have breath or mindfulness practices that are culturally appropriated? Do you know their origin, if people of European descent have been given permission to practice them? If not, find breath or mindfulness practices from your lineages, they exist in almost all, if not all of our ancestries and pasts.

Part of the concrete action that needs to be taken today is to no longer succumb to white silence within ourselves and instead call it out when we see racism around us, not being in denial, doing our work, and using our mind to confront these issues within and without instead of silencing and ignoring them. The next three chapters of this book will go more in depth looking at the importance of practices of embodiment, connecting to nature and inner creativity in this unsettling work.

Chapter 7

Water

Helms's Second Stage of White Racial Identity Development: Disintegration

The second stage of Helms's model of white racial identity development is the stage she called "disintegration." In this stage, an individual has been confronted with a racial encounter and their previous belief that racism is not a significant societal issue has been challenged (p. 58). They may experience feelings of guilt and shame surrounding their racial ignorance which they may attempt to block out, repress, and ignore (p. 58). "Entry into the Disintegration stage implies conscious, though conflicted, acknowledgement of one's Whiteness. Moreover, it triggers the recognition of moral dilemmas associated with being White" (p. 58).

In this stage, individuals may start accepting the reality that people of colour are not treated the same as white people and that people of colour are unfairly discriminated against in a variety of ways (p. 59). Individuals in this stage can also begin to experience "feelings of guilt, depression, helplessness, and anxiety" (p. 59). They will be experiencing uncomfortable cognitive dissonance at this point when their new realisations are in conflict with their behaviour, how they have been living most of their lives; how they interact with people of colour; how they discuss or do not discuss race relations with their peers; and perhaps even their political leanings. Helms explained that there are three ways to deal with cognitive dissonance in these circumstances: "(a) changing a behaviour, (b) changing an environmental belief, and (c) developing new beliefs" (p. 59). If the individual tries to fix this cognitive dissonance by changing their actions, instead of going back to denial of the realities around them, then they will slowly start to shift into the next stage of white racial identity development: reintegration (p. 60).

In the disintegration phase one's old ideas, beliefs, and ways of understanding the world start to fall apart, being dissolved into new revelations about the world and how others are treated within it. In this way, it can be thought of as a *solutio*, a dissolving of one state of being into another.

Introduction to *Solutio*

This chapter will investigate the colonial psyche's focus on the sublimation of the body and sexuality. Earlier, the Christian underpinnings of this disconnect were explored, and its associations with the body as something evil (Sirach 17:3, NRSV), sinful (Romans 7:25, NRSV), and perverse (Jeremiah 17:9, NRSV). In this chapter, we will investigate how alchemy offers a counterbalancing antidote to this part of the colonial psyche by honouring the sacredness of the body and sensuality. We will explore how alchemists conceptualised water and its corresponding alchemical operation *solutio*, imagine into *solutio* as a metaphor for a part of the distorted alchemical journey to the New World and look at how we can now consciously engage with this operation and element in our unsettling journeys today.

Water

Nearly half of the Earth's population lives by the sea and 50–80% of the Earth's oxygen comes from the ocean. The ocean's cycles partnered in an endless dance with the moon impact weather systems around the globe. We humans are 80% water, and thus should drink an average of 3 liters of water daily (most of us don't).

Jung, as well as many other authors, scholars, and poets throughout time, described the unconscious as the sea. Life emerged out of water, which is why the sea symbolises the unconscious, the matrix of all life/consciousness. The ocean represents the watery depths of our dreams, where a plethora of unknowns, sea monsters, and dark waterlogged deaths could await us. Only 3% of the water on Earth is freshwater. This freshwater flows as creeks and rivers, pools in lakes, cascades down waterfalls and evaporates into the clouds to rain, hail, snow and mist down upon us. Every plant, animal, and living creature (except for those in the sea) depend on freshwater for survival. The incredible diversity of life in tropical forests depends on its constant humidity, and the highest levels of biomass in the world are in rainforests, which I get to call home. At the same time, the United Nations predicts that by 2025, two-thirds of the world's population will be living with water shortages of some kind and that 1.8 million people will live in dire water shortages. Between 1993 and 2019, around 279 billion tons of ice melted and was lost in Greenland, and in this same time period, Antarctica lost about 148 billion tons of ice per year (NASA, 2021, § 7). Sea levels globally rose eight inches over the last century, and the rise is accelerating every year (NASA, 2021, § 10).

Intertidal zones are some of the most biodiverse zones in the world, the liminal meeting between shore and sea. All geography on Earth can be shaped by water. Rivers wear through rock until great canyons are formed; creeks shape the contours of the land; endless sand beaches are formed by the ocean crashing rocks together for millennia until millions of sand particles exist from what was once only a few rocks. A young child who has never seen the ocean recently asked me in a sandplay therapy session, "Is it named sand because it is where the *sea* and l*and* meet?"

Water covers 75% of the planet. All life on Earth originated from the ocean 3.5 billion years ago. Today, there are more pollutants in the sea than there has ever been before and these pollutants are poisoning all life within it. Every year 14 billion pounds of garbage are dumped in the ocean 200 billion pounds of life is caught from the ocean for human consumption, and 63 billion pounds is wasted and discarded. Of all the humans who have died in the ocean's untamed wildness, the death that travelled across the sea with the first colonial voyagers had the highest toll.

When we are told stories about the early colonial explorers, voyagers, and settlers, they all begin with the sea. Captain Cook and George Vancouver, aboard the Resolution, set sail, resolved to discover and claim land in the name of the Queen. We are told stories of stormy seas, endless horizons, painfully slow and inefficient distillation systems onboard to get precious drops of freshwater from the salty expanses, and rain barrel collection systems. The ships became rolling homes on the water for the colonial explorers, the seasickness becoming at times unbearable as the ocean buoyed these explorers about, crashing them into 30-metre-high waves, not decided yet if it would allow these colonists to make it across its reach. Many times, it decided against it and many sailors and ships sank into the ocean's depths.

Cook's body was dismembered after his death, cut apart in the ceremonial manner only great leaders in Hawaii received, the dismembered body parts distributed among the chiefs of Hawaii. Over the days after his death, his crew received pieces of him back bit by bit to lay to rest at the bottom of the sea. Today, the dismembered remnants of him have long since disintegrated and dispersed into its depths. The sea was a place which defined Cook's life and ultimately, his death. The effects of his actions around the globe still persist and are not as prone to disintegration as his physical self. Today, many places around the world still bear the names he gave them, as well as the tragic colonial history and the many diseases he spread around the globe.

Cook's Journals

Both fresh and salt water affected every part of Cook's travels, from weather to waves to drinking water to survive.

> *August 16th, 1776: Between the Lat. of 12° and 7° N the weather was generally dark and gloomy, with frequent rains of which we saved as much Water as filled the most of our empty water casks. These rains and the close sultry weather they accompany but too often bring on sickness in this passage, one has at least every thing to fear from them, and cannot be too*

much on ones guard, by obliging the people to dry their cloathes and airing the Ship with fires and smoke at every opportunity. This was constantly practised on board the Resolution & Discovery and we certainly profited by it, for we had fewer sick than on either of my former Voyages. (Cook, 2003, p. 486)

Solutio's Relationship to Psyche: Positive and Negative Potentials

In the alchemical laboratory, the process of *solutio* is characterised by water, by the dissolving of solid to liquid. "*Solutio* often meant the return of differentiated matter to its original undifferentiated state—that is, to *prima materia*" (Edinger, 1991, p. 47). Jung saw the shadow and water as inseparable. He imagined the shadow as a watery expanse, understood it as the world of "water, where all life floats in suspension; where the realm of the sympathetic system, the soul of everything living, begins; where I am indivisibly this and that; where I experience the other in myself and the other-than-myself experiences me" (Jung, 1934/1954, § 45).

The negative expressions of the alchemist's *solutio* can be imagined as an individual flooded by the unconscious, overwhelmed and unable to face or regulate their emotions, or regressing back into infantile emotional states, which can be imagined as the longing to be back in the waters of the womb and might look like selfishness or tantrums (Edinger, 1991, p. 49). The negative expression of solutio can also manifest as the resistance to being in the flow, changing and allowing oneself to be transformed (p. 50). *Solutio* can be like a sudden rushing of a river and can be twofold: "it causes one form to disappear and a new regenerated form to emerge" (p. 51). In this way, *solutio* can be deeply transformative in washing away what is no longer needed. However, there can be a lot of fear and resistance experienced by the personality in the face of the changes *solutio* brings.

An example of how we can imagine the negative aspects of *solutio* in the colonial context is in the institutional attempt to dissolve the connections of Indigenous people from land, family, culture and spirituality. This can be seen as a distorted *solutio* process in the colonial shadow's expression of its violence. We can perhaps see it manifested as colonial attempts at dissolving Indigenous connection to place by forcing their dislocation to other spaces and lands. It may also be seen in the dissolving of colonialists' own traditions, connections, and roots as they left what they knew as home and never returned.

In contrast, the positive potential of *solutio* is a return to wholeness, a melting, an undifferentiation and unifying: "The soul stirs things back to life by moistening" (Rossi, 2017, p. 44). The psychological processes associated with this are calling into question the rigid, fixed aspects of the personality so that there can be an opening and possibility of them dissolving and allowing for something new to form (Edinger, 1991, p. 48). *"Solutio* comes from the Self. What is worth saving in the ego is saved. What is not worth saving is dissolved and melted down in order to be recast in new life-forms. Thus, the ongoing life process renews itself" (p. 81). The positive potential of *solutio* is a dissolving of ourselves and our position and privilege in the world as we know it, a melting of our power and equalising of it among all parts. Psychological *solutio* can be a dissolving of our complexes so that something can reform from them anew.

In alchemy and depth psychology, there is an association between water, the body, and sexuality. "Water finds purchase in the tiniest of fissures and beings to flow. Venus' sensual eroticism, aesthetic pleasure, in our fantasies. And as aqua vitae, water has the power to revivify what has become dry and calcinated" (Rossi, 2017, p. 44). Jung often highlighted the importance of condensation from spirit to the return of the watery body (Jarrett & Jung, 1988, p. 368). Jung recognised and honoured the body as essential to the wholeness of our selves and psyches. He recognised the vitality and wisdom of the body as a neglected aspect of the Western psyche and emphasised the importance of our return to it and its tending. Using the alchemical understandings of water and body in this way contextualises this chapter's focus on how the colonial complex relates to body and sexuality, the harm it has inflicted on bodies and sexuality in the violence of colonisation and the decolonising potentials going forward in terms of settler relationship to body, gender, identity, and sexuality.

As previously discussed, this exercise of looking at colonialism alchemically is to open our minds to the change required of us in a way unique to metaphors and stories. In this process, I often engage in psychologising physical symptoms and events. Hillman (1975) advocated for the usefulness of the psychologising of symptoms and treating concrete expressions of archetypal realities. He believed that this psychologising places emphasis and value on the story, the idea, the narrative behind our psychologies, mythologies, and worldviews (p. 117). Hillman believed that the value of this approach was that it allows the psyche to engage in self-reflection upon "its nature, structure, and purpose" through myth and stories (p. 117). Psychologising is the storytelling of our lives and place in the world. It is a connection between the individual life and the story with which that life is engaged, as "ideas allow us to envision, and by means of vision we can know. Psychological ideas are ways of seeing and knowing soul, so that a change in psychological ideas means a change in regard to soul and regard for soul" (p. 121). Psychologising is the writing of myth for the soul, and the hope is that it allows for deep change of perspective, humility, and openness to change.

In this vein of psychologising, this chapter will continue engaging in the narrative of the colonial alchemical longings for the rebirth of a new inner world and its gold. We have imagined that this longing was externalised, and the colonisers then engaged in a disturbing, distorted search to fulfil these longings in the physical world. Analytical psychologist Marian Woodman explained this kind of externalisation of one's inner needs and how this can lead to addicted behaviour which may "result from distorted and desperate attempts to fulfil our genuine needs" (Sieff, 2015, p. 66). Woodman continued, explaining that in these states of externalising our inner longings, "we may find ourselves craving food that brings no nurture, drink that brings no spirit or sex that brings no union. Our hunger is for food – but it is for soul food" (p. 66). She described how in these states of craving and addiction we are actually longing for our deep creative expression and a connection to our own soul (p. 66). She described how, "when we are unable to fulfil our buried emotional and spiritual needs, we turn to concrete substitutes, which then poison us" (p. 66). This kind of addiction and externalisation of our needs is what we are investigating here in colonial consciousness, while using the metaphor of alchemy to look at the possibilities of the deeper needs and longings being expressed and sought after in such destructive ways.

In considering this narrative, we can look at one aspect of alchemical processes, and imagine how it may have featured in this distorted colonial alchemical journey: *solutio*. Like all alchemical operations, *solutio* has negative and positive, light and shadow potentials. In this chapter, we will explore how the colonial psyche seems to have manifested many of the shadow aspects of *solutio* in its negative stance toward the body, the feminine, and sexuality. We will also look at how working toward the positive aspects of *solutio*'s water element might be a useful way to shift our colonial relationship with the body, the feminine, sexuality, and water today. We will begin by imagining into some of the aspects of colonialism's history in what is now called Canada as expressions of the negative potentials of *solutio*.

How the Colonial Complex Enacted the Negative Potentials of *Solutio*

We can imagine the colonial complex enacting the negative aspect of *solutio* in many ways throughout the colonisation of so-called Canada. An ironic example of this was the colonials judgement of First Nations people, who they called "savages" for getting naked and bathing every day, while many of them themselves only bathed once a year. In Europe, people lived in such close proximity to livestock, often sleeping in the same rooms as them, that they had all sorts of diseases the likes of which had never existed in the "New World" (Crosby, 2015, Location 4326). This was why Indigenous tolerance to the new diseases of the unsanitary colonialists was so low (Location 4326). So many bouts of pestilence and pandemics had swept through Europe over the centuries in part because of the unsanitary and overcrowded living conditions of the poor.

The class systems in Europe had created such extreme wealth gaps that a huge percentage of the population was direly impoverished. There were also frequent public beheadings and the binding of others to pyres to burn (Menakem, 2017, p. 59). These were pained people coming over from Europe, filled with what Menakem calls "Dirty Pain," or as "the pain of avoidance, blame, and denial. When people respond from their most wounded parts, become cruel or violent, or physically or emotionally run away, they experience dirty pain" (p. 20). Settler-colonials came to the New World hoping to be cleansed of this dirty pain that they carried within them. They hoped to have their painful histories washed away and find the newness of the life possible across the sea.

The following sections will imagine into how the negative aspects of the *solutio* processes enacted through the colonial complex could have affected bodies and sexuality. This metaphor of water is being used to categorise and sort through the vast horrors of colonialism, and as a metaphorical container for these extremely difficult subject matters. The hope is that it can aid in our ability to process, face, and reckon with it all in our own ways before taking the concrete actions necessary from there.

White Body Trauma

We begin this investigation by looking at the trauma imbedded in white bodies themselves, before looking at the trauma white bodies then inflicted on bodies of colour. Menakem (2017) posited that fleeing medieval England may have been a trauma survival response for many settlers, where terrible violence had been inflicted on white bodies by white bodies in Europe for centuries (p. 76). Menakem cited a description of some of the harm inflicted in medieval England:

> The tortures and punishments of civil justice customarily cut off hands and ears, racked, burned, flayed, and pulled apart people's bodies. In everyday life, passers-by saw some criminal flogged with a knotted rope or chained upright in an iron collar. They passed corpses hanging on the gibbet and decapitated heads and quartered bodies impaled on stakes on the city walls. (p. 76)

These Europeans then brought their intergenerational trauma to the "New World" and inflicted it on the people of colour they interacted with here. Menakem (2017) wrote that he believed the trauma that now lives in Black Americans, can be traced back through the generations of white bodies all the way back to medieval Europe (p. 76). Menakem believed that European settlers brought this thousands-of-years-old intergenerational trauma "stored in the cells of their bodies" and that it is this trauma that continues to perpetuate more violence, harm and oppression throughout

North America today (p. 294). He argued that the act of moving across the seas did not heal the settlers' trauma; rather it continued to live through them, and the settlers "blew much of their trauma through the bodies of Africans and their descendants. This served to embed trauma in Black bodies, but it did nothing to mend the trauma in white ones" (p. 294). I believe that this trauma also fuelled the colonial violence inflicted and perpetuated toward Indigenous people. I also want to acknowledge that the white trauma that has been discussed at length in this research is not the same as the trauma that settler-colonials have inflicted on Indigenous people and the intention here is not to trivialise it or suggest its equivalence. And the trauma that was held within white bodies was not left on European shores when settlers tried to escape it and sailed across the seas hoping for a fresh start and a new world for themselves. Instead, this trauma was brought across the waters and its devastating impact was spread.

Colonial Ideas about Cleanliness, Hygiene, and Disease

A deeply disturbing irony of the colonial relationship with water was how much settler-colonials condemned Indigenous people as "dirty" and "savage" when it was the colonials themselves who were far less hygienic and clean. Stannard (1993) wrote that this irony was emphasised especially because, for example, during the sixteenth century, a third of England was so impoverished that they lived at the "bare margin of subsistence" and the hygiene, health, and sanitation of the entire population was so poor that it was a rarity for people in England to survive past their mid-thirties (p. 136). Maracle (2017) described how at the time Europeans believed that washing the body naked was unacceptable and that in fact it was a "dirty, filthy sin against God. No one stripped naked in England to wash. Public bathing occurred once a year in town fountains. Garbage was thrown out the windows into the gutters, along with faeces, urine, and dead babies" (p. 31). In the mid-1700s, epidemics of cholera and typhus were so severe in settler Canada that Toronto covered its rivers to try to stop the spread of it. Both of these diseases are caused by unsanitary living conditions (p. 31). It was only in the late 1800s that doctors started washing their hands between patients and thereby started to lessen the spread of diseases between them (p. 31). And yet, Maracle reminds us that despite all of this, at the time it "was Indigenous people who were referred to as filthy savages precisely because they stripped naked and washed every day" (p. 31). These colonial ideas of bodies being "dirty" continue in the vein of a distorted *solutio* expression, of shaming the body and thinking of it as inherently sinful, instead of acknowledging and honouring its importance and value to the wholeness of our selves and as a part of, and connection to, the beauty of the natural world.

Colonial Violence toward Indigenous Bodies

The colonial violence inflicted on the bodies of Indigenous people took many forms and continues to be seen in the disproportionate levels of police brutality inflicted on the bodies of Indigenous people, black people, and people of colour. Charles Darwin wrote: "Wherever the European has trod, death seems to pursue the aboriginal. We may look to the wide extent of the Americas, Polynesia, the Cape of Good Hope, and Australia, and we shall find the same result" (1839/1989, p. 322). In so-Canada, there have been many ways that colonial violence has been directed at Indigenous bodies. This included malnourishment experiments and other studies that were inflicted on Indigenous people, mostly on children. These experiments were done to study the effects of malnourishment on Indigenous children at residential schools and throughout Northern Indigenous communities. Thousands of Indigenous people were unconsentually a part of these experiments. In some cases, children were malnourished for five years and suffered severe physical and emotional harm all while under observation of scientists (Mosby, 2013, p. 161). In 1907, Dr. Peter Bryce started to realise the extent of the horrors within residential schools. When he went to the superintendent of Indian Affairs to report the harm being done and the astonishingly high death rates in schools, Maracle (2017) reported that the superintendent responded: "If they are dying, isn't that the point?" (Location 15160).

Part of the agreements the European sailors had on the explorers' vessels travelling the world was that rations for food, water, and alcohol would be given to them (Cook, 2003, p. 430). Then there was the additional agreement that the sailors would be let ashore whenever possible and another kind of ration would be available for them in the villages that they came upon. Men threatened mutiny when their rations were low or if they had been at sea for too long and had been unable to get ashore frequently enough. Before Cook was killed, he had been sailing for months near shorelines without landing, the crew on the Resolution was on short rations and they were restless to land ashore. Cook journaled at this time that the crew was "mutinous" and "turbulent" (p. 430). The white sailors saw Indigenous women's bodies as an entitlement in exchange for their work on the ships. They saw it as a given that those women were there for their taking and they mutinied when denied access.

The repercussions of this entitlement to Indigenous women's bodies have been devastating on many levels. Cook wrote in his journal of his men's "connections with women," and that these "connections" provide "one of the greatest securities amongst Indians, and it may hold good when you intend to settle amongst them" (Cook, 2003, p. 452). It was thought that sailors having intercourse with, or raping, the women made settling the communities easier. Many of the men brought over venereal diseases from

Europe that had not existed anywhere else in the world. Even when they knew that they had these diseases, they continued to sexually engage with and rape women in the villages that they came upon. Cook knew of this behaviour and half-heartedly tried to limit it. However, without real consequences for the men, this had little effect (p. 532).

Some communities that Cook and his crew came upon had different, and at times more liberal, ideas around sex than the heavily Christianised concepts of sex that the English sailors were accustomed to. And so, it could be that some of these women did engage consentually in sex with the sailors and I do not want to discredit their own agency. But we know, even from Cook's own journals that many of the cases were not consentual and none of the women were aware of the terrible diseases that these sailors had and were not disclosing as they slept with those women. In which case, it is questionable if any of the sex could be considered consentual, and arguably it all could be considered rape.

In his book *Ecological Imperialism* (2015), Alfred Crosby, professor of history and geography, described the dire consequences of the sexually transmitted infections (STIs) spread by European voyagers on Indigenous communities (Location 720). He wrote about how these European STIs spread quickly in those Indigenous communities around the world, in almost all the communities "visited" by the voyagers, he wrote the STIs "spread widely, killing some adults and many fetuses and babies, destroying fertility, and sending populations into steep decline" (Location 720). Many of these infections, especially syphilis which was rampant in Europe during the fifteenth and sixteenth centuries, quickly started to shorten Indigenous women's lives in the communities the voyagers went and drastically affected their fertility as well (Location 1658): "Venereal disease can be decisively important in the history of a people in jeopardy, because it cripples their ability to reproduce" (Location 3582). Crosby wrote that the birth rates of many of these small, vulnerable communities took a sharp decrease after the haunting arrival of the voyagers. These ships travelling from community to community were "crewed by malnourished, often poorly clothed, often maltreated men who, as sailors in the slow age of sail, had no possibility of a normal family life. Tuberculosis and venereal infections were for them occupational diseases" (Location 3595).

Evidence shows that the spread of STIs from Cook's ships was especially devastating around the globe: "In 1769 the British saw nothing of it ashore, but in 1772 the French found it among the indigenes at the locations on the New Zealand coast where the British had touched. Indeed, the French acquired the infection left behind for them by their fellow Europeans" (Crosby, 2015, Location 3595). When Cook retraced his course in 1773, he found widespread suffering from venereal diseases in many of the places they had visited the year before, and the few of his men previously unaffected by the diseases caught them ashore during this second voyage (Location 3595).

In the 1850s, Francis D. Fenton researched the steady decline of the Maori population and found that "venereal disease was destroying the procreative powers of the whole race," he wrote that "Of the 444 [research participants], only 221 had any living children, and 155 were completely barren" (Crosby, 2015, Location 3974). During this same period, a colonial surgeon in Wanganui noted that out of "a sample of 230 Maori women, 124 either had no children or had no living children" (Location 3974). These doctors were clear as to the cause of the steep decline of the birth rate: "the worst villain in the tragedy was surely venereal disease" (Location 3974). The spread of European venereal diseases, often from rape, was a devastating aspect in the genocide of Indigenous populations around the world, killing adults, or making them infertile, and devastating communities emotionally with the resulting heartbreak.

On Cook's ships, rations for food, water, and booze were given as well as the expectation that the sailors had of being able to have access to women's bodies, with or without their consent. This would have been a part of the agreement that the men undertook when they agreed to work aboard the ships and travel the world. Today, "Indigenous women and girls are 12 times more likely to be murdered or missing than any other women in Canada" (NIMMIWG, 2019, p. 7). Statistics Canada reported that "between 2001 and 2015, homicide rates for Indigenous women were nearly six times higher than for non-Indigenous women" (p. 7). Somewhere in our psyches, it seems this colonial entitlement to Indigenous women's bodies still exists. The idea still seems to putrefy in the colonial psyche that Indigenous bodies are there for the taking of white men and that there is an aspect of disposability of those women and their bodies. Indigenous women's bodies are still being found left in ditches, garbage cans, pig pens, and at the bottom of rivers across Canada to this day. There is no excuse for this and the horror of it must stop.

Psychologically, we have been uncomfortable with the corporeal, earthly, and the feminine, which have all been split from the Western psyche for a long time (Jung, 1943/1968, § 26). If we do not heal this split within us, we will only continue to project our hatred of our internal feminine onto the world around us. This colonial hatred and fear of women and their power had profound impacts on Indigenous people during the colonisation of so-called Canada and the rest of the world. Paula Allen (1992) believed that this patriarchal fear was one of the core causes of colonial violence:

> The physical and cultural genocide of American Indian tribes was and is mostly about patriarchal fear of gynocracy [woman-centered social systems]. The Puritans particularly, but also the Catholic, Quaker and other Christian missionaries, like their secular counterparts, could not tolerate peoples who allowed women to occupy prominent positions and decision-making capacity at every level of society. The colonizers saw

(and rightly) that as long as women held unquestioned power of such magnitude, attempts at total conquest of the continent were bound to fail. (p. 3)

Whether it is true that this patriarchal fear and hatred of women was the central impetus of colonial harm inflicted or just one of the many factors in colonial violence, it needs to be addressed in our settler decolonising efforts today. What is undeniable is that colonialism has been violent to people and bodies of colour: "all our phrasing—race relations, racial chasm, racial justice, racial profiling, white privilege, even white supremacy—serves to obscure that racism is a visceral experience, that it dislodges brains, blocks airways, rips muscle, extracts organs, cracks bones, breaks teeth" (Coates, 2015, p. 10).

Today, a dissolving, a *solutio* of our old ways of thinking around sex, the body and feminine is needed. We must heal rape culture within the Western psyche. This requires the prioritisation of respect, consent, an emphasis on female sexual satisfaction, the de-stigmatisation and celebration of gender, and sexual freedom of expression and identity. It needs to highlight settler decolonising and healing our sexuality so that these devastating parts of our psyches that disparage and desecrate bodies—especially women's bodies of colour and queer bodies of colour—stops, once and for all. There needs to be a complete dissolving of the old, so that something new and healthy can begin to form and take hold.

European Sexual Repression

The deep repression of sexuality in Europe during the colonial voyages was profound and consequently, it affected the world at large. During the 1470s in Europe, bath houses and brothels were being closed by authorities (Stannard, 1993, p. 224). The approved clothing for women was the black mantle that covered the whole female form, only leaving a small peephole to see through (p. 224). Iron and lead bodices and plates were worn to flatten and impede the development of women's breasts so as not to incite temptation in men (p. 224). This regression back "to traditional Christian denial of the body and rejection of things sexual [...] was the persistent ideology that woman is the blind instrument for seduction of nature, the symbol of temptation, sin, and evil" (p. 224). At this time, witchcraft was synonymous with women's bodies and sexuality: "Natural femininity, overflowing, voluptuous, and sinful is categorised as unlawful. Henceforth only witches will dare to have wide hips, prominent breasts, conspicuous buttocks, long hair" (p. 224). Stannard wrote that during the time that Columbus was about to sail to Cathay, witches were seen as the home of nudity and eroticism for the whole of the European psyche (p. 224). Both the *Malleus Maleficarum* written in 1486 and the *Tratado de las Supersticionesy Hechicherias* in *1529*, the two major texts of European witchcraft of the time, wrote that "all witchcraft comes from carnal lust" (p. 224). (A short note on this topic, to say that though not many female alchemists are referenced in alchemical texts, I believe that many women who would have been engaged in similar ventures would have been labelled as witches at the time and persecuted for their work. These women were often out tending the people in their communities as healers, making medicinal remedies, and being midwives. Their history is often erased or tainted in stories of evil and demonic activity. I think of alchemy then as also including these women and their work as being a part of the ancestral heritage that can be reclaimed in this alchemical lineage.)

These fearful Christian ideologies deeply affected settlers' judgement and fear of Indigenous people as they associated them with witchcraft, which they were told encompassed all the most evil aspects of the world. Maracle (2017) wrote of the devastating outlawing and attempted erasure of Indigenous plant knowledge, medical knowledge, and midwifery knowledge caused by this settler hatred and fear of what they considered witchcraft (p. 32). A great irony is that during the seventeenth to the end of the nineteenth century, many settler women preferred and sought out Indigenous midwives instead of settler physicians (p. 32). Eventually, this led physicians to fight for the banning of midwives (p. 32). Only in the last few decades have midwives in Canada started to regain any rights. Despite having to keep that knowledge secret for generations, many Indigenous traditional healers fought to preserve and pass down their knowledge, keeping it alive today.

This shadow side of *solutio* manifested as these colonial ideas surrounding the body and the feminine have wreaked global damage and have affected millions of lives around the world. Colonial settlers must face this part of our psyche so scared and hateful of sex, the body and the feminine if we are to begin our work of reparations for these harms today.

Colonial Fear and Hatred of Female Sexuality

Naomi Wolf (2012) studied the connection between patriarchal societies and their widespread fear of sexual liberation, and specifically female sexual liberation (p. 59). She wrote of the neuroscience that shows that sexually satisfied and empowered women and people with vaginas experience continuously more dopamine through their journeys of sexual liberation (p. 59). With more dopamine, women are more assertive, empowered, confident, and less likely to stay silent to abuse and injustice (p. 59). Wolf calls dopamine "the ultimate feminist chemical" (p. 59). Dopamine is the link between women experiencing pleasure and empowerment in their sexuality leading to their assertiveness, motivation, energy, focus, and confidence in the rest of their lives as well (p. 59). Wolf believed that patriarchal society has always in some way known this and that this is part of the reason that patriarchal societies have been so scared of, and tried to control and repress, female sexuality; on some level they knew that sexually repressed or traumatised women are easier to control (p. 59). "If a woman has optimal levels of dopamine, she is difficult to direct against herself. She is hard to drive to self-destruction, to manipulate and control" (p. 59). Wolf contended that this societal fear of women's empowerment through their sexual liberation can be seen in the nineteenth-century obsession with "the dangers of female masturbation" as women were starting to gain more rights in society (p. 144).

This same kind of European fear and hatred of female sexuality can also be seen in the case of Dr. Brown in the 1850s, a gynaecologist specialising in clitoridectomies for young women who were too fiery and lively (Wolf, 2012, p. 147). Dr. Brown promised to cure these girls of their lively state and return them post-procedure to the families in a state of "docility, meekness, and obedience" (p. 147). Wolf emphasised that we can now understand this change in behaviour of the young women as the trauma associated with genital mutilation and also the interruption to their neural activation (p. 147). These young girls would have had their access to pleasure and sexuality severely interrupted and thus would have had lessened dopamine levels and thereby experience less confidence, inspiration, motivation, and overall feelings of aliveness and joy (p. 147). These same kinds of mutilation were practiced all across England in the 1800s in an attempt to subdue its young women (p. 147).

Wolf hypothesised that the continual and various ways of inflicting trauma to vaginas, either through genital mutilation, rape, or other kinds of sexual abuse, serve as an act of war because it oppresses women so deeply. "Injury or trauma to the vagina and the pelvic nerves materially interfere with the neural pathway's delivery of those intoxicating chemicals to the female brain" (Wolf, 2012, p. 88). Wolf understood this subjugation of female sexuality as a means to repress and control over half the population (p. 88). Wolf argued that patriarchal society understood the advantages in subjugating women even if they did not understand the science of the "biologically-based link between a sexually traumatised woman and a lowered ability to muster happiness, hopefulness, and confidence" (p. 89). This violence can be thought of as a reflection of the shadow of *solutio* consciousness in Western consciousness, and the Western hatred, fear of and subjugation of the body, the feminine, and sexuality. Wolf conceptualised this violence as the actual original sin of the West: not Eve's exploration of her own sexuality or curiosity but instead Wolf saw the sin as the repression, subjugation, and domination of Eve's sexuality.

Today, data shows that Western women are reporting "lower and lower levels of happiness and satisfaction" in bed and in their lives (Wolf, 2012, p. 238). A study done by the National Health and Social Life Survey found that in the United States in 2009, 43% of women and 31% of men reported sexual dysfunction of some kind (p. 340). Sexual dysfunction and dissatisfaction can lead to depression, lack of confidence, vitality, and motivation (p. 59).

In contrast, people who are satiated sexually are more open, social, active, happy, confident, and motivated (p. 59). For us to be active participants in the world and to be a positive influence within it, our sexual wellbeing is a vital player in our ability to do so and our well-being while we do it. And it is our responsibility to tend and heal this vital part of ourselves today.

Daniela Sieff (2015), biological anthropologist, wrote about the basic human somatic fear of retraumatization, which she wrote "is burnt deeply into our brains and bodies" (p. 1). She says that this basic fear leads to dissociation from our bodies, emotions and "any parts of our personality which have attracted disapproval" (p. 1). She explained that this dissociation leads to finding ourselves stuck in "the distorting framework of shame, believing that we are fundamentally defective and inadequate. As a result, the way that we relate to ourselves, to other people and to the world around us is compromised and distorted" (p. 1). This work argues that this distorting framework of shame, fear, and dissociation of which Sieff detailed has been taking place in the colonial relationship to sex and the body. In addition, this shame, fear, and dissociation has been compounded and exacerbated by the violence that colonialism has wreaked in its distorted framework of trauma.

Our colonial sexual repression has harmed the world in profound ways. Whole familial lines have been infused with our intergenerational trauma passed to them unconsentually through the abuse that occurred in colonisation and residential schools. It has inflicted profound harm on lesbian, gay, bisexual, transgender, queer, and others(LGBTQ+) communities and two-spirit Indigenous communities. As unlikely as it may sound, healing our colonial sexual repression, and disconnect is our duty and responsibility. True unsettling requires us to heal our own relationship with our sensual natures in order to stop inflicting our sexual trauma, repression, and fear onto the world around us.

The Impacts of Settler-Repressed Sexuality on People of Colour

Menakem (2017) wrote of the racialized trauma within the bodies of white Americans, which I argue lives in the bodies of white Canadians as well. He described how the projections of this trauma can allow white individuals to bury this trauma by dehumanising, attacking, and then blaming the victim (p. 94). Settler repressed sexuality deeply affected (and continues to affect) people of colour as settlers' violent expression of these repressed energies were projected onto them.

Part of this violence toward First Nation's bodies and sexuality came in the form of the Eugenics Board, which mandated compulsory sterilisation for certain individuals (Stote, 2015, Location 1098). This legislation was enacted throughout Alberta and British Columbia (Location 1098). In Alberta, from 1928 to 1972 the Sexual Sterilisation Act was in effect (Location 1098).

The Eugenics Board sterilised thousands of people during this time (Location 1103). Marginalised people were more likely to be forcibly sterilised, and Indigenous people were disproportionately impacted (Location 1103). In 1937, an act was passed that allowed for sterilisation to occur without consent for anyone with "mental defectives": "This amendment allowed the Eugenics Board to compel the sterilisation of any patient it defined as mentally defective and who was likely to transmit this defectiveness to his/her progeny" (Location 1121).

One of the main methods used to diagnose mental deficiency was IQ testing. "Records indicate that patients whom the Board wished to sterilise were often subject to more than one test in hopes that their score would fall within the criteria for mental deficiency" (Location 1121). It is widely accepted that IQ tests are unequally biased toward Western European knowledge and therefore those who were not raised in Western culture tend not to do as well on them (Location 1127). Through this and other unsound and unjust testing, Eugenics Board deemed most immigrants of colour and Indigenous people were not of "sound intelligence" and thus were "mentally defective" (Location 1127). Seventy-seven percent of the Indigenous patients whose cases were reviewed by the Eugenics Board were given this label of "mentally defective" (Location 1127). Once diagnosed as mentally defective, individuals could be sterilised without any consent required, and often were (Location 1157). Seventy-four percent of all Indigenous people presented to the Eugenics Board were sterilised (Location 1157).

The violence carried out by the colonial state on Indigenous bodies is widespread and the effects are ongoing. Widespread belief in racial eugenics shows severely disturbing beliefs, and these beliefs were, and in many cases still are, considered colonial cultural norms. These ideas are rooted in white supremacy and colonial attitudes toward the body, in general and especially toward bodies of colour. Investigating how these mindsets continue to express themselves within our culture and biases is a crucial part of decolonising and the positive *solutio* process of dissolving old toxic ways of being.

Abuse in Residential Schools

Thousands of children were physically and sexually abused in residential schools. The Truth and Reconciliation Commission report showed that the Canadian government had received "37,951 claims for injuries resulting from physical and sexual abuse at residential schools" (TRC, 2015b, p. 106). This represents approximately around 40% of the survivors of the schools (p. 106). However, this number does not account for those who underwent abuses and did not file claims, and for those who did not survive the schools or who were no longer living at the time of the legal report. Therefore, the number of children who were physically or sexually abused in residential schools is, in all likelihood, far higher.

Various researchers have studied the motivations of perpetrators of child sexual abuse. Most have determined that we cannot reduce the complexity of this violence to a simple cause (Thomas et al., 2012, p. 188). However, research has shown some trends and commonalities among perpetrators. One of these factors is a conservative religious upbringing: "research on child sexual abuse and religion suggests that poorly integrated, conservative religious beliefs may contribute to higher rates of sexual offending than well integrated or more liberal religious beliefs" (Hidalgo, 2007, p. 101). Examples of this can be seen in the high numbers of cases of child abuse perpetrated by members of clergy. For example, studies show that in some denominations, 5.8–19% of ministers have admitted to "inappropriate sexual behaviour with church members." This percentage includes adult as well as child victims (p. 31).

Another factor, as shown by Thomas et al. (2012) is that many—but not all—perpetrators of child abuse had been abused as children, but that most had experienced negative sexual experiences of some kind (p. 188). Negative sexual experiences as described here can include extreme sexual shame from highly conservative religious values (Hidalgo, 2007, p. 88). One study found that: "priest offenders are significantly more likely to profess conservative sexual values" (p. 101). Hidalgo quoted studies that looked at sex offenders who were incarcerated for abusing children of the same sex as themselves, which found that the Catholics in this group were "more likely to be moderately or highly devout than Catholics in any other group in the study" and represented a "highly devout subset of the Catholic population" (p. 35). The repression and shame around innate sexuality when one's religion tells you it is shameful can be an ongoing sexual trauma. Hidalgo made clear the connection between "sexual shame, or passive sexual trauma, as a source of many adult sexual disorders" (p. 88). Unfortunately, this kind of extreme shaming of sexuality and sexual orientation can often come from the church, especially in Catholic denominations (Location 1127).

The more rigid and conservative a child's religious upbringing, the more detrimental it can be on their relationship to sex in general and their sexual identity and expression: "Often, the sources of trauma associated with these experiences in childhood and adolescence stem from sexual shame and intolerance derived from rigid, conservative, religious, and cultural beliefs" (p. 88). This sexual shaming is also very prevalent in evangelical churches, though these churches did not have the power or following during the residential school era that they do now or that the Catholic church had during this time period.

Western Christianised repression of sexuality had devastating consequences for Indigenous communities, seen particularly in the devastatingly high numbers of children who were sexually abused and raped in residential schools by the nuns and priests who were supposed to be caring for them. Healing our connection to sensuality and sexuality in general is of the utmost individual and societal importance.

Aside from those on the asexuality spectrum, human beings are sexual creatures and when our connection to our innate sensuality and sexuality is repressed, shamed, and inhibited, we can become very ill and a danger to the world, others and children around us.

Oppression of Two-Spirit People

Another devastating consequence of the colonial Christian relationship to sexuality is its homophobia, transphobia and persecution of the (LGBTQ2) community in Europe and in what is now known as North America. Lynda Gray (2011) from the Tsimshian Nation wrote about the inclusivity of Indigenous cultures pre-contact: "Everyone had a place in the community despite their gender, physical or mental ability, sexual orientation, or age. Women, Elders, Two-spirit, children, and youth were an integral part of a healthy and vibrant community" (Cull et al., 2018, p. 21). Two-spirit is an Indigenous concept that many, but not all, Indigenous people within the LGBTQ2 movement have reclaimed to describe themselves and their sexual orientation. A two-spirit person is a gender and/or sexually fluid Indigenous person who identifies as two-spirit. The name refers to a traditional belief that two-spirited individuals have a masculine and feminine spirit.

Pre-colonisation, two-spirited individuals were often revered as spiritual leaders in their communities (Jacobs, Thomas, & Lang, 1997, p. 4, 14). Blu explained the important societal role two-spirit people held in Indigenous communities in what is now called Canada: "Our Two-Spirited people, our trans people, they've always been in community. They were ostracised through colonisation. They were told that their lifestyles were not appropriate, that they couldn't carry on the way they were. But, we're still here" (NIMMIWG, 2019, p. 40). Indigenous communities are still trying to heal from colonial interference with concepts of gender, sexuality and identity today: "the lasting colonial influence on gender norms and relations, and perspectives on gender identity and sexual orientation, leading to increased misogyny, homophobia, and transphobia in Indigenous communities" (NIMMIWG, 2019, p. 113). As settlers, healing our colonial misogyny, homophobia, and transphobia is another responsibility in our settler decolonisation processes. The suffering that Christian colonial bigotry has enforced in so-called Canada has harmed the entire LGBTQ2 community, and especially the Indigenous and people of colour within those communities.

Current Colonial Relationship to Water

Transitioning from more abstract ideas around water and body/sexuality to the colonial relationship with the element of water itself, we will now examine how water has been weaponized as a longstanding form of colonialism. In so-called Canada today, many Indigenous communities do not have potable or running water and many of the water sources around them have been contaminated and polluted by industry making them dangerous and undrinkable (Shimo, 2018, § 10). It is shameful that in a country with one-fifth of the world's total freshwater and 60% of the world's lakes that so many people could be without running or drinkable water. Yet many are, and it is not in white neighbourhoods—it is First Nations reserves that are without potable water (§ 12). In Canada in 2018, a minimum of 50 First Nations communities had long-term boil water advisories. In some of these communities, this has been ongoing for decades (§ 10). Other communities have no running water at all (§ 10). This has had severe health impacts: "The lack of water has been linked to health issues in indigenous communities including hepatitis A, gastroenteritis, giardia lamblia ("beaver fever"), scabies, ringworm and acne" (§ 10).

Many corporations are taking advantage of Canada's abundance of freshwater and our poor federal protection around water sources. Nestlé extracts 3.6 million liters of spring water a day from a well belonging to the Six Nations with no compensation to Six Nations (Shimo, 2018, § 13). This injustice is exacerbated by the fact that the Six Nations reserve does not have access to this water themselves (§ 22). Martin-Hill, a McMaster University professor, is studying the lack of running water and contaminated water on Canadian reserves and its impact on communities, individuals, wildlife, and fish (§ 37). He has noted that Six Nations is not in agreement and disapproved strongly of Nestlé pumping: "They told Nestlé that they wanted them to stop. Of course, they are still pumping as we speak" (§ 14). For every million liters of water that is extracted from the Six Nations, Nestlé pays the province of Ontario $390.38 US (§ 22). However, the Six Nations receives nothing from Nestlé or the province for this water (§ 22).

Ken Greene, who lives on Six Nations without running water, spoke of the necessity of water to all forms of life: "Everything has to do with the water ... Because it has to do with the land. Land needs water. We need water. We can't survive without it" (§ 25). Since the pumping of this well by Nestlé, the well and surrounding water table has been struck by drought, which has "decimated the local populations of salmon, trout, pike and pickerel" (§ 26).

In a 2005 documentary, former CEO of Nestlé Peter Brabeck-Letmache celebrated the commodification of water and dismissed the perspective that water was a human right. He said:

> One perspective held by various NGOs – which I would call extreme – is that water should be declared a human right ... The other view is that water is a grocery product. And just as every other product, it should have a market value. (Shimo, 2018, § 35)

Martin-Hill reflected on Canada's water situation and how it values corporations' access to water over Indigenous communities' access to water:

"What is happening with our water is a systemic, institutional assault on Indigenous people's lands and rights over those lands to protect and preserve them" (Shimo, 2018, § 37). Martin-Hill directly attributed many issues among First Nations communities to this lack of drinking water, including the devastatingly high suicide rate among First Nations youth, which is five to seven times higher than that of other Canadians (§ 38). "For a Six Nations person, water is sacred and a symbol of life. But the lack also has metaphorical significance, as it becomes representative of the myriad ways that indigenous Canadians are treated as second-class citizens" (§ 38). Martin-Hill continued, "The young people are upset, pissed and demoralised … There's a strong element of depression, sadness and hopelessness because it's been going on for so long. Young people don't see a future" (§ 39). Thomas, who lives without drinking water on the Six Nations reserve, explained that she sees the inequality around water on First Nations reserves as "the latest example of an ongoing cultural genocide" (§ 44).

There is a deep irony that when Europeans first came to these lands, they bathed once a year and many Indigenous people bathed daily. And now, through colonial displacement of Indigenous reserves far away from natural water sources and the industrial pollution of waterways, we have taken away access for many Indigenous to running water, and settler Canadians have adopted the habit of bathing freely and regularly.

Venus and Cook: The Killing of a King

Psychotherapist and biologist J. Bruce Lloyd wrote that to process and heal shame, we must reckon with our stories from our emotional selves "from the heart and from the body, not from the head. We must tell the stories of our original wounding, of our Lost Journey and of our misguided attempts to find healing," and he continued that "it is how we tell our stories, and what we feel as we are telling them, rather than the actual content that is crucial to healing shame" (Sieff, 2015, p. 35). I will finish this section on the colonial relationship with the negative expressions of *solutio* with one such mythic story and some narrative connections. I hope it may help in shifting this distorted story and in the transition into the next section, where we begin imagining into how we may shift into a healthier relationship with these elements today.

One ancient alchemical text tells a tale of a king demanding water to quench his thirst, but when the water is brought to him, he drinks so much that soon "all his limbs were filled and all his veins inflated, and he himself became discoloured … 'I am heavy and my head hurts me, and it seems to me as though all my limbs were falling apart'" (Edinger, 1991, p. 52). Jung commented on this text and wrote that the king's thirst is due to his egotism and need to endlessly consume, when the king drinks, he is so overpowered by his thirst and the water (the unconscious) that he is inundated by it

(p. 52). The king eventually dies. Edinger saw this tale as being about the "swollen ego" which is "dissolved by its own excess. Its dissolution leads the way to a possible rejuvenation on a sounder basis" (p. 53). In this tale, the king (or the old ruling power) dies by *solutio* so that a new, better ruling power can take his place (p. 53).

In ancient alchemy, Venus, the sensual goddess of love born from the sea was linked to *solutio* (Edinger, 1991, p. 54). She was thought to embody "dangerous powers of *solutio*," which were represented in her associations with "seductive mermaids or water nymphs who lure men to death by drowning" (p. 54). This goddess born of the sea is perhaps a dangerous embodiment of *solutio*, or perhaps a retributive one. I think it no wonder that she is sometimes seen as the dangerous force which seduces powerful men into watery deaths when the body, the feminine, sex, and sensuality, all things sacred and central to her very self, have long been shamed, feared, and made evil in Western culture and the church. In *Aphrodite's Complaint*, Hillman personified Aphrodite saying:

> If you had been put in a closet for hundreds of years by priests, philosophers, and prudish women who loved their religions more than their bodies ... finding no societal frame in which to fit into the literal realities of medieval piety, reformational capitalism, iron-age industrialism, ceremonial colonialism, scientific progressivism ... if there simply was no dignified place for you in the big literal world, what avenue would be left except fantasy? (Hillman, 2007, Location 3959)

Captain Cook was killed on February 14th, 1779, what we now think of as Valentine's Day (Cook, 2003, p. 430). If we have any modern-day celebration of Venus, it is February 14th. On this day a few hundred years ago, Cook was dismembered, and his body parts were taken by the sea. Before his death, Cook's ships spread around the globe STIs, Christian ideas of sex being shameful, as well as harsh judgements around women's subordination.

There was much imagery of the king surrounding Cook's death. His second lieutenant was named King and he took control of Cook's ship, the Discovery, after Cook's death (p. 431). Cook's death was ordered by the king of Hawaii and his death was carried out in the ceremonial death only kings received. This ceremonial death of a king that Cook received involved complete dismemberment and then his body parts were put out to the sea where they eventually dissolved: death by *solutio* (p. 430). Perhaps this can be seen as a symbolic moment of Venus' revenge, the *solutio* of a violent, patriarchal king, given a king's death, replaced by Mr. King, on Valentine's Day of all days.

In our narrative, perhaps we can understand this moment in time as the beginning of a metaphorical death of an old, outdated ruling power. The power that replaced Cook has not improved over the last few hundred years;

it may have even worsened. But maybe today, the ruling power can finally start to be dissolved, reborn, and utterly replaced, for good.

A poem written by the alchemist named Valentinus, in 1717:

> A stone there is, and yet no stone,
> In it doth nature work alone.
> From it there welleth forth a fount [Venus]
> In which her Sire, the Fixed, is drown'd:
> His body and life absorbed therein
> Until the soul's restored agen.
> (Edinger, 1991, p. 54)

How the Colonial Complex Can Now Enact the Positive Potential of *Solutio*

Embodiment: Landing in and Caring for Our Bodies as Home

Reconciling our relationship with body, sexuality, sensuality, and the feminine and engaging in the positive potentials of *solutio* are of the utmost importance in the healing and decolonising of the Western psyche today. Values regarding embodiment, caring for our body, and being aware, mindful and present in our bodies are central to Jung's theories as well as to the field of depth psychology. Von Franz and Jung both saw alchemy as a profound modality to help us return to our bodies, the world, and an appreciation of our somatic, earthly natures (Goodchild, 2006, p. 64). Jung often wrote of the intelligence of the body: "[I]nasmuch as the living body contains the secret of life, it is an intelligence" (Jarrett & Jung, 1988, p. 360). He condemned the West's denial of the body and emphasised that healing for the Western soul must include reconciling with the aliveness and intelligence of the body (p. 64). "Remaining true to the earth would mean maintaining your conscious relationship to the body" (p. 66).

Jung also maintained that the connection between our treatment of the body and our treatment of the Earth are vitally intertwined, that to reconcile with our body is to reconcile with the body of the Earth, and vice versa (Jung, 1918/1970, § 19). He stressed the importance of remembering our connectedness to our body, to the earth and to our "kinship with all things" (Jung, 1963, p. 359).

Menakem (2017) also emphasised the importance of this work for white people and stressed the need for them work through their own cultural trauma (p. 295). Menakem also stressed the importance of this work being embodied and to avoid our efforts being solely focused on policy changes, he wrote that this transformation cannot rely "primarily on new laws, policies, procedures, standards, and strategies" he went on "We've already seen how these are no match for culture. For genuine transformation to take place, white Americans must acknowledge their racialized trauma, move through clean pain, and grow up" (p. 85). Menakem also believed that for now, we need to do this work primarily in our respective racial groups and that our healing must come from our own historical backgrounds. Only after that healing has been done separately can we come together to heal as a community (p. 85).

As Wolf's (2012) research shows, this process must also include the healing with our sensual, sexual natures. Not only because of how much trauma our repressed sexuality inflicts on the world, but also because of how much our sexual awakening can benefit our positive and enlivened participation in societal change. "Social conservatives have always feared real sexual awakening because erotic aliveness has the power to lead people into other kinds of resistance to deadening norms and rigid political, class, and social oppressions," Wolf continued, "Eros has always had the potential to truly rouse people, spiritually and politically as well as physically" (p. 234).

In our unsettling work today, it is vital that healing our connectedness to our own bodies is emphasised. If we continue to inflict the colonial harm we have imbued on our own bodies we will not have a good chance of stopping the infliction of this harm on the world around us as well. We will not have a good chance of becoming better stewards of the land if we continue to hate, deprive, and abuse our own bodies. Nor will we have a good chance of stopping our infliction of violence on bodies of colour when we have not healed from the trauma of violence of our own histories.

Positive Potential of Solutio

The negative aspects of *solutio* can look like watery indecision and formless inaction, whereas the positive aspects of *solutio* can be a dissolving of what no longer serves us, a softening of stuckness, hardness, and a permeability and an openness to new ideas and change (Rossi, 2017, p. 44). "The soul loves moisture, and its proclivities of emotion, reverie and reflection are imagined in watery ways" (p. 44). In the positive expressions of *solutio*, "what has become fixed, habitual, literal, then starts to dissolve and take a softer shape" (p. 44). In the alchemist's laboratory, the Bain Marie, a hot tub shaped like a double boiler, was an alchemical tool allowing for fire and water to combine to melt away unnecessary substances. In the Bain Marie, "the heat is gradually raised thereby loosening and relaxing what was stubborn and tightly bound. The Bain Marie allows for the creation of the right kind of languid heat that keeps the temperature up, melting what resists change" (p. 44). This watery warmth is what might be needed in part for the colonial psyche to warmly melt away the constrictions that keep us tightly bound in our colonial complex.

One positive aspect of *solutio* entails a rebirth; it represents baptismal waters, the alchemical bath: the way in which we return to a primal water state in order to be born again (Edinger, 1991, p. 47). Some voyager expeditions, such as that of the Spanish conquistador Juan Ponce de León in 1513, had as their conscious missions a search for the Fountain of Youth in the New World (Martin, 2019). I think it likely that somewhere in the unconscious of European psyches, this was what all the expeditions were seeking, to be washed and cleansed and born again, back to the innocence and vitality of life: they longed for paradise across the seas. They sought the fountain of youth and the New World. Water played a vital role in this dream, the dream to be made new in the waters. Settlers came to what is currently known as North America looking for the Fountain of Youth, and this pursuit still drives a large portion of capitalism today. In 2019, the beauty industry with its emphasis on eternal youth and antiaging products was worth 49.2 billion dollars in the United States (Ridder, 2020, § 1).

Solutio is a process in the psyche that craves the return to mother, the watery rebirth of the womb, and craves the safety of that primal water world, of its eternal newness. In the colonial psyche, perhaps this manifests as the desire to be washed clean of our societal sins, dirtiness, of hundreds of years of torture, oppression, and class systems. This freedom can manifest in people expressing their genders, identities and sexualities in ways that would have been forbidden from them in the past and in many places are still forbidden or oppressed today. Even just in the phrase *gender fluidity,* there is water. The gender fluidity revolution happening today is maybe in part in protest of the restrictive, oppressive dichotomy and binary of genders and sexualities from the past and a celebration for gender freedom, sovereignty, and fluidity today.

The industrial revolution was going on during some of the largest European migrations to so-called Canada. There were literal black clouds of coal over England, the dirtiest of energy sources burned into the air constantly only to come back to land on children's faces in the streets and thickly coat those faces of the children who were chimney sweepers. Societally, we craved, needed, water to wash it all away; we took to the sea. We set sail toward a longed-for cleansing on our way to the promised New World: a place to restart, an Eden, a paradise, home to cities of gold, endless space, as of yet fresh, unpolluted streams, lakes, rivers, and wide-open sea.

Solutio/Water Concrete Actions and Reflection Questions

Perhaps now, part of the long overdue cleansing we have craved can look like intentionally reconnecting with the cleansing of our daily interactions with water as we drink it, bathe in it, visit it, are precipitated on by it and by accepting the fluidity of sexuality and gender, in those around us, or within ourselves and honouring the sacredness of our own bodies and sensuality. The colonial relationship with water is not only historical but continues today. The pollution of waterways from industry and lack of protection for water put freshwater sources around the world and here in so-called Canada at incredibly high risk. We have been desecrating what we most need and crave. Today, it is our duty to re-establish a healthy relationship with the waters.

In this chapter, we looked at the colonial complex's sublimation of the body and sexuality. Through the metaphors of the alchemical water element we looked at alchemy's tending and honouring of the sacredness of the body and sensuality, which we can begin to carry out in our own lives through the following unsettling practices and direct actions:

- Take a stand against the continuation of the colonial practices oppressing Indigenous people and communities concerning rights to water and the lack of potable water in so many reserves today. Write to your elected officials, march, and educate yourself and then others on these issues.
- *Reflection questions*: Where do you hold shame in or concerning your body? What is your relationship to pleasure, to listening to your body's needs, to respecting it as a beautiful, worthy, living creature, and to sexuality as a healthy, sacred expression of your body and soul? Are there parts of your body that you have learned to hate as they do not fit into impossible colonial beauty standards? Where can you bring healing to your relationship to your body or your relationship to your sexuality and openness, acceptance, and celebration of others' sexualities and gender expressions?
- Read and work through the exercises and journal prompts in Resmaa Menakem's (2017) *My Grandmother's Hands: Racialized Trauma and the Pathway to Mending Our Hearts and Bodies*. Do the work and exercises he gives; do not just intellectualise them, but rather allow your body to process and heal where racialized trauma, fear, and racism reside within you.
- When you think about colonialism, what sensations arise in your body? Is there constriction, holding, tension in any specific places? Is there any openness or ease? When you sit with these sensations and breathe into them, what happens? Does anything shift? At the end of this exercise, see if you can name or put language/words to the sensations you were experiencing—what were the feelings attached to them?
- Do you feel any signs of a fight, flight, or freeze response being activated in your body in response to discussions of colonialism? Does this shift if you return to following your breath and sensations in your body?
- How do you feel colonialism in your body? How has it affected your relationship to your body? What practices help you repair that relationship? Are there self-care practices, activities outdoors, dancing, stretching, or embodiment practices that particularly resonate with you?
- Does it feel possible to feel settled or grounded in your body and to have a regulated nervous system while discussing colonialism? Can you feel the possibility of holding the tension of opposites when acknowledging

the horror of colonialism and simultaneously the possibility of healing and transformation?
- Continue to work through the exercises in *Me and White Supremacy* (2020). Again, focus on truly reflecting, processing, and integrating the prompts instead of just reading through them and not doing the actual work.
- Work on healing your connection to your sexuality; Naomi Wolf's *Vagina: A New Biography* explores women's sexuality throughout time and the healing necessary for many Western women in relationship to their sexuality today.
- Sheri Winston's (2010) *Women's Anatomy of Arousal: Secret Maps to Buried Pleasure* is a more in-depth look at women's sexuality and offers paths of reconnection within it.
- For conversations surrounding the development of healthy masculinity, see *Fire in the Belly: On Being a Man* (1991) by Sam Keen, as well as *He: Understanding Masculine Psychology* (1974) by Robert A. Johnson.
- See Christine Downing's (1996) *Myths and Mysteries of Same-Sex Love*, bell hooks's *All about Love* (2018), and *Trans Like Me: Conversations for All of Us* (2018) by CN Lester to deepen understandings, appreciations of, and celebrations of all types of love, sexuality, and identity in the world.
- Carrie Phillip, (Shxwenatqwa) a Sto:lo counsellor, recommends a practice for First Nations and settlers alike to engage in: a daily water cleansing. This involves giving thanks for the water in the shower, as you wash your face morning and night, or when you take your first sip of water in the morning. It is a simple act of cleansing and gratitude that offers a momentary reminder of connection and interdependence, a sacred ritual in a short everyday moment. Phillip wrote: "A Water Ceremony I was taught many years ago: Consciously place a cup of water by your bed at night. In the morning, immediately say a prayer for the new day, and drink the water. The water not only cleanses our external ... it is key to our internal health as well" (Carrie Phillip, Sto:lo Nation, Personal Communication June 2021).
- And finally ... dance. Dance in your living room, move your body, find a Five Rhythms group near you and dance with others. No need for professional dance training; as humans, we can tune into and listen to how our bodies want to move, follow rhythms, and express themselves. Learning to feel connected to our bodies and allowing themselves to express themselves through us is a profound act of embodied somatic healing and a profound part of learning how to show up fully in this world.
- Do you have water or sexuality practices that are culturally appropriated? Do you know their origin, if people of European descent have been given permission to practice them? If not, find practices from your lineages, they exist in almost all, if not all of our ancestries and pasts.

Chapter 8
Earth

Figure 8.1 Emblem II: "The Earth Is Nurse".

Source: Michael Maïer, *Atalanta Fugiens*, 1618. Etching from an alchemical text depicting Earth as mother and nurse.

DOI: 10.4324/9781003296546-9

Helms's Third Stage of White Racial Identity Development: Reintegration

Following disintegration, we reach the third stage of Helms's (1993) white racial identity development, "reintegration." Though Helms believes reintegration often occurs in this process, she does not perceive this stage as necessarily a positive evolution forward in white racial identity development. In many ways, reintegration can mirror the negative expressions of *coagulatio* a hardening into a firm, resolute stance of perceived rightness, defensiveness, or anger (p. 60). Helms believed this to be a common reaction to the vulnerability of having one's opinions about race dissolve in the disintegration stage. Helms explained that an individual in the reintegration stage "comes to believe that institutional and cultural racism are the White person's due because he or she has earned such privileges and preferences" (p. 60). Unfortunately, at this stage, rather than a positive reintegration that forms, or a new identity taking shape from the emotional waters of disintegration, at first there is often a solidifying of one's racist ideas (p. 60). This can look like a reforming of the primary racial attitudes of superiority and potentially hatred, in a last attempt of the ego to avoid the inevitable reshaping of outlook, personality, and experience of the world that must be undertaken for true integrity to be possible (p. 60).

Nonetheless, Helms (1993) found, this hardening of the reintegration phase must be dealt with and passed through before transformation into the next stage can occur (p. 60). Something that can only begin once an individual recognises that racism does in fact exist, that society does indeed privilege some over others because of their race and that there is no basis for the delusion of white superiority. It is only once an individual starts to let down the reactive, defensive walls of denial, anger, and fear seen in the reintegration stage that they can begin to move into the pseudo-independent stage (p. 61).

Introduction to *Coagulatio*

This chapter investigates the colonial psyche's perceived separation from, and superiority over, nature. We have explored the Christian underpinnings of this disconnect were explored, which included looking at Christianity's focus on ascension and its attitudes towards the earthly being fleshy, sinful and "corrupt" (Genesis 1:22; 6:11, NRSV). In this chapter, we will investigate how alchemy offers a counterbalancing antidote to this aspect of the colonial psyche. We will discuss how alchemists conceptualised earth, its corresponding alchemical operation *coagulatio,* and its emphasis on honouring the living earth and land. This chapter will imagine into *coagulatio* as a metaphor for a part of the distorted alchemical journey to the New World and explore how we can now consciously engage with this operation and element in our decolonisation journeys today.

Earth

Thirty percent of the land on Earth is forested. Globally, 1.5 acres of forest are cut down per second, which equals roughly 36 football fields of forest every minute (The World Counts, 2021, §1). At this rate of deforestation, there will be no rainforests left on Earth in 100 years (§6). Moreover, one million species that we share this planet with are at risk of extinction due to human-caused climate change (United Nations, 2019, §1–3).

When they landed upon these shores, we can imagine that colonisers were longing for a new world within and yet they concretised, literalised their longing, and sought it physically instead of internally. While seeking this physical new world, they brought about all the wreckage and destruction from making physical that which was always meant to be internal. We continue to seek the healing for our discomforts externally today: 79% of Americans say they engage in retail therapy (Schultz, 2018, §9); and 38% say they eat unhealthy foods or binge eat when stressed (American Psychological Association, 2013, §3). As North Americans, we continue to seek the answer to heal the immaterial void externally when it has been waiting for our tending of it internally for the last 500-plus years.

Part of healing this distorted alchemical relationship to Earth and the physical, material world is having the courage to face our emptiness and longing within. From there, we can work towards a true relationship with the aliveness of the world around us, rather than seeing it as the raw material for the products that we hope will fill the voids within us. This would mean valuing it for its inherent beauty, vitality, and aliveness.

Cook came to this land raping and pillaging people and the Earth. As his cultural descendants, settler-colonials have only continued this way of relating to land. It is now our turn to steer the narrative in a new direction, working towards the honouring and tending of life in all its forms.

Cook's Journal

> *December 25th, 1776: I found the shore in a manner covered with Penguins and other birds and Seals, but these were not numerous, but so fearless that we killed as many as we chose.* (Cook, 2003, p. 492)

> *May 11th, 1777: Finding that we had quite exhausted the island of all most every thing it produced I this day got every thing off from the shore, intending as soon as the Discovery had recovered her best bower anchor, to proceed to an island called Happi.* (Cook, 2003, p. 529)

Coagulatio's Relationship to the Psyche: Positive and Negative Potentials

Coagulatio refers to the Earth element, and in the alchemical laboratory, this process occurs during a reforming of a solid from a liquid, a solidification of something back into a solid state, perhaps even after a *solutio* (Edinger, 1991, p. 84). Some images associated with *coagulatio* are Earth, soil, body, rootedness, rigidity, boundaries, literally, and embodiment.

In colonial power, there was a hardness, rigidity, and heaviness that could not be penetrated, and it allowed colonialists to be so hardened that they were able to commit the deepest acts of terror. The more negative expressions of *coagulatio* in colonial history might have looked like territorialism, claiming possession of land as they came upon it or delineating false boundaries in the landscape in the creation of unjust reserves.

The positive potential of the *coagulatio* stage that individuals can work toward achieving within themselves can be seen after a productive *solutio* process (Edinger, 1991, p. 85). Once the hardness has been dissolved, the liquid can reform into something new (p. 85). This is the process of putting ourselves back together in a new way after we have let ourselves be humbled and melted open (p. 85). The positive potential of it can be seen as ego development after parts of the personality have gone through *solutio* and dissolved; it is a rebirth and a reforming of newness (p. 85).

In alchemy, *Coagulatio* can also refer to the incarnating process, whereby there is a descent and an enlivening of flesh and an embodiment of the earthy corporeal nature of the body. This can be a redemptive embodiment to counteract the colonial Christian ascension away from—and punishment of—the body and earth (p. 87). This may also look like remedying white fragility, finding the strength and grounding for this work, and remembering the forgotten parts of ourselves.

How the Colonial Complex Enacted the Negative Potential of *Coagulatio*?

Stealing of Indigenous Land

When *kweèt'į̀*, rock seekers, arrived on what is now known as Canada, they quickly claimed ownership of the land and denied Indigenous sovereignty by asserting false sovereignty of the British crown. Manuel and Derrickson (2017) wrote that the only thing that allowed the dispossession of Indigenous people from their lands was "the quicksilver of racism, that black magic of white supremacy" (p. 92). There was no justice in the taking of Indigenous lands, and dispossession of Indigenous land continues today in the disenfranchisement of Indigenous sovereignty and land claims that continue to be widespread and active throughout so-called Canada.

Thomas King (2013) wrote of how his ancestors perceived the colonialists arriving at their lands as "armed with the divine imperative to subdue the earth" and that the colonialists were "annoyed that the virgin lands they had imagined, the empty wildernesses they had been promised, were occupied" (Location 410). The lands that the colonialists came upon were occupied by King's ancestors and the Indigenous Nations throughout what is now called North America (Location 410). And so, British and later Canadian forces started confiscating land, and dispossessing Indigenous people from their rightful and traditional territories (Adams, 1997, p. 30).

Coulthard (2014) saw this dispossession of Indigenous land as the foundation of settler-colonialism (p. 15). He defined settler–colonialism as "structured dispossession" and argued that this was the defining feature of settler–colonialism (p. 15). For Coulthard, the settler–colonial relationship is fundamentally based on a power of dominance which continuously works to dispossess Indigenous people of their lands (p. 15).

Further, Coulthard (2014) argued that the violence of dispossession of Indigenous people from their lands is at the core of Canadian history. He wrote that Canadian state domination continues to be committed to maintaining ongoing colonial Canada's access to stolen land and resources for the proliferation of capitalist development through "force, fraud, and more recently, so-called 'negotiations'" (p. 15). This development perpetuates the ongoing disenfranchisement of Indigenous people from the land which provides the "material and spiritual sustenance of Indigenous societies" (p. 15).

The extent to which the violent dispossession of Indigenous people from their land was central to the colonising of what is now called Canada cannot be overstated. This ongoing process is genocidal. Not only has the physical dispossession of land been central to colonial violence, but it is also intertwined and inseparable from the emotional and psychological abuse of the colonial laws and policies that continue to oppress Indigenous people. Maracle (1996) wrote from her Sto:Lo experience of colonialism that, "like miners in a shaft we are weighed down by the oppressive dirt which colonialism has heaped upon us. Unlike with miners, the dirt is heaped upon us deliberately and no one is terribly interested in removing the load" (p. 11). The colonial psyche's relationship to land and how it has projected this onto the world around it has had devastating consequences. In unsettling pursuits, this colonial relationship to land and the ongoing rigid colonial policies surrounding it must be investigated, interrupted, and transformed. A part of this process necessitates a thorough investigation into the colonial psyche's distorted relationship to land, imagined here as a shadow expression of the alchemical operation of *coagulatio*.

Smallpox and Bodies: The Spread of Disease

As discussed in the last two chapters, looking at these physical events and symptoms through an alchemical lens is not meant to suggest alchemy was the cause of colonialism. Instead, it is an exercise in psychologising symptoms, in imagining into the events that took place and sorting them into the four elements as a way to categorise and sort through all the wrongs committed. It is also a depth psychological tool of looking deeper into myths and history to attempt to find remedies for it today.

An example of Jung (1929/1967) psychologising in his work is his statement that "gods hav[e] become diseases." He wrote that we in the West "are still as much possessed by autonomous psychic contents as if they were Olympians ... The gods have become diseases; Zeus no longer rules Olympus but rather the solar plexus, and produces curious specimens for the doctor's consulting room" (§54). Jung identified these mythic figures within the psychological symptoms and troubles that we contend with. In doing so, he encouraged imagining into how these myths of the past and this period of history continue to shape and affect our lives. He does this as a way of inviting soul, meaning, and mythological perspectives into our everyday modern existences. He was not suggesting here that Zeus was literally in our solar plexuses, but instead it was a way of inviting the depth of the mythic into his investigation of our complexes and illnesses. In a similar vein, in the following section, we look briefly at smallpox. I am not suggesting that smallpox was actually a manifestation of colonialism's distorted relationship with *coagulatio* and its relationship to the physical and earthly. However, we can conceptualise it instead as one more expression of the violence of colonialism on the earthly and the corporeal.

As discussed in the previous chapter, around the time of contact, European and settler ideas about hygiene were very different than our ideas about hygiene today. Doctors did not have any understanding of germs and so sterilisation practices as basic as hand washing, let alone anything more complex, were not utilised. Because Europeans lived in such close quarters with their livestock in England, they had a whole host of diseases that they carried with them that Indigenous people had had no exposure to (Crosby, 2015, Location 4326). As such, rates of smallpox killed close to 90% of many Indigenous people across all of what is now known as Canada (Stannard, 1993, p. 87). In some places, like Peru, the death toll from smallpox was 94%, meaning somewhere between 8.5 and 13.5 million Peruvians were killed by it before the sixteenth century (p. 87). We also know that at various points during colonisation, this spread of smallpox was intentional with colonisers knowingly distributing small-pox-infected blankets to Indigenous people (Fenn, 2000, p. 1554).

The Bible speaks of pestilence that will befall those who disobey or displease God (Deuteronomy 28:15, NRSV). Europeans saw pestilence as a punishment from God for the disobedient and heathens. As such, they justified the widespread death not as consequences of settlers' own unhygienic, disease-ridden lifestyles, but instead as acts of God. These European diseases spread from body to body and had a profound and disastrous effect on the inhabitants of what is now known as North America, ending in the excruciating deaths of millions from this disease. We can understand this horror as one more expression of colonialism's violence toward Indigenous bodies as well as one more aspect of history that the colonial psyche must reckon with in its efforts towards decolonising, healing, and unsettling today.

In 2020 a new plague began its spread around the globe, one that in so-called Canada and North America is disproportionately affecting marginalised people and Indigenous communities. Unlike the smallpox pandemic, there were effective vaccines to protect against COVID-19 available early on in this pandemic. However, many settlers chose not to get vaccinated and stop the spread of this plague that is disproportionately affecting people of colour and Indigenous communities (Mashford-Pringle et al., 2021, p. 2). We cannot pretend colonialism is not still alive and well today. Many settlers say about the horrors of the past "well I wasn't there committing those horrors, or spreading those smallpox blankets, it wasn't me, I'm not responsible!," to which I usually respond: as white settlers we are the cultural descendants of those people, benefitting greatly from the horrors they committed and that we as a society continue to commit in different forms today. Now I also add, we were not there spreading smallpox blankets, but we are here during this plague today, and if we are not taking an active role in trying to curtail the spread of it then we are actively participated in its continuation. There are perhaps not many ways we could be more colonial than beingwhite on these lands and actively contributing to the spread of a plague disproportionately affecting and killing Indigenous people.

A note to say, this critique is directed specifically at white settlers who chose not to get vaccinated. This book reviews just some of the abhorrent medical abuses towards Indigenous people in so-called Canada. However, the history of these medical abuses is extensive and horrific, and for some Indigenous individuals this history has created well-founded distrust of medical institutions. There are many very legitimate reasons within Indigenous and BIPOC communities to chose not to get vaccinated. This critique is directed specifically at white settlers.

Degradation of Nature

Over the last two millennia, and dramatically in the last 500 years, Western civilisation's relationship to nature has become more and more mechanistic and utilitarian. Jung (1935/1976) felt that the Western soul had lost its connection with the natural world and that much environmental and societal damage that occurred was because of this lost foundational connection (§585), "in spite of our proud domination of nature we ... have not even learnt to control our own nature, which slowly and inevitably courts disaster" (Jung, 1935/1976, §597).

Colonial exploits were marked by their objectification of nature and seeing nature as something to extract for resources. "White supremacy and white privilege and white lies—[is] a history that has often been buried deep in the dark, rich, black American soil" (DiAngelo, 2018, p. 17).

Hillman (1997) described how in the seventeenth century throughout North America, forests were being cleared for resources. One justification that was used for the practice of cutting down whole forests was in part that they were seen as "dark and damp geography" and because settlers believed that within them there lurked evil spirits as well as all kinds of feared "pagan communities" (p. 13). When colonisers arrived on what is now known as North America, for economic as well as superstitious reasons, they immediately started drastically changing the physical landscape and ecosystems. Crosby (2015) described this as a "continual disruption" that included major deforestation; stripped resources; ever-growing settlements and cities; overused soil and pasture; the creation of large fields necessitating the destruction of entire ecosystems that existed there before and the introduction of completely new and invasive species at every level of existence (Location 4478). This disruption continues today.

Crosby (2015) compared settlers to weeds, an apt metaphor. For, as he explains, Europeans weeds brought to what is now known as North America also played a devastating role in the colonisation of the land (Location 2686). These settler weeds fed European livestock and also quickly covered "the raw wounds that the invaders tore in the earth," thus pushing out native species and dramatically altering the landscape and ecosystem (Location 2686). The patterns of destruction that those early colonisers wreaked with the help of their invasive ecology have only intensified over the last 500 years, culminating today in an environmental catastrophe the likes of which the human species has never seen.

The extreme expression of the shadow side of *coagulatio*, which we can imagine manifested as a distorted colonial relationship with the Earth, has changed a whole continent's ecology. It is unlikely that this can ever be undone. However, in investigating where these colonial ideologies still live within the colonial psyche and doing what we can to change, transform and heal them both in the collective and within ourselves, we can work towards the hope of changing the future of this distorted colonial tale. We move closer to right relationship with every invasive scotch broom pulled and native *Lhásem,* chocolate lily, replanted.

Ungroundedness

Orphan Wisdom, an organisation founded by Stephen Jenkinson aims to heal some of the trauma and harm done by settlers over the centuries. It is centred around the idea that settlers are orphaned from their own cultures, histories, and selves. Jenkinson (2021) taught that much of the destruction and suffering settlers cause and experience, stems from their disconnect from heritage, ancestry, place of origin, and rootedness to ancestral land (§6). "Ours is a culture built upon the ruthless foundation of mass migration, but it is more so now a culture of people unable to say who their people are. In that way we are, relentlessly, orphans" (§6).

Edgar Villanueva (2018), of the Lumbee Nation, amplified Jenkinson's idea of settler-colonials as orphans, agreeing with the sentiment that it is the cause of a great deal of settlers' dysfunctional impact on the world (p. 105). Villanueva described how settlers "broke the ties to their lands of origin, to the bones of their ancestors, to their old ways" he continued "the grief that this has caused is enormous, yet it is almost never acknowledged" (p. 105). He wrote that it was the historical choice of settlers to "abandon, to sever, to forget" their connection to their history and ancestral territory in Europe (p. 105). He believed that the only way to heal this profound disconnection is for settlers to acknowledge and properly grieve this interruption from their purpose and ancestry (p. 105). Villanueva acknowledged that viewing settler-colonials as orphans in this way may seem as though it is calling for too much compassion or understanding for them. However, Villanueva argued that in efforts to heal abusers, the point is not to excuse their behaviour or negate the consequences of their actions, but instead it is to address the causes of the oppressive behaviour in the goal of working towards its transformation for the benefit, safety, and wellbeing of all (p. 105).

Williams, Owens, and Syedullah (2016) also wrote about white culture's disconnect from the groundedness of culture and the repercussion of this for one's connection to self and one's origins (p. 126). Being divorced from one's heritage is like an alchemical *seperatio*, the cutting off of matter in some way. Williams et al. believed that white people today have "the same hearts fundamentally" as the people of the past who are to blame for the horrible crimes of history (p. 149). The authors asked what happened to those white individuals that allowed them to become so ungrounded from their own humanity, separated from their hearts, compassion and morality (p. 149). They asked how white people could have treated bodies of colour in the way that they did, enslaving, raping, and killing them: "what kind of cut-offness had to happen" to white people for them to have been able to commit such violence (p. 149). The authors advocated for white people to undertake an internal investigation into these questions themselves and seek to understand how such dysfunction exists in their lineage and may continue in their behaviours today. Williams et al. encouraged white people to restore themselves to wholeness by calling out and questioning systems that have harmed everyone: both the marginalised as well as those who are privileged by them (p. 149).

That we settlers carry so much trauma and are divorced from our heritage and sense of belonging to land has deeply affected more than just ourselves. In unsettling processes, healing this trauma and decolonising relationships to land has to be centred. This includes letting go of colonial beliefs that justify the possession of stolen land and even further, the return of that land.

Capitalism and Consumerism

Kendi (2019) described capitalism and racism as "conjoined twins" and claimed these twins inseparable (p. 156). Kendi explained the progression of the twins of capitalism and racism throughout the centuries of colonialism, through global slavery, forced labour, and the industrial revolution (p. 156). For settlers, the world that was being created by these conjoined twins of racism and capitalism promised great "adventures" in the "New World" and the potential of new lives awaiting them.

Veracini (2010) described how these promises of settler–colonialism failed to deliver for settlers: rather than personal independence and wealth we see crippling debt amongst the majority of the population, there were promises made of vast swaths of land for all and instead most North Americans today barely have yards, and the continent as a whole operates on unsustainable land management practices and the necessity of environmental degradation (p. 96). Ultimately, the promise of a better life for settlers was never fulfilled. Veracini wrote of how this "better life" ended up looking like the isolating, modern lives of dissatisfaction seen throughout so-called North America today (p. 97).

A world of hyper-individualism and loneliness helped create the conditions that capitalism has fed off of, by creating dissatisfied individuals through advertisements and new impossible definitions of success. Capitalism has fed settlers the story that the answer to their dissatisfaction is to buy and consume more. The "American Dream" is the story that success and happiness depend on the accumulation of possessions and having more than those around you (Veracini, 2010, p. 77). All of these settler–colonial beliefs and promises laid the groundwork for the culture of conspicuous consumption we have in North America today.

Social psychologist Erich Fromm (1976) criticised North America's culture of consumerism and attributed it to deep psychological disturbances within the population: "The attitude inherent in consumerism is that of swallowing the whole world. The consumer is the eternal suckling crying for the bottle" (p. 27). He saw the colonial longing for endless accumulation of material goods as the attempt to fill the void of dissatisfaction within. He saw this longing as the craving for "speed and newness," fulfilled only temporarily by one's next purchase (p. 177). He believed this pattern reflects a deep settler restlessness, ungroundedness, and "the inner flight from oneself" (p. 177). Fromm saw settler psychological malaise and consumerism as unequivocally connected, saying that this anxious need to accumulate and buy more and more was only a temporary protection from the longing within for something deeper (p. 177). He believed that the only hope for the world is for colonisers to stop focusing on consumption and the act of having and instead focus on a deep sense of solidarity and care for the world of which they are a part (p. 189). Fromm advocated that an inner transformation that changes how settlers relate to the world around them is the only thing that will change their course of action, and thus the world, in a meaningful and sustainable way.

The distorted colonial relationship with the Earth has led to its inextricable connection to capitalism and dependency on consumerism. This has wreaked havoc on the natural world with its mass deforestation, high greenhouse gas emissions, and pollution. For justice, as well as the health of our planet, these colonial attitudes and behaviours must change, and the urgency to do so is extreme.

White Environmentalism

Colonial attitudes have also seeped into our care for the environment. White environmentalism often perpetuates colonial ideas of subjugation of Indigenous peoples and has privileged those who benefit from colonial powers and disenfranchised those who do not. Thomas King (2013) described various projects by white environmentalists who were seemingly only concerned with their own well-being and preservation of the environment affecting their own communities and did not care about projects that were not in their own backyards. He relayed an example of plans for a landfill that was to be built on a reserve by big multinational companies, white people nearby were not pleased. King said he found it amusing "watching environmentalists and concerned non-Natives lecture Indians on traditional beliefs and ethical standards" (Location 2767). King explained that he has only seen white individuals get passionate about projects happening on reserves when those white individuals will in some way be affected by the development themselves (Location 2767). King explained how health in First Nations communities has often suffered immensely from industrial operations that have at times operated for decades on or near reserves, with or without those communities' consent with no outrage from white communities. However, as soon as projects come along that will affect the white communities, preaching environmentalists have come to lecture Indigenous people on Indigenous traditional beliefs of communion with land, trying to dissuade them from allowing such industrial projects to go forth.

It is imperative that settlers care about and defend environmental issues. However, this caring must look vastly different than it has looked within many white environmental groups. Colonialism has been woven throughout the white environmental movement since its inception. The blame for environmental damages occurring has also, at times, been put on Indigenous groups by white conservationists. For example, the focus of the blame for declining caribou numbers in the Northwest Territories has been minimally focused on the expansive clear-cuts and mining operations throughout the caribou's territory (Sandlos, 2007, p. 44). Instead, the blame has been focused on the hunting of the caribou by Indigenous groups, which has been happening sustainably without issue since time immemorial (p. 44).

In 1976, Greenpeace, backed by many white Canadian environmentalists, launched a massive campaign to end the seal hunting in Nunavut because they "felt it was immoral for anyone to kill a seal, even the Inuit of the Canadian north" (Moore, 2013, Location 2434). Although the seal was not an endangered species, Greenpeace wanted to end its hunt because the hunting of young seals was "unethical" (Location 2439). This campaign resulted in legislation being passed that devastated the Inuit's subsistence hunting practices, their ability to be food sovereign as well as their economic livelihoods. This campaign also went global and led to the United States banning all seal products and the European Union banning anything made from white seal coats, furthering the devastation of the local Inuit economy even further (Kerr, 2014, §9).

In 1985, Greenpeace issued an apology to the Inuit for their role in the resulting cultural damage (Kerr, 2014, §10). In 2014, Greenpeace issued another apology to the Inuit. The name of the released article said that it was an apology, although they actually do not give an apology in the article. They did say: "We acknowledge the role we played in the unforeseen consequences of these bans" (§10). Greenpeace did not acknowledge the effects that their environmental campaign continues to have on the Inuit communities, ways of living, and economic opportunities. Nor did they specifically apologise for their colonial practices infusing their environmental agendas, but they said that they have a desire to learn more about decolonising their environmental practices (§4).

Greenpeace, an organisation made up of mostly white, "well-meaning" people, has devastated whole communities with their ethics around what is right and wrong. They seem to be trying to make steps toward investigating how their colonial beliefs have impacted their understanding of right and wrong. However, they still have a long way to go. These examples are products of a much larger issue: White environmentalism. White environmentalists think that they know best, and this has been as the expense of Indigenous people and their sovereign rights. If these groups do not cast blame on First Nation people, these groups have instead often participated in fetishization of First Nation culture. This fetishization can be dehumanising for First Nations people and often leads to these white environmentalists taking part in appropriative behaviour to attempt to shed their own colonial ties.

Perhaps a more recent example of white environmentalism may be seen in what are being called the Fairy Creek protests on Huu-ay-aht, Ditidaht and Pacheedaht ḥahahuułi, (ḥahahuułi means traditional territory). All three of these Nations are a part of the Nuu-chah-nulth Nation, whose lands Cook and Vancouver first landed on in so-called BC, on so-called Vancouver Island. The Fairy Creek protests began in August 2020 without the explicit consent from the First Nations of the area (Winter, 2021). These protests are now considered the largest act of civil disobedience in Canadian history with over 882 arrests made (Larsen, 2021). These protests began after Teal-Jones, a logging company, signed a revenue-sharing agreement with the Pacheedaht Nation. From there, protestors started creating blockades for months impeding the forestry from taking place against the wish of the First Nations.

On many different occasions the Huu-ay-aht, the Ditidaht and the Pacheedaht whose lands the Fairy Creek protests occurred on, have all asked the protestors and outside activists to stand down and allow their First Nations communities to make the decisions around how their lands are cared for and managed, "Third parties—whether they are companies, organisations, other governments, or individuals—have no right to speak on behalf of the Nations," the joint announcement from these three Nations continued, "Moreover, for third parties to be welcome in their ḥahahuułi, they must respect their governance and stewardship, sacred principles, and right to economically benefit from the resources within the ḥahahuułi" (Thomson, 2021). Many activists and protestors have continued to defy these requests; one group of protestors named "the Rainforest Flying Squad" would not leave the area even after the requests of the First Nations as the rainforest flying squad said they had to protect the trees no matter what cost (Pawson, 2021).

These protests are occurring in the context of settlers having logged most of BC; the reason there are so few old-growth trees left is because settlers have logged them and the province has profited greatly from it. However, when First Nations want to try to support their communities out of colonially imposed poverty, we settlers do not feel that they should have that right, and we protest. "In the past 150 years, we have watched the resources being stripped from our unceded lands with little to no recognition of our rights, and we are proud and excited to be finally restoring involvement, governance and control," said Rod Bealing, Pacheedaht First Nations' forestry manager (Tait, 2021).

Some members of these three Nations are a part of the blockades, but the protestors are predominantly non-Indigenous (Winter, 2021). Pacheedaht hereditary chief Frank Queesto Jones also condemns the protestors staying against the wishes of the Nations whose lands they are occupying: "Pacheedaht needs to be left in peace to engage in our community-lead stewardship planning process so that we can determine our own way forward as a strong and independent Nation" (Winter, 2021). This kind of paternalistic interference with First Nation decision-making can be seen as colonial in nature, defying First Nations sovereignty and asserting a patronising idea of "we know best, not you," or "these trees are more important than your decisions and sovereignty."

There are also more complex discussions to be had here around it being chiefs and councils of Nations making the decisions about land use, that the chief and council system is a colonially imposed system and that many argue that it is the hereditary chiefs who should be listened to instead. The Fairy Creek protests are complicated by the fact that chief and council as well as Pacheedaht hereditary chief Frank Queesto Jones do not support the protests whereas Pacheedaht elder who is also a hereditary chief Bill Jones is a supporter of the protests and advocates for their continuation (Winter, 2021). This situation is complicated, and as such it is difficult to say if the settler protestors participating are engaged with white colonial environmental practices. However, if I was participating in protests I would be wary of ones where to participate I had to disrespect the majority of the First Nations leaders involved, elected and hereditary, who were asking continuously for me to stop my blockades and to respect their sovereign rights by leaving.

Environmental critiques of big oil, unsustainable logging practices, and especially government regulations surrounding environmental issues are important in the process of finding sustainable paths forward. However, the consciousness that allowed for these structures to gain such power must also be examined in these investigations. The question of who is complicit in these systems and who privileges from them must be examined. When these white groups proclaim that they are back-to-the-landers, there is rarely a process of enquiry into whose land it really is that they want to return to or their historical and cultural connection to it. Colonialism perpetuated the environmental destruction occurring today. And the colonial psyche and its relationship to land is what has allowed this destruction to occur. Thus, to be in integrity as a white environmentalist, our complicity in colonial structures must be acknowledged, and we must be willing to do a thorough inventory of colonial attitudes within ourselves that impact our relationship to consumerism, wealth, ideas of success, land, and Indigenous people and their land sovereignty.

There is hope in environmental movements—there has to be. Many of the settlers who are engaged in the environmental movement have the foundational beginning needed, which is genuine care for the Earth. The next necessary next step is for individuals involved in environmentalism to become clear on their own positionality, privilege, and inherently colonial relationship to the land. The biggest thing white environmentalists need to accept is that they need to respect what Indigenous people want to do with their land. It is their land, and we need to respect their decision of their territory, whether we agree with them or not.

McCallum (2008) wrote about our innate need and desire to reconcile with the environment and save endangered animals, and he believed we do it "because we know that at some deep level their fate has something to do with us; that any step toward reconciliation with the land, with whales, wild dogs, and butterflies is a step towards our own healing" (p. 175). This kind of reconciliation would be a positive expression of *coagulatio* and would entail responsibly tending a healthy relationship with the earth element and Earth itself. If what McCallum advocated for is true and that desire for reconciliation with the environment is innate, then we must also continue working on making sure that the protection of the environment is not just a continuation of our colonial regime in our problematic white environmental movements and instead is a true step towards global healing, repair, and justice today.

How the Colonial Complex Can Now Enact the Positive Potential of *Coagulatio*?

We have reviewed the ways in which we can imagine that the colonial psyche has enacted the negative potentials of the *coagulatio* in its distorted attempt at an alchemical process. We have seen these themes in the colonial psyche's hardness, rigidity, and its toxic relationship to Earth, land, and the corporeal. Perhaps now we can imagine into how enacting the positive aspects of *coagulatio* could help restore balance, healing, and reparations for these toxic aspects of colonisation.

In alchemical imagination, the positive potentials of *coagulatio* may lead to a reverence and respect for land and the earthly. *Coagulatio* can be thought of as a descent, embodiment and incarnation to the earthly, corporeal and immanent. It can be a process of remembering the parts of ourselves that have been cut off and exiled from our psyches, like our connectedness to the aliveness of the world around us. It can also aid in connecting us to the strength and groundedness that are required to face the horrors we have committed and remain rooted and firm in our commitment to justice and reparations today. *Coagulatio*, after a healthy *solutio*, is a process of reforming ourselves anew into individuals with more integrity, solid moral compasses, and the ability to face the difficult parts of our pasts and histories. The following sections outline how this conscious *coagulatio* could be envisioned for the colonial psyche and its unsettling efforts today.

Becoming Soil Soaked

Hillman (1985) wrote about the relationship between the myths of a place and the land itself. He also explored what this connection means for the complex relationship settlers have to the lands they live on. He emphasised settlers' task of honouring the myths of the land they live on without appropriating them, while also tending to the myths of their own ancestral lineages: "if you live in the Pacific Northwest, you must see through the literal pavement into the literal Native American myths and styles" (p. 7). As settlers, it is important to honour these myths. However, we cannot appropriate them or take them as our own. Nor can we forget the myths and stories in our lineages that have shaped us and our own complex relationship to land. Hillman described settlers as perpetual immigrants, and how in North America we cannot "hear the rocks speak" because of all the psychological baggage we continue to carry with us from the "Old World" (p. 7).

Hillman (1985) advocated for the importance of looking at the baggage of our own lineage, and the myths, history, and horrors within our own past "Doesn't it take centuries for a settler to hear the earth of a place, to become soil-soaked" (p. 7). He explained that he understood his task as a depth psychologist as "unpack[ing] the immigrants' trunks" of settlers and helping other settlers investigate what they are psychologically bringing with them to these new lands as well (p. 7). He pointed to the investigation of how Christianity continues to affect settlers and how they relate to this land as an especially important enquiry for settlers today (p. 7).

Healing Our Relationship to Nature Heals Us

Not only is restoring our relationship to land important for its protection, but it is also good for us to tend this foundational relationship. Research in recent decades in fields such as conservation psychology have been able to show the mutually beneficial symbiotic relationship between people and nature. Studies such as Beringer (2000) have shown the many positive effects on individuals that occur when they connect to nature,Beringer's research findings suggest 12 different ways that nature heals individuals, which are that it conveys: a "sense of continuity and stability; support; positive feedback, perspective, exploration of self and body; slowing- down effect; freedom from social judgement; self-worth; transcendence; and calming and euphoria" (Clayton & Myers, 2015, p. 172). Studies also show that time in nature can lead to feelings of connectedness, a deep sense of belonging to something greater than oneself, and transcendent experiences outside of one's ordinary experience of the world which allow one to feel a deep sense of meaningfulness (p. 353). Naess' (1989) work showed that in nature, "one experiences oneself to be a genuine part of all life" (Clayton & Myers, 2015, p. 174).

Various conservation psychologists have studied the phenomenon of an ecological self, which suggests that our relationship with nature is an integral part of ourselves (p. 351). They show that when people feel connected to their ecological selves, their time in nature is not just enjoyable but also "self-relevant and potentially transformative, affecting the way we define ourselves to ourselves as well as to others" (p. 351). Further research shows that when we are more connected to nature we take better care of it as it becomes a part of our own self-identity and its preservation is understood to be a part of our own (p. 354). Nurturing this connection to nature is vital for settler decolonisation, and it must also be done thoughtfully with deep, continual enquiry into what it means to connect as settlers to Indigenous stolen land.

In her work, Blackie (2018) wrote indirectly about the ecological self and described "the ever-unfolding, alchemical process in which the land constantly makes and shapes us" (p. 272). She believed that connecting to this deep alchemical experience of the enchantment of the land is a part of connecting to our place in the world (p. 272). Maybe connecting to the land and healing our relationship with it is not only our responsibility as humans but even more so right now our responsibility as white people when we have wreaked so much destruction in our disconnect from it. However, to truly undergo a conscious *coagulatio* here, this reforming of connection must be approached with the utmost caution and enquiry about what it means for settlers to connect to land that our cultural ancestors stole and how that shapes our personal connection to that land today.

Caring for the World Around Us Is Good for Us

Authors such as Ruth King (2018) have advocated for mindfulness practices in our journey toward antiracism. King compared meditation or mindfulness practices with composting and said with these practices, you might not see changes happen, but that deep within "the heap of your practice," transformation is occurring and with time, she says, "you will have rich, nourishing soil to feed and seed kindness" (Location 1387). King believed mindfulness practices are very useful in transforming racism and she calls them an "antidote to racial ill will and aversion. It uplifts the heart and deepens the capacity to bear witness to racial distress without war" (Location 1387). King advocated that mindfulness is an embodied, tangible practice that can be done to transform racism within and to support us in our direct action (Location 1387). I would also caution that mindfulness or meditation on its own will not cure our settler-colonialism or ingrained delusions of white supremacy and that believing so would be a very dangerous spiritual-bypassing belief to fall into.

Healing Colonial Disconnect from Land: Unearthing Trauma, Cultivating Care

Some authors and scholars believe that there has been too little emphasis on the unearthing of the trauma of white people in this movement. Saad (2020) wrote "As you root out your internalised white supremacy, your body, mind, and spirit will be affected," and she encouraged that as this work is done, deep self-care is prioritised so that we stay grounded in self and body and stay emotionally well as we undertake the work (p. 24). Williams (2016) advocated for the need to unearth the trauma of white people living in such a racialized society before any transformation and forward-moving action as a collective is possible (Williams, Owens, & Syedullah, p. 158). King (2018) advocated for planting seeds of racial consciousness in our lives, after this unearthing of racialized trauma (Location 3529).

King (2018) believed that though we cannot change the fact that racist seeds were planted in the past, we can work today to plant and cultivate new seeds, until they are the ones thriving in our societal gardens. "Now, with more wisdom and care, we can plant new seeds of well-being in the same soil of consciousness, which will make prior seeds of ignorance and harm more difficult to blossom" (Location 3529).

Coagulatio/Earth Concrete Actions and Reflection Questions

In this unearthing and replanting of seeds of racial justice and equality, we can begin to imagine a different future. In this chapter, we delved into the colonial complex's perceived separation and superiority over nature, and through the earth element, we looked at alchemy's encouragement of the honouring of the living earth and land. These are processes that we can initiate in our own lives through the following unsettling practices and direct actions. Though a re-examination of our own relationship to land, Earth, and nature is vital, it must be followed up with direct action: concrete action here today is urgent.

- Action here can begin by looking up Land Back movements near you. Donate to them (financially or with land), support them, join them if you are welcome.
- Read and work through all the exercises in the workbook *Decolonise First, a liberating guide & workbook* (2020) by Ta7talíya Michelle Nahanee.
- Make sure that any environmental groups or activities you engage with are not perpetuating white environmentalism, white saviour behaviour, or perpetuating Indigenous disenfranchisement from land rights, or their sovereignty.

- Join or form a community group dedicated to extracting invasive species of plants harming the native ecosystems around you.
- Continue learning about the Indigenous land on which you live and any negotiations/ land claims/activism/protests near you. Find ways to contribute, through donation of money and/or volunteering of your time.
- Further reading: Arthur Manuel's *The Reconciliation Manifesto: Recovering the land rebuilding the economy* (2017); *My conversations with Canadians* (2017) by Lee Maracle; Leanne Simpson's *Dancing on our Turtle's Back* (2011); *Braiding Sweetgrass* (2015) by Robin Kimmerer; *Mindful of Race* by Ruth King (2018); and the collection of essays entitled *Resurgence and Reconciliation Indigenous-Settler Relations and Earth teachings* (2018).
- Journal prompts: What is your relationship to land? Are there places where you feel disconnected, and separated from nature? What sensations do you explore as you feel into the separation? Is there a place in the world or an activity where you feel especially connected to nature? What is that like? How does your body respond to this connection? What is your historical connection to that place? What is the story of that place?
- Get to know one plant in the forest you have not spent much time with before—a moss you haven't paid particular attention to or Devil's Club, whose thorns you have only ever scowled at. Spend some time in silence with the plant. You may want to sketch it, or write a description of it, or create a little ode to it. What does it mean for you to relate to this plant? Is it a native species to this ecosystem? Are you?
- Do you have practices in this theme of Earth/body/land that are culturally appropriated? Do you know their origin, if people of European descent have been given permission to practice them? If not, find and start learning practices from your lineages, they exist in almost all, if not all of our ancestries and pasts.

Chapter 9
Fire

Figure 9.1 Emblem XXII.

Source: Michael Maïer, *Atalanta Fugiens*, 1618. Etching from an alchemical text, depicting a pregnant alchemist tending the hearth fire and cookstoves.

DOI: 10.4324/9781003296546-10

Helms's Fourth Stage of White Racial Identity Development: Pseudo-Independence

Helms's (1993) fourth stage of white racial identity development is pseudo-independence. Helms sees this stage as the first movement towards a potentially positive white identity (p. 61). In the previous stages, individuals primarily needed to work on acknowledging the racialized harm they were committing and then working to undo their negative racist white identities. In this fourth stage, individuals begin to actively acknowledge the harm being done to people of colour from individual and systematic racism. The flame of justice is sparked in their minds, and their hearts start warming with empathy for the other as well as the heat of anger as they acknowledge the harm that the delusion of white supremacy has caused. The fire of passion for the cause gets flamed. However, in this stage, there will still be confusion at times as to how to take right action and what this process entails.

Helms (1993) described how in this stage, individuals may also start acknowledging how they have perpetuated racialized harm either consciously or unconsciously in the past. They might also begin acknowledging the responsibility of white people, including themselves, to work towards the mitigation of racial harm. These individuals thus no longer feel comfortable with their previous racist identities, and they start to find new ways to redefine their relationships to their whiteness (p. 61).

Though individuals in this stage may be heading in an antiracist direction, they often still hold many conscious and unconscious biases and beliefs and still perpetuate harm in their actions. Their interactions with people of colour may at times look like trying to play white saviour and paternalistically help people of colour. They might attempt to assimilate people of colour into the white culture more fully to try to "help" them from being discriminated against (Helms, 1993, p. 61). This is racist as it attempts to assimilate people of colour into white supremist culture rather than realising the inherent racism, and deeply problematic natures of these systems of "success" in the first place (p. 61).

Helms (1993) wrote that many people of colour will be rightly suspicious and uncomfortable with white people engaged in this kind of inappropriate and misguided saviour behaviour. Therefore, the pseudo-independent person "may not feel entirely comfortable with her or his White identity, but overidentification with [people of colour] is also not likely to be very comfortable. Thus, the person may come to feel rather marginal where race and racial issues are concerned" (p. 62). At this stage, there needs to be enough either internal or external motivation to continue undoing the harms of the white racial identity and to continue the uncomfortable process of forging a new one in the fires of inner reckoning. Only when one continually seeks out "the quest" for a better white identity and definition of whiteness will they begin to transition into the immersion/emersion stage of white racial identity development (p. 62).

Introduction to *Calcinatio*

Earlier, we investigated the colonial psyche's disconnect from a personal experience of the soulful, passionate or sacred, the Christian underpinnings of this disconnect, including the Christian ideals perceiving that which is too personally passionate as frivolous, fleshy and sinful (Colossians 3:5, NRSV). We also investigated how, in the Catholic tradition, the relationship between the individual and the sacred has been interrupted with the church mediating between the two (Leviticus 5:12, NRSV). This separation of the individual from the soulful is foundational to the shadow of colonial consciousness. Its estrangement from embodiment, experiences of connection, and the fullness of the experience of life has deeply impacted its psychic health and actions in the world. We will now investigate how alchemical metaphors may offer an antidote to this part of the colonial psyche by encouraging the tending of one's own connection to the soulful and creative.

This chapter will explore how alchemists conceptualised fire and its corresponding alchemical operation *calcinatio*. It will imagine into *calcinatio* as a metaphor for a part of the distorted alchemical journey to the New World and explore how we can now consciously engage with this operation in our settler decolonisation journeys today.

The Sacred

Throughout this work, the term sacred is used without referring to specific religious or denominational entities, but instead refers to a human experience of something greater, such as an experience of a mundane task suddenly feeling full of purpose or having an experience of awe or wonder as we look at a landscape or loved one which we have looked at thousands of times before. The definition of sacred here is inclusive of any human experience that an individual deems sacred.

The experience of the sacred is a human experience unrelated to religious affiliation. This experience may occur at the birth of a child or the death of a loved one. It occurs in the places in life where we encounter that which brings us out of our ordinary experience of the world or to a deeper experience of it, where the ordinary becomes extraordinary. Some studies which have conducted research on the experience of the sacred describe it as "a sense of identity that transcends the individual and encompasses one's position as part of a living ecosystem" (Clayton & Myers, p. 351). Conservational psychologists stress that this idea of exploring the sacred in connection with nature involves a felt sense of "'identification' not in the sense of indistinguishability with life processes, but in terms of our capacity to see something of the other in ourselves, to experience a sense of similarity or shared community" (p. 351). Some people experience this feeling while making art, listening to or playing music, making love, running, being in nature, eating beautiful food and sharing it with others, or participating in their religious practices. Whatever and however this is experienced is included in this research's definition of the sacred.

Some people experience the sacred as a feeling of connectedness to that which is around them, a feeling of rightness, wholeness, wonder, aliveness, joy, hope, fullness, expanded consciousness, a sense of stillness and aliveness within silence or sound, of fulfilment, or peace. I understand these human moments as sacred. It has felt important for me in this work to reclaim these words outside of a religious context.

Fire

The alchemical operation of *calcinatio* was thought to be purifying or deeply destructive, just as fire can be regenerative or devastating. Some of the images associated with the alchemical *calcinatio* are fire, blood, rage, passion, burning, desire, and the heart. Alchemists believed that in its negative potential, *calcinatio* expresses itself emotionally as frustration, anger, rage, feeling thwarted, scorched, or as heat rising to your cheeks in shame. In a *calcinatio,* positive guilt is what leads to greater consciousness and accountability, whereas debilitating shame leads to inaction, distorted rage, and violent outbursts. "We are the primal chaos that the fire is illuminating and heating. Alchemical fire is the heat of the soul cooking, consuming, transforming itself" (Rossi, p. 43).

In recent years we have seen these metaphors being manifested literally in a global, heated reckoning with race and a boiling confrontation with systematic racism. George Floyd's murder in 2020, was a spark that ignited a new level of societal reckoning with racial and racist issues. In North America in 2020, there were physical burnings as shops were set on fire with the rage of no longer being willing to live in such an unjust and racist society.

Not only are our collective emotions heated—the Earth is physically warming up as well. Nineteen of the warmest years on measurable record have occurred in the past twenty years (NASA, 2021, §1). Our industrial capitalist complex has us constantly pulling black blood from deep veins of the earth to burn and stoke atmospheric heat, heating the enveloping ethereal hold around us. Wet'suwet'en and Lakota chiefs along with Indigenous activists throughout the continent have tried to apply pressure to the wound to staunch the flow. In 2020, massive wildfires ravaged Australia and California, in part, a result of this global warming. Our bodies too have been on fire—a fever has been burning across the globe, from lungs to lungs as COVID-19.

Calcinatio's heat has smouldered on what is now known as North America for centuries. During the smallpox epidemics, villages across the continent were burned in a futile attempt to stop the spread of the disease. Before that, Captain Cook spread the searing, burning pain and death of sexually transmitted infections with him and his ships across the globe, including what is now known as North America (Crosby, 2015, Location 3583).

Cook's eventual death was in part a result of his attempt to kidnap the Hawaiian king. He also offended the Hawaiians by taking the palings of a shrine dedicated to the god Ku and using them as firewood (Cook, 2003, p. 628). Cook and his crew relied on firepower and with it they often felt undefeatable (p. 657). In the end, firearms failed to protect Cook against the Hawaiian vengeance for his sacrilegious and violent behaviour (p. 657).

Cook's Journals

> *February 14th, 1779:* On Cook's death Clerke, now seriously ill, was in command of Resolution and the expedition, and Gore was given the command of Discovery. Clerke got the fatal mast on board, and set about recovering the bodies of Cook and those who were killed with him. The bodies of the marines were never recovered. Cook's body had been dismembered and divided among chiefs: this was normal reverential treatment of the body of a great chief. However, some parts of the corpse were slowly brought back – with the bewildering inquiry as to when Lono would return and what would he do to them when he did. The remains were committed to the waters of the bay. Clerke did not want retaliation or vengeance, but not all were of the same mind. When a watering party was stoned there was a violent reaction; the houses of a whole village were burned to the ground and those who could not get away were bayoneted or shot, and two heads were severed and placed on poles. (Cook, 2003, p. 480)

Cook and his crew misused fire seemingly every step of the way, even after Cook's death, Fire was used in violent, horrific ways over and over again.

Calcinatio's Relationship to the Psyche: Positive and Negative Potentials

The alchemical process of *calcinatio* corresponds to the element of fire. In the alchemist's laboratory, it is characterised by the heating of a solid in order to evaporate the water, leaving a dry powder. For example, the alchemists heated limestone to evaporate water and produce quicklime (Edinger, 1991, p. 17). "The alchemist must learn all there is to know about fire, the various kinds, its sources and its fuels for not all fire is to be fed the same way" (Rossi, 2017, p. 22). Jung saw alchemical fire as representational of libido-life energy (p. 18). *Calcinatio* is anything to do with fire, heat, or burning. Hillman (2010) discussed fire's primary role in our lives and psyches by its "radiance, its flickering instability, its warmth, and its rage" (p. 20).

Fire, fever, and burning played horrifying roles in the colonising process of so-called North America. The distribution of smallpox blankets was a devastating genocidal act of terror. Colonisers tried to burn whole nations up in fevers. In many places across North America, 90% of Indigenous populations were killed in the fevers and blistering heat of smallpox's boils. There was also the colonial introduction of "firewater" or alcohol into Indigenous communities after the forcible removal of their children to residential schools. Some see the introduction of this often deadly addiction in the face of such trauma as a deliberate act of attempted genocide.

Conversely, the productive process of *calcinatio* that we can engage in today is the burning off of what no longer serves and leaving behind productive psychological material to work with. The burning of the body of the king is a classic alchemical image signifying "the death of the ruling principle of consciousness, the highest authority in the hierarchical structure of the ego" (Edinger, 1991, p. 19). Today, the ruling principle and dangerous aspects of the colonial psyche that have been in charge for far too long are what we can begin to burn away.

The productive side of *calcinatio* can also entail learning the art of fire. Hillman (2015) wrote that this art "means learning how to warm, excite, enthuse, ignite, inspire ... the state of one's nature so as to activate it further into a different state" (p. 20). For settlers, learning the art of fire might look like burning the patriarchal ruling, power-hungry complexes within and being ready for something new to be reborn from the humility and vulnerability of the ashes. As it is necessary today, it was necessary 500 years ago. Instead, the discomfort of burning these hierarchal structures within was thwarted and the burning happened externally and violently instead.

The alchemical lens understands fire as the heat required for transformations. Metaphors for the heat of cooking and the transformation that happens in matter, food, and cooking are used to describe the changes that can happen to our psyches as well. Hillman (2010) wrote, "in alchemy, we are what is being cooked. We are the vessel and the stuff within it, as well as the lab in which it all happens (p. 20). Fire is seen as the changemaker, the flame needed to begin the cooking, the changing, the creating: it is the passion and anger that takes action (Rossi, 2017, p. 43). Hillman (2010) described inertia and resistance to change as innate to human nature (p. 127). Heat is what gets the atoms of molecules moving, it is what can change water from frozen to liquid to gas; it is the great transformer. Only intense heat can get us moving and unstuck from these frozen places (p. 127).

Our job is to work with this fire, not to resist it, suffocate it or let it spread untended, destroying everything in its wake. We must, as Hillman (2015) wrote, learn the art of the fire (Location 274). Fire is what fuels our passion, our curiosity, imagination, love, excitement and joy. Fire is the creative spark of life which calls us forth asking us to show up and live our lives to their fullest capacities. To live fully, we must meet and come into a relationship with this fire: "We have to meet fire with the fiery material of our passions, our inspirations. Fire is the spark and thrust of our desires, our longings, and our vision. To come to terms with our fire, we have to imagine into our fire" (Rossi, 2017, p. 43). As Jung (1915/2009) wrote, there is an aspect of inescapability with fire—to live, to show up on this earth, we will be confronted with our inner fire, we will not be able to escape it, we must learn to face it and not to cower from it: "There is no escape ... You'll think up clever truisms, preventive measures, secret escape routes, excuses, potions capable of inducing forgetfulness, but it's all useless. The fire burns right through you. That which guides forces you onto the way" (p. 291).

How the Colonial Complex Enacted the Negative Potential of *Calcinatio*

> "The main islands were thickly populated with a peaceful folk when Christ-over found them. But the orgy of blood which followed, no man has written. We are the slaughterers. It is the tortured soul of our world."
>
> —William Carlos Williams (Stannard, 1993, Location 177)

As we have explored in the last three elemental chapters, first with Ziegler's archetypal medicine, then Hillman's psychologising symptoms (seeing the narrative and mythic underpinnings in works), and finally Jung's seeing the gods manifesting as diseases, we continue in this same vein of psychologising symptoms in this chapter. We will continue looking at the archetypal underpinnings of colonisation and imagining into them as a part of a distorted alchemical journey gone terribly wrong. Where the settlers were seeking internal gold and the rebirth we imagine that they thwarted the process and sought it externally and destructively instead. Hillman (1997) reminded his readers that this kind of externalisation of inner processes was the most dangerous risk of alchemy (p. 9). In this final elemental chapter, we can imagine into how this distorted alchemical journey could have been undertaken in the specific *calcinatio* operation and colonialism's relationship with the element and metaphor of fire.

Blood, Colonialism, and Fire

In the conquering of what is now known as North America, we can imagine the alchemical operation of *calcinatio* being embodied in its relationship to fire and blood. This included the violent shedding of blood in the colonial killing of millions, and, in later policy development, with its focus on blood quantum as a means of continued assimilation and extinction of Indigenous people.

Ruth King (2018) described how white people continue to justify and deny the violence they are complicit in by avoiding the heat of confrontation with the shame, anger, and rage at the injustices, and the general heat of the emotionality surrounding these realities (Location 961). "The world's heart is on fire, and race is at its core" (Location 111). She wrote that when white people "collude, they maintain privilege by avoiding the intense heat and creative chaos that is required to compost racial avoidance into racial awareness and honesty" (Location 961). Here, she described the avoidance of the fire of racial reckoning as the perpetuation of these racist patterns. She argued that hiding in the cold of white silence is part of what has kept white individuals feeling safe from having to face the realities of their complicity in these racialized injustices. She called instead for the necessity of letting ourselves be transformed by the fire of racial reckoning.

The Danger of Being Scared of Fire

Many Indigenous nations on what is now known as North America have historically practiced controlled burns as a vital tending of land, food sources, and healthy ecosystems (Boyd, 1999, p. 2). These prescribed, managed burns were interrupted with colonisers implementing fire suppression management techniques (p. 3). The consequence of the change in fire management drastically altered the landscape and ecosystems of what is now called North America (p. 3).

When we repress fire due to fear, the fire can actually get out of control and be more dangerous. In contrast, small, controlled burns at frequent intervals clears off the top layer of debris on the forest floor, halting accumulations of tinder and fuel. Many First Nations understood "the beneficial effects of understory and spot burning in several forest types [which act] as a preventive to wildfires, disease outbreaks, and extensive forest burns" (Boyd, 1999, p. 3). It is the bioaccumulation of debris on the forest floor that, without smaller, more frequent burns, can accumulate and lead to vast and dangerous wildfires.

The prescribed burns practiced by some Indigenous Nations were vital in the health of many ecosystems. These prescribed burns helped to create flourishing environments for food sources such as camas and other root crops, and many different kinds of wild berries (Boyd, 1999, p. 2). However, settlers put an end to these controlled burn practices during colonisation and instead settlers implemented "the ill-advised, unnatural (and culturally specific) practice of fire suppression" (p. 3). Fire suppression continues as the main way of managing fires in so-called North America today and its modern and historical effects have had drastic and devastating impacts on plant diversity and ecosystems across the continent. The value of the traditional methods of prescribed burning is only now beginning to be recognised.

The Gary Oak ecosystem is one that needs occasional fires to thrive. These ecosystems are now nearing extinction and are listed as "at-risk or endangered" throughout North America (Pellatt, McCoy, & Mathewes, 2015, p. 1621). In so-called Canada, these ecosystems are home to over a hundred endangered species (p. 1621). Conservation studies have confirmed that "fire suppression, cessation of aboriginal land-use, climate change, western colonisation and subsequent intensification of land-use has greatly altered Gary Oak ecosystems" (p. 1621). Partly as a result of colonial fears surrounding controlled fires, Gary Oak ecosystems and the hundreds of species that they house are endangered. Many other ecosystems supporting vast plant diversity which depend on the natural cycles of small fires every now and then are also now endangered because of fire suppression management (p. 1621).

First Nations knew that they could not stop forest fires completely and so they would let fires burn, or start them intentionally, and as a result of their relationship with fire, ecological diversity thrived. Their smaller controlled burns prevented the massive fires we see wiping out millions of hectares of forests today. Currently, the build-up of tinder, paired with rising heat temperatures and decrease in precipitation due to human-caused climate change, has led to devastating wildfires throughout the continent (Pellatt, McCoy, & Mathewes, 2015, p. 1636).

We cannot live in fear of fire, nor can we live in fear of the internal fires of passion, desire, anger, or rage. When these emotions are repressed, like fires, they become most dangerous. Colonial fear of fire has been dangerous, and its repression has not been working. Like the alchemists, we must now learn to navigate the tending of inner and outer fires and learn not to smother them, nor let them rage and burn out of control.

How the Colonial Complex Can Enact the Positive Potential of *Calcinatio*

The Positive Potential of Calcinatio

The previous sections have investigated how the colonial psyche can be seen as having enacted the negative aspects of the alchemical *calcinatio* operation over the centuries, in what we are imaging as a distorted alchemical journey. We will now imagine into the potential of the colonial psyche engaging with the positive expressions of *calcinatio's* fire today.

Alchemists understood one of *calcinatio's* positive potentials as its relationship with creative life energy, or what Jung called libido (Edinger, 1991, p. 18). When tended, this energy manifests as passion, vitality for life, creativity, and engagement with the world. Fire in this sense is also related to desire: sexual desire, but also desire for life itself. Hillman (2015) wrote of this relationship between desire and fire: "For desire to be consummated, for the opus to come to fruition – in art, in love, in practice of any sort – learn all you can about its fire: its radiance, its flickering instability, its warmth, and its rage" (Location 274). This same fiery desire is also related to the warmth and passion in life and the world (Location 294). The positive aspects of *calcinatio* can look like an embrace, devotion, and engagement with this passion, love, desire, and energy in the world. This fire can burn away that which no longer serves us, and we can rise from it anew: Hillman reminded us of the cookstoves of the alchemists and how these cookstoves are really found within us:

> You are the laboratory; you are the vessel and the stuff going through the cooking. So, too, the fire is an invisible heat, a psychic heat that clamors for fuel, breathing room, and regular loving consideration. (Location 281)

The metaphor of the alchemical *calcinatio* encourages us to let go of our colonial ways of being, let them be burned away by the heat of our own inner fire and allow our passion, vitality, love for the world, and justice to now lead our way.

The Fiery Passion Needed to Combat Racism

In *Mindful of Race*, King (2018) equates racism to heart disease, an illness circulating through the veins of America (Location 187). She also saw a cure for this disease—the transformation of the hearts and minds of individuals across the continent. She advocated for sitting with the emotions in our own bodies that racism can bring up and transforming our emotional relationship to them so that we can better go out into the world and advocate for the changes that need to be made without our own unprocessed emotions (fear, anger, denial, defensiveness, and trauma) hijacking those attempts: "Allow racial distress to teach you how to be more human. Sit in the heat of it until your heart is both warmed and informed, then make a conscious choice to be a light" (Location 3603). She entreated, "May we understand and transform racial habits of harm. May we remember that we belong to each other. May we grow in our awareness that what we do can help or hinder racial well-being" (Location 3603).

Menakem (2017) also stressed the importance of connecting to our own souls and processing the trauma that keeps us disconnected from our selves in the journey of advocating for and embodying antiracism in the world. He talked about how the divisions we see between races are not the core conflict that needs to be addressed: "These divisions are all reflections of a much older and more elemental conflict. That conflict is the battle for the bodies and souls of white Americans" (p. 295). Menakem continued discussing how this battle has been "fuelled by trauma as old as the Middle Ages, and it has been simmering in white American bodies since long before we became a nation. Now the heat has been turned up, and the conflict has reached critical mass" (p. 295). Menakem believed that what happens next is that "this trauma will either burst forth in an explosion of dirty pain, or provide the necessary energy and heat for white Americans to move through clean pain and heal. Only this second outcome will provide us with genuine safety" (p. 295). To undertake this unsettling antiracism journey, we must learn to tend these inner fires, stoke them to create enough passion to engage in the work, but not let them overwhelm us in what Menakem calls dirty pain: unprocessed rage, aggression, hatred, etc. This fine line of stoking the fire but keeping it under control was central to the alchemists work and must be central to our unsettling and antiracism work today as well.

Activation of the Nervous System in Antiracism Work

Another way to conceptualise this inner fire is to look at our own nervous systems. Many traditions associate the nervous system, or activation of the spinal cord, with the words heat, electricity and fire. Menakem (2017) wrote about the nervous system in terms of "the soul nerve" (p. 295). He wrote that as part of the racial reckoning needed today, our bodies and soul nerves are being activated in profound ways, and that our racialized traumas are continuously getting triggered through these times (p. 295). Menakem explained that to fully process these experiences and move forward in integrity, we need to fully feel and sense our soul "'nerves' constriction and expansion; the pain, fear, hope, and dread; the sense of peril; and the sense of possibility," he continued "to tolerate the discomfort of this activation, we all need to carefully observe ourselves, slow ourselves down, settle our bodies" (p. 295). This kind of nervous system dysregulation requires our tending, soothing, and healing so that we can show up in this work without our triggers constantly hijacking our behaviours, beliefs, and actions.

Activated Nervous Systems and Activists

Modern polyvagal theory of the nervous system explores the profound connection between the impact our nervous system has on our mental health and vice versa. The autonomic nervous system has three pathways of response to sensations and environmental signals (Dana, 2018, p. 4). The vagus, a critically important part of the parasympathetic nervous system is divided into two pathways: the ventral vagus and dorsal vagus (p. 8). In ventral vagal activation, it is possible to achieve the most deeply relaxed state and feelings of safety within the nervous system. This state has been described as the full-bodied warmth of relaxation—"the ventral vagal pathway responds to cues of safety and supports feelings of being safely engaged and socially connected" (p. 8). In contrast, the dorsal vagal pathway responds to cues of "extreme danger" and is what we know of as the freeze response (p. 8). Dorsal vagal reactions will take us "out of connection, out of awareness, and into a protective state of collapse. When we feel frozen, numb, or 'not here,' the dorsal vagus has taken control" (p. 8).

Perhaps we can draw some parallels between the dorsal vagal response of a shut down, dissociated freeze response and white inaction on racial issues. Desmond Tutu once said that "if you are neutral on situations of injustice, you have chosen the side of the oppressor" (King, 2018, Location 1763). The dorsal vagal response leading to an inability to move or to take action is perhaps part of what is happening at the nervous system level when there is a freeze response in antiracism work. It is not effective having people stuck in these freeze responses, and the polyvagal lesson here is that we cannot get people out of these states by shaming them or yelling at them, for they are in deep survival threat responses to what is being perceived as the highest level of threat. At that point, threatening them with anger or blame will only make them retreat more into this survival response.

The sympathetic nervous system governs the fight or flight response to cues of danger and prepares us for action (Dana, 2018, p. 8). When activated, it triggers the release of adrenaline (p. 8). Perhaps we can see this response as occurring in the image of the radical, angry activist who is poised for a fight and confrontation. Today, this angry activist is often thought to be the most committed and effective activist. This type of activism certainly has its place and has contributed to necessary changes that might not have been possible without its righteous anger. Anger is absolutely often the most appropriate immediate response to injustices. However, I wonder if it would be possible to look at this from a nervous system level and see this type of activism as an example of the fight response of the sympathetic nervous system that is stuck in an activated state.

Dana (2018) explained that if the different parts of the nervous system were able to write their own stories, "the sympathetic nervous system will write a story of anxiety, anger, and action," whereas "the dorsal vagal description will be one of collapse and a loss of hope" (p. 175). It is only "the ventral vagal story [which] will include elements of safety and care" (p. 175). If we are only engaging in our activism from the sympathetic nervous system, we will burn ourselves out. It is not sustainable to remain in the sympathetic nervous system response for long periods of time, as it is only supposed to be a temporary response to acute danger, and it will burn us out if it is always activated. It is harmful to us to have our nervous systems in such stress, flooded with adrenaline and always activated. It is a huge drain on our emotional and physical resources.

When we believe that being the fighting, angry activist (that is, being in a state of constant sympathetic nervous system engagement) is the only way for us to contribute to causes, we overlook how the ventral vagal system can contribute to advocacy work. "If we are not safe, we are chronically in a state of evaluation and defensiveness ... It is a ventral vagal state and a neuroception of safety that bring the possibility for connection, curiosity, and change" (Dana, 2018, p. 7). How beautiful emphasising bringing in regulation, calm, and an expanded ability to use more areas of our brains—including those regions capable of empathy, deep listening, and reasoning—would be to our activism work. And yet somehow this idea can feel contentious as there is an idea that we should not be calm in the face of these horrors. I agree that anger and rage are often very healthy and often the healthiest first response to injustice. That being said, I think there is also a place for regulation as a resource for us to draw on and act from, as this leads to nourishing ourselves and others for the long, sustainable advocacy path ahead and not just quickly burning out our nervous systems by constant, sustained dysregulation.

Dana (2018) explained more ways that we can nurture these ventral vagal pathways in our lives. She elucidated that polyvagal theory shows that the "brain and body systems that process social warmth and physical warmth share common pathways" (p. 162). Dana explained how our brain's wiring of physical and interpersonal warmth are connected: when we feel physically warm, we feel interpersonally safer and more connected (p. 162): "Warm environments, hot showers or baths, holding hot drinks, or holding hot packs changes people's impressions of others and brings a positive shift toward connection" (163). Dana discussed how we can use the brain's interconnected wiring of physical and social warmth to aid in feelings of connectivity, safety, and self-regulation. "People who are perceived as warm send autonomic cues of safety, inviting approach and connection" (p. 162). She wrote how even holding a hot cup of tea or having "a hot shower or bath can reduce feelings of social exclusion. Wrapping up in a warm blanket can moderate the sense of isolation. Heart-warming is both a physical and psychological experience" (p. 163). She wrote that another resource for living from the ventral vagus is nurturing self-compassion for ourselves (p. 43).

We can think about learning to tend, strengthen and regulate our nervous system as acts of embodiment, ways to connect to our inner vitality, our birthright of bodily health, calm, and the inner fire of our regulated nervous systems. As one resource for this work, we can remember that warmth helps us self-regulate and activates brain regions of safety and a sense of connection with others. We can also remember the resources our breath and body-based awareness can have in helping us learn to guide our nervous systems into regulation and calm, active engagement. Somatic therapy or polyvagal theory can help support learning this kind of regulation.

Healing the Nervous System from Christian Trauma

Having the Catholic church be a conduit between an individual and God can be compared to preventing an individual from self-regulating their own nervous system or tending and connecting to their own inner fire themselves. In the Catholic tradition, individuals need to confess to a clergy member before forgiveness can flow through and calm their hyperactive sympathetic nervous systems. "With the offerings by fire to the LORD; it is a sin offering. Thus the priest shall make atonement on your behalf" (Leviticus 5:12, NRSV). Jesus said to his apostles and those who would go on to found the church: "Receive the Holy Spirit. If you forgive the sins of any, they are forgiven them; if you retain the sins of any, they are retained" (John 20:21, NSRV). It is an impediment to learning how to stoke, care, and tend one's own nervous system, not being able to access this self-regulation of self-forgiveness oneself. The Catholic church has inserted itself as necessary in this kind of regulation instead of allowing individuals to learn to self-regulate and soothe their nervous systems themselves. Reclaiming responsibility for our own nervous systems, connection to the soulful and access to our own forgiveness and regulation has the potential to be an empowering reclamation of the direct access to our own internal regulation, inner vitality, and aid in our unsettling pursuits.

Pendulation and Titration

This book is attempting to support the centrality of the ventral vagus, and honour it as the foundational, grounding well from which our activism can grow and be nourished. While acknowledging a healthy nervous system as a necessary part of activism and unsettling, this research has attempted to embody the theory of pendulation and titration in its content and writing style. Pendulation in polyvagal theory is "intentionally moving between activation and calm" and titration is "using tempo and parsing of experience to monitor and manage response" (Dana, 2018, p. 29). Both of these techniques can help the nervous system stay regulated while processing difficult information or memories. These techniques can help so that the "autonomic nervous system stays out of protective survival responses and maintains enough ventral vagal influence to bring curiosity to the process" (p. 173). The theory of pendulation and titration is used in the writing of this book in its attempt to move between more difficult, activating topics and then back to drawing on resource places, with more storytelling bits or more poetic language and then back into what is difficult. In this way, the hope is to avoid flooding the nervous system, and at the same time help it to build tolerance for the discomfort of this material:

> We live a story that originates in our autonomic state, is sent through autonomic pathways from the body to the brain, and is then translated by the brain into the beliefs that guide our daily living. The mind narrates what the nervous system knows. Story follows state. (p. 35)

If we change our state, then we can change our story for the better, and from there, continue to change our state. Hopefully, this change can be out of a colonial state of being and can move toward unsettling, decolonising and antiracism behaviours, actions, and states today.

Creative Expression and Antiracism

Another means of cultivating positive expressions of *calcinatio* in our lives is tending to our creative expression. If this inner fire and personal connection to the soulful was part of what the colonial Catholic church attempted to limit, then reclaiming it is an alchemical counterbalance to that historical oppression. Creative expression, and nurturing our passions, no matter if they are deemed "skilful" by society or not, can connect us to our sense of self, our joy, and the sense of our creative personal relationship to the world. King (2018) suggested that all art forms, including storytelling, are "healing art form[s]" (Location 3254). She advocated for telling our stories and listening to the stories of others as a way to "keep our hearts well lubricated and our ears attuned to humility and care. And it is an artful way to plant seeds that help us wake up, remember our belonging, and serve well" (Location 3254). King (2018) strongly believed that both the work of antiracism and the world "[need] people who have come alive" and she emphasised the importance of tending our inner aliveness in our antiracism and decolonial work and journeys (Location 3365). She suggested that we explore if there is something in us longing to write novels, essays, poems, sing, perform, play music, create art or "dance like wildfire" (Location 3365). She wrote that creative expressions of any kind are key parts of tending our own inner vitality and she emphasised the importance of contributing that vitality to the betterment of our communities and the heart of the world at large. "Consider your artistic expression, no matter how large or small, a gesture of affection that cultivates a culture of care. Offer it generously, as ceremony, and without apology" (Location 3365).

Niessen (2017) argued for the importance of art in decolonisation: "Art has the power to bring together people from all ages and all walks of life. It can bring about awareness and understanding, promote critical thinking, and can also work towards healing;" she continued, advocating that creating art will "never erase the horrors of residential schools or reverse the damage done to families and communities, but it can bring about hope—hope that we can some day eradicate the perils of hatred, racism, and ethnocentrism" (p. 31). Connecting to an art practice in an intentional way can be an important part of connecting to our inner fires and melting the colonial rigidity, hardness, and disconnect within. When done with justice and healing in mind, it can also be a part of our unsettling journeys and activism today.

Calcinatio/Fire Concrete Actions and Reflection Questions

Concrete actions must be taken with respect to our unsettling processes. This includes working on tending our nervous system regulation, whether that is with the help of a therapist, a body-based practice, breath practice, or other forms of intentional somatic-based work. This could also entail an examination of how we can embody the passion for these issues into direct action: what groups could be joined, what financial support could be offered and whose voices and work we can amplify. This could also entail cultivating passion for these issues if you are feeling numb or withdrawn or dissociated from them. Consider Joanne Macy's "Work That Reconnects," in her book *Coming Back to Life: The Updated Guide to the Work That Reconnects* (2014). This work helps guide individuals from numbness and dissociation in the face of social and environmental justice issues through the psychological processing often necessary to reconnect to empathy, passion, and the energy and strength necessary to face these difficult issues while nurturing a fiery passion and vitality in one's life and advocacy work.

In this chapter, we investigated the colonial complex's disconnect from a personal experience of the soulful or sacred and the potential balance of looking at the alchemical understandings of the fire element and alchemy's valuing of the importance of tending one's own connection to one's passions and the soulful. There are many ways that in our own lives we can begin to recover that connection, and the practices below can provide a useful starting point for that work.

- Connect to an art practice, express your creativity and your soul work to warm and burn away the colonial deadening, dissociation, and apathy within. Nurture that which is most alive, vital, engaged, and connected within you.
- Journal questions: Do you feel a resonance with the idea of the "Inner Flame"? Do you have a sense of this connection within yourself? What do you see as the relationship between this inner vitality and colonial consciousness?
- Pay specific attention to your body, breath, and nervous system after and during reading this chapter and when you complete these readings. Can you stay in a zone of regulation while you engage with these topics? Does having a warm cup of tea or hot water bottle with you help calm your nervous system down and allow you to feel safer and more present while doing the work?
- Spend some time in a movement practice that is new or familiar to you, paying special attention to your embodiment in the practice. Can you stay aware of your breathing, of the sensations in your body and on your heart throughout the practice? What makes your body feel most alive? Choose at least one song to dance to, where you spend the whole song as present as you can be in your body, following the movements your body, not your mind, wants to make. Can your movement practice happen outdoors? How does it change it if this is normally something you do indoors? Where have you learned not to

be embodied, alive, vital? What are the messages you received about your passion, enthusiasm, and energy early on in life?
- Continued reading: Finish reading *My Grandmother's Hands* (2017) and *Me and White Supremacy* (2020). For a continued conversation around healthy masculinity and regulation, finish *Fire in the Belly* (1996) by Sam Keen. For a look at mindfulness as a tool for regulation in antiracism work, continue reading and finish *Mindful of Race* (2018) by Ruth King. And for more powerful works and continued calls to action by Indigenous authors in so-called Canada, see: *Islands of Decolonial Love* (2013) by Leanne Simpson; *A Mind Spread Out on The Ground* (2019) by Alicia Elliott; and *Seven Fallen Feathers* (2017) by Tanya Talaga.
- Do you have practices in this theme of fire/soul that are culturally appropriated? appropriated? Do you know their origin, if people of European descent have been given permission to practice them? If not, find practices from your lineages. For example, if you smudge with sage look up practices of cleansing from your own ancestry and heritage, almost all, if not all lineages will have cleansing practices. In Gaelic traditions, burning juniper was used to cleanse, bless or protect a space. For people of Scottish descent, saining would be a more appropriate non-appropriative alternative to smudging.

Chapter 10

Conclusion

Part I. Albedo (and a Little *Citrinitas*)

Helms's Fifth Stage of White Racial Identity Development: Immersion/Emersion

Helms's (1993) fifth stage of white racial identity development is immersion/emersion. In this stage, an individual starts forming what Helms called a positive white identity. In this new stage, they see through and replace the race myths that they have been raised on in colonial culture (p. 62). Individuals in this stage immerse themselves in the learning and unlearning necessary for the letting go of negative white racial identities and the development of positive white racial identities. Individuals in this stage may ask themselves: "'who am I racially?', 'who do I want to be?' and 'who are you really?'" (p. 62). In this stage, these individuals are no longer attempting to change people of colour and they can see the racism within themselves in their past behaviours (p. 62). During this period, the emphasis is on unlearning the racism within oneself and encouraging other white people to do the same: "He or she may participate in White consciousness-raising groups whose purpose is to help the person discover her or his [or their] individual self-interest in abandoning racism and acknowledging a White racial identity" (p. 62). Deep emotional and cognitive processing, unlearning and relearning is taking place during this stage, there is a reckoning with all the racial harm one has personally committed in the past as well as the endemic historical and political racialized harm and violence in our culture (p. 62).

Eventually, a sense of relief can emerge during this stage, which can occur after finally being honest with oneself and taking accountability for one's privilege and one's responsibility within community. A sense of motivation and encouragement can come along with the relief of knowing the path forward towards integrity. These more positive feelings "not only help to buttress the newly developing white identity, but provide the fuel by which the person can truly begin to tackle racism and oppression in its various forms" (Helms, 1993, p. 62). This stage is a true reckoning with whiteness

DOI: 10.4324/9781003296546-11

and a coming to terms with one's role within it. And so, we transition now to looking at the alchemical stage which reckons with whiteness as well, the *albedo*. The above description of Helms's stage of immersion/emersion correlates with the positive potentials of the *albedo* in unsettling processes. This includes the opportunity for emersion into integrity and humility in our work that the *albedo* stage can provide. However, like all the other alchemical operations and stages, the *albedo* also has negative potentials that will be explored in this chapter.

Peace, Reconciliation, and Assimilation: Navigating the Perils and Potentials of the Albedo

For the last four chapters, we have been examining the elements in four alchemical operations. As previously discussed, in addition to relating to elements alchemically, alchemists also worked with colours. Indeed, alchemical stages are often thought to begin in the *nigredo* (darkening), progress into the *albedo* (whitening) and *citrinitas* (yellowing) and finally to the *rubedo* (reddening). The previous chapters of this book may be considered part of the *nigredo*. Alchemists believed this stage could be so intensive and the work so deep that it was often the only stage that many alchemists would have been able to complete in their lives. In this chapter, we will now transition from the *nigredo* to the *albedo*.

Like all the other operations we have examined so far, the *albedo* has both positive and negative potentials: it can be engaged responsibly or irresponsibly, generatively or destructively. The *albedo* can be seen as a movement towards unity where "all becomes one" (§ 388); as such, the *albedo* in its negative expression can be understood as a form of spiritual bypassing. Perhaps the reader can already start to see the potential problematic nature of this stage, especially when it is believed to be the achievement and end goal.

The negative potentials in this stage can include arrogance, as individuals believe that they have figured the world out and are superior to those around them. They dive into the negative expressions of *albedo*, "all the while believing oneself having achieved the opus, one is actually back again at the ignorant beginnings of the *prima materia*. Delusions induced by supremacy" are not uncommon in such individuals (Hillman, 1986, p. 37). This relates to earlier chapters which examined colonial aversion to and hatred of the dark and reverence of the light. In the negative potentials of the *albedo*, the delusion of white supremacy can rear its head again. White people may become so deluded in what they believe to be their vast knowledge on these topics that they become arrogant racial educators believing that they are the experts and will no longer listen to or respect BIPOC leaders and their voices in the field.

Hillman continued describing some of the negative aspects of the *albedo* stage as the possible "spiritualisation of innocence" paired with the "arrogance of the spirit regarding its own ignorance" and that the *albedo* consciousness deluded in these two polarities could become "numbed by its own light" (p. 35). In this stage, there can be a sense of 'I can do no harm', and this can lead to an arrogance of perceived perfectionism and achievement of "purity" (p. 35). Hillman explained that this white consciousness thrives on "repression and idealised projections" (p. 35). This can be a deluded sense of having reached a "purity" which can result in a holier-than-thou, distorted expression of the *albedo*. As such, it can be a profoundly dangerous stage and can, in its delusions, continue the perpetration of the delusion of white supremacy and the violence of racialized harm.

Conversely, when the earlier stage has fully been engaged in integrity, the positive potential of the *albedo* can be humility. After learning so much, we can be humble in the realisation that we still know so little and it can lead to a continued commitment to learning in a world where we realise we know so little about the vast majority of all the earthly things to learn about and that the opportunities for more learning will always abound. Just as when light passes through a prism and we see that it contains all the colours within it; the *albedo* stage too can hold and contain all of the different stages and be a place of spiralling back to all of our areas of growth, change, progress, and healing as needed. If approached responsibly, this stage can be an openness to what is next and a humble dedication of oneself to the vital work needed.

Albedo *and the Politics of Reconciliation*

There are many dangers found in the negative expressions of the *albedo*, as there are with spiritual bypassing and the declaration of peace under false pretences. In the following section, we will be examining this idea of a distorted *albedo* and its colonial manifestation as attempts to enforce a "false peace" in the form of colonial reconciliatory attempts.

The concept of peace necessitates its opposite. Cultures have words for peace only if there is a history of warring or wartime in their past. The fight for peace can be a bloody one. Throughout history, perhaps the most powerful political platform has been peace and the fight for its reign. The aspiration for peace may also be one of the most profound human longings, for it includes feelings of security, interconnectedness, good relations, abundant and fruitful connections, contentedness, and community. In this section, I will examine the West's historical relationship to the concept of peace as an expression of the negative potentials of the *albedo*. This will include looking at the phenomenon of longing only for the *albedo* stage of relief and contentment and the unwillingness to engage fully and honestly with the process of the *nigredo*: the process of the acknowledgement of and tending of the difficult, gruelling, and painful within oneself. The aim is to offer an alchemical understanding of the relationship between the longing for peace and the longing for the *albedo* stage of alchemy, the longing for the transcendence of suffering, and how all of this relates to the Canadian state today: its relationship with peace treaties, longing for reconciliation, and efforts to transcend the pain of the past with simply a handshake and hurrah.

For a historical look at the politics of peace in the Western colonial lineage, we will turn our focus for a while to Rome. The Roman Empire's conquering of territory was the largest and most extensive the world had ever seen. Much of Rome's conquering efforts were ostensibly in the name of peace. Armies would get inspired and their blood would boil for conquest in the pursuit of peace and peace-victory. In her book *Pax and the Politics of Peace*, Hannah Cornwell (2017) quoted Tacitus's writing in the first century CE. As he described the Roman Empire's pursuits. He detailed the empire's aims "to rob, to slaughter, to ravage under false names they call 'empire', and the desolation they create, 'peace'" (Location 516). In naming the "desolation they call peace," Tacitus spoke here of how in the Roman Empire, the brutality of conquest and imperial rule were disguised in the name of peace and left horrible bloodshed and devastation in their "peaceful" wake (Location 516). Tacitus wrote of the concept of Pax-Romana, Roman Peace, as a weapon of war and imperial ideology in empire forming. He described how deceptive it was to name it peace when really it aimed to achieve power, aggression, and imperial domination (Location 527). Cornwell wrote that the concept of peace became a political tool of domination, and efforts towards peace became centred on conquering and political control (Location 569).

In his book *Pax Romana: War, Peace and Conquest in the Roman World*, Goldsworthy (2016) wrote that the peace in the Roman Empire was one of domination, where a people were defeated and then forced to "love" Rome and accept the "peace" of being conquered; it was a peace of domination, not one of respect or equality (Location 454). The Roman tactic was that after a war, attempts would be made to create peace treaties so that the territory could be profitable and the taxes gained from it could be higher (Location 460). These profits and gains were driving forces for the efforts towards peace after the Romans conquered new territories (Location 460). Goldsworthy wrote: "Peace, whether Roman or created by a modern power, is a veil to conceal conquest and domination. This is not a new idea" (Location 284). In Rome, after the taking of a new land, peace treaties were created, and reparations were agreed upon: tiny settlements in comparison to the loss of territory and bloodshed of the conquest (Cornwell, 2017, Location 624). These are the origins of the concept of peace in the Western world, and it has deep ties to war and conquest. Herein lies the Western roots of colonial powers of domination, and its false pretence of peace.

Current Canadian and Indigenous Discussions Surrounding Reconciliation

Coulthard (2014) wrote of the modern Canadian political landscape and the peace treaties and reparations being attempted within this colonial state. Specifically, he addressed the relationship between the Canadian state and Indigenous Nations and the ongoing efforts to reconcile the Canadian colonial conquering of Indigenous people. Coulthard described many of the current political moves towards "reconciliation" as continued tools of colonisation. In *Red Skin, White Masks: Rejecting the Colonial Politics of Recognition*, Coulthard described the Canadian politics of reconciliation as the political effort to have Canadian and Indigenous politics unite and come together in shared values and goals (Location 135). Coulthard asserted that what this really means is the Canadian state coercing Indigenous Nations to reconcile themselves with the state and assimilate into the values and politics of the colonial rule (Location 135). As Tuck and Yang (2012) argued: "The desire to reconcile is just as relentless as the desire to disappear the Native; it is a desire to not have to deal with this (Indian) problem anymore" (Tuck and Yang, 2012, p. 9).

The politics of reconciliation remain entrenched in colonial values of assimilation under a liberal-appeasing, politically correct new guise (Coulthard, 2014, Location 137). Coulthard believed that Canada's current political platform of reconciliation is not "ushering in an era of peaceful coexistence grounded on the ideal of reciprocity or mutual recognition" (Location 146). Instead, he believed "the politics of recognition in its contemporary liberal form promises to reproduce the very configurations of colonialist, racist, patriarchal state power that Indigenous peoples' demands for recognition have historically sought to transcend" (Location 148). Coulthard wrote that Canadians' current interest in reconciliation and peace-making is no more than continued colonial efforts to assimilate Indigenous people and Nations into the colonial state.

Coulthard's (2014) analysis of the current Canadian political landscape harkened back to Tacitus's 2000-year-old analysis of Roman tactics of peace-making, where he denounced Rome for making peace and reparations solely for the purpose of continued domination. The same tactics of peace-making continue on, perhaps under new guises, within Canada's political parties today. Coulthard made clear that this colonial mentality has also worked its way into the modern guise of politically appropriate liberalism, of do-gooders believing that we settlers are working towards peace while only working towards the colonial rewards of reconciliation.

On June 11, 2008, Stephen Harper (Government of Canada, 2008), then Prime Minister of Canada, issued the first apology on behalf of the Canadian state to First Nations people for the devastating impacts of the Indian Residential School System. This apology was regarded as the first big step towards reconciliation in Canada. Astonishingly—or perhaps, for some, not so much—a year later, on September 25, 2009, at a G20 summit,

Harper said in a speech that Canada has "no history of colonialism" and that Canada is free from the dark history shared by other developed countries (Coulthard, 2014, Location 2242). This ability of the Prime Minister to negate the reality he had already publicly acknowledged as truth exemplified the superficiality of the apology and the insincerity behind Canadian political efforts towards reconciliation today. The current talk of reconciliation is for show, for strengthening political platforms, and is reminiscent of the same aims harking to Roman times of wanting a state where all, including the conquered, can be sated, given the bare minimum of reparation so that all the conquered citizens can coexist, and the society can be more easily managed. Coulthard described this insidious aspect of the Canadian politics of reconciliation as "rendering consistent Indigenous assertions of nationhood with the state's unilateral assertion of sovereignty over Native peoples' lands and populations" (Location 2276). In Coulthard's analysis, it becomes clear that the dominant settler narratives surrounding reconciliation perpetuate the subjugating forces behind our concept of peace.

Cash Ahenakew (2016) also found that Canadian conceptions of reconciliation necessitate Indigenous assimilation and continued erasure of sovereignty (p. 336). He explained that reconciliation and "Indigenous logics" are welcome in Canadian politics only when they do not in any way threaten the status quo (p. 336). Ahenakew emphasised the sheer magnitude of going about the task of reparations responsibly and of "imagining beyond our colonial historical legacies" (p. 336). The magnitude of this task feels especially immense when colonial powers will do anything to avoid decolonising efforts and instead take part only in reconciliatory efforts that are safe ways of "keeping power" and that focus only on tolerating, including, and integrating others (p. 336).

Ahenakew (2016) upheld Coulthard's critiques of Canadian politics of recognition and inclusion as "liberal discourses" (p. 323). Ahenakew also believed that capitalism must be addressed in our conversations surrounding reparations, as capitalism in so-called North America is completely dependent on Indigenous lands (p. 330). As Rome profited from its conquered lands, so Canada has been created off the profits and resources of Indigenous land. In true unsettling efforts, these ties and dependencies on capitalism which have flourished off Indigenous land and resources while marginalising Indigenous people must be critically examined. Ahenakew explained that with all the work there is to do, we must be willing to stay committed for the long haul and not expect quick fixes when we engage in decolonising efforts (p. 329). He believed that this long-term commitment is how we will have any hope of "decentring and disarming" settler-colonialism and its iron grip on its privilege and colonial domination (p. 329).

Ahenakew (2016) also highlighted the importance of acknowledging interdependent thinking, honouring of the land, and emphasis on poetic and storytelling language in Indigenous worldviews and decolonising work (p. 337). He advocated for the importance and decolonial potentials of "using metaphor and poetry to disrupt sense-making and prompt sense-sensing in the experience of readers" as well as "turning our attention to and historicising the referents that circumscribe Western frameworks of reasoning so we can recognise these referents in our researcher-selves and in our writing" (p. 337). Ahenakew emphasised that Indigenous research methodologies and perspectives cannot be adopted as "quick-fix solutions or escapes from deep-rooted and ongoing (neo)colonial thinking" (p. 323). This is also true for alchemical ways of seeing the world; imagining into the world alchemically is not inherently decolonial. Deep investigations and changes in colonial thought, behaviour, and socio-political structures must also take place in conjunction with alchemical musings for them to meaningfully contribute to unsettling processes. In addition, Indigenous worldviews must not be appropriated by settlers. However, connecting to worldviews from our ancestries, such as alchemy, can help us foster deeper understandings of our interconnectedness with the natural world in support of, and in conjunction with, our settler decolonial work.

Maracle (2017) wrote about her cultural understandings of peace, forgiveness, and reconciliation and how they differ from those of colonial Canada. Specifically she shares her stance on Indigenous resurgence and reconciliatory efforts today (p. 91). The peace Maracle described is one inherently different from the Western concepts of peace built upon 2,000 years of conquering and colonialism. In our efforts as settlers to learn and unlearn what is needed for our unsettling processes, we need to bring a curiosity, humility, and openness towards learning about a different understanding of peace from ours. After one of her talks about the current genocide of Indigenous women and girls in Canada, Maracle was asked what she sees as important for reconciliation in Canada, and she replied: "Well, stop killing us would be a good place to begin" (p. 137). The audience broke out into nervous laughter and when it finally trickled off, she continued, "then maybe stop plundering our resources, stop robbing us of our children, end colonial domination—return our lands, and then we can talk about being friends" (p. 137). Maracle's fierce reply made clear that we cannot just continue to speak about reconciliation, offer heartfelt (or not so heartfelt) apologies, and expect to attain harmonious relations without doing the real reparations and work required of us.

Maracle (2017) continued her analysis of Canadian attempts at reconciliation by writing how the conciliation which is required for a reconciliation to take place never occurred in Canada, so the very concept is flawed. She wrote, "Canada views itself as the nicest coloniser in the world. It does not ask the colonised if they agree with this, Canadians just keep repeating it to each other like bobbleheads that can't stop bobbling" (p. 133). She called this view a part of the "mythological madness" of

Canada and the distorted story we tell ourselves about our history (p. 134). Canada's lack of emphasis on making tangible political and social changes to right the wrongs of the past, the current abuses of power, and the present-day genocide of Indigenous women and girls are all markings of the continued colonialism occurring in our political and social spheres.

In Maracle's (2017) responses to the politics of reconciliation, she criticised settlers' emphasis on being forgiven in the process of reconciliation and how she believed that this is also a colonial approach to reparations. She wrote of how the concept of forgiveness is a Christian one and how Indigenous people learned this when they were forced to attend and convert in Christian residential schools. Maracle wrote, "to accept forgiveness as a concept, I would need to convert, as forgiveness fits into the context of European belief systems. It does not fit into mine" (p. 74). The concept of forgiveness places the onus of reparation onto the group that has been hurt. In forgiveness models, the group that has been wronged must find it within themselves to forgive the oppressive force. The emphasis within models that necessitate forgiveness is not on the reparations the oppressor needs to make for healing to occur. During the apology Harper made to the First Nations people of Canada, he placed the onus on First Nations people to forgive Canada: "The Government of Canada sincerely apologises and asks the forgiveness of the Aboriginal peoples of this country" (Government of Canada, 2008, § 9). In this speech, we see the Canadian politics of recognition and reconciliation at play, where the settler state can offer words of apology and expect peace to manifest instantaneously.

Maracle (2017) made clear that the premises on which we are grounding concepts of reconciliation—such as conciliation ever having previously occurred—and models of forgiveness are themselves based in colonial values. As Coulthard (2014) explained, if reconciliation means we are all on the same page, and that page is one from the Canadian state, then that reconciliation is one of assimilation. As Maracle (2017) argued, if reconciliation has to do with one group finding it in their hearts to offer forgiveness to the other then that is a Christianised reconciliation, which does not place expectations of change on the oppressor and remains colonial in nature. Maracle explained how her cultural understanding of recovery after harm is very different from our colonial ideas surrounding reconciliation, she wrote: "We do not have forgiveness as a recurring theme in our culture" (p. 75). Instead, she explained, "if you hurt someone, own it, look at yourself, track where it came from, learn from it and make it right, continue to learn from it, continue to deepen your understanding, and grow from it" (p. 75). This process Maracle described of recovery from harms done is a much more active and embodied process than we have seen in Canadian understandings of reconciliation. It is a process of showing up and facing all of the parts of ourselves that have done wrong and are hurt, seeing how they became hurt, and then working to heal them, the consequences of our actions and working to unravel and the repair the harm done. The decolonial process Maracle suggested is a process of committing to deep self-honesty and reflection, continuous self-growth and understanding. This process has the potential to occur in a positive manifestation of the alchemical metaphor of the *albedo* stage.

The Politics of the Albedo

The *albedo* is an important part of the alchemical process, in its positive potential it is a long-awaited breath of relief in achieving contentedness and peace after a difficult journey. However, Hillman (2015) wrote of how more Christianised writings surrounding alchemy emphasise the glory of the *albedo*: a triumph over the darkness and blackness of the *nigredo*. These writings look forward to the *albedo* as salvation, as Hillman (2015) wrote, "Christianised readings seem unable to avoid salvationalism" (Location 1673). Here we see the earlier discussed themes of valuing the delusion of the supremacy of whiteness over darkness and this delusion's potential to remanifest at this stage. In the alchemical journey, there can be the danger of wanting to achieve the *albedo* too soon, of pretending one is through the *nigredo* when one has not done the work required of them, or of doing all that one can to achieve the *albedo* quickly, whether it is real, earned, or not. Pretending one is in the *albedo* before it is achieved through the real and hard work of the previous stages of the work is the equivalent of today's spiritual bypassing, of acting enlightened but having skipped over the real and often difficult introspective work needed to get there. It is like Rome saying to one of its newly conquered provinces, while it still pools with bloodshed, devastating poverty, and loss of life from the war: Here is a token reparation gesture, let us sign treaties and peace will forever reign.

I believe we can also see this attempted process of bypassing into a perceived *albedo* in current Canadian politics with its hyper-focus on reconciliation. It feels similar to Rome's tactics, where we apologise and expect the immediate gratification of peace. This attitude disregards the hard work necessary to begin to make amends. In honest reparations work, there must be an immersion in the discomfort of facing the horrors of the past to work through the emotional processes necessary for their resolution. Maracle (2017) wrote of how she perceived denial to be central to Canadian identity and its history, and she perceived Canadians' denial as a continual pursuit to defend our innocence (p. 75). With Canadians' insistence on our goodness, innocence, and our denial of anything dark or uncomfortable, we ground ourselves further in the denial by claiming to be in the purity of the *albedo*, of having achieved innocence, and no longer having any work to undertake in the process of reparations with the Indigenous people of this land. This being said I do not mean to equate settlers fixing themselves as inherently leading to reconciliation. White people working on themselves will not directly lead us to resolution, decolonisation, or reparations. It is only a beginning of the process, with the intention of allowing further work to happen from a place of accountability and integrity.

In the period of time since Harper's apology to survivors of residential schools, I believe Canada has falsely believed itself to be in *albedo*. There seems to be a desire for the long, arduous *nigredo* to have completed itself during Harper's 8-minute speech. The shadow had not been acknowledged properly before, the shadow was barely acknowledged for those 8 minutes, and then there was a self-congratulation as though the shadow would not have to be faced again. However, a true *albedo* process is profoundly different, and it does not involve being blinded by the light. To truly be in the *albedo*, one must have deeply undergone the transformative process of tending the hurting, tending the uncomfortable, and facing the pain of the shadow. One cannot feel the sense of healing of the *albedo* without having truly and justly faced all that needed to be faced in all the alchemical processes and work beforehand.

Hillman (2015) wrote that the honest *albedo* process does not negate the suffering of the past and instead allows for a space large enough to contain all of it, with an ample expanse for breath and peace to begin to re-join it. Hillman wrote that in the *albedo* "sadness is felt in the world itself, as if held together and wrapped round by sorrow" (Location 2016). Both sadness and spaciousness can be experienced in the positive expression of the *albedo*, and there is a balancing, a grounding of the entirety of the experience that can begin to occur. Racialized investigations within oneself and one's unsettling processes never finish. The commitment to this work is lifelong, and so if there is ever the belief that an individual has attained perfection and has no more work to do, it can probably be assumed that they are in a false *albedo*.

Before we can begin to truly and honestly speak of reconciliation, we settlers must get through the process of working through the millennia-old colonial ideas of domination within us. Maracle (2017) wrote, "most Canadians think it is enough to know something, but this is not enough—you must commit to the continued growth and transformation of whatever you claim to know" (p. 78). Today, we must work through the 2,000-year-old narratives that tell us that peace is a way of sublimating and ruling, that peace can be achieved only when one holds all the power and creates the rules. We must first truly and deeply undergo the transformative experience of facing the pain and the suffering we hold within ourselves and have inflicted on the world at large. Only then will we achieve the true spaciousness of the *albedo*. Only then may conversations surrounding reconciliation and allyship hold some meaning, some truthfulness, some integrity. Perhaps then, for the first time in 2,000 years, we settlers may begin to learn something of the true meaning of peace and the complexity it contains.

All alchemical operations, including *albedo,* have both a positive and negative side, just as peace has both a negative and a positive side. We have seen the destructive and uncompromising colonial use of peace over the last two millennia. We have seen how, in the building of the Roman Empire, peace was used as a weapon of war in the gathering of troops, then necessitating its implementation post-war for those conquered if they wanted to survive. Since the violent creation of the Roman Empire, the practice has been that if the colonised want to survive, they can assimilate, and only then can there be peace. We have seen the same occurring for the last centuries of colonial rule and today, in modern colonial assimilation politics of reconciliation. However, there is another side to peace, another side to the *albedo* that we have the potential to nurture within our political system and us: a side of peace that we settlers must now devote ourselves to learning. In these matters, we can look back to our past and try to decipher the places where we can see a precolonial understanding of peace. In this, we can take direction from Maracle (2017) and others in their decolonial description and knowledge of true peace.

Albedo Conclusion

Within the alchemical *albedo* lurk all the dangers of the delusion of the supremacy of whiteness. In the last few millennia, it seems we have become trapped in relating to peace only in its connection to war and in the domination and assimilation of the people conquered post "victory." However, there is an expansive and beautiful potential of peace and the *albedo*, perhaps almost forgotten in our Western psyche. This quality is one of true coexistence, interrelationships, mutual respect, and the quiet joy of being in integrity and harmony with life. In the settler decolonising and healing of the settler psyche, we must now tend these positive potentials and qualities of peace for our own well-being and in our tending of our relationships with Indigenous peoples today. This, along with the honest and intentional processes of facing and tending the colonial shadow are what could allow us to truly experience the peace of the *albedo*, and ready us for the reddening and aliveness of the alchemical *rubedo*.

Citrinitas, a Yellowing Transition

In later alchemical texts, the stage of yellowing, or *citrinitas*, is often omitted (Hillman, 2015 Location 4477). In this research, we will not spend significant time on it either, except to acknowledge the many layers and depth of unsettling and alchemical work. The *citrinitas* is considered a transition from the *albedo* to the *rubedo* (Jung, 1937/1968, § 333). "Where white unifies all colours into a monotheism of subjective reflection, the yellow clarification is also a dawning of multiple vision, seeing each thing as it is, beyond subjectivity, and thus bridging to the *rubedo's* sanguine" (Hillman, 2015, Location 4656). There are many places of transitions like this one before the next step in our work, and there are constantly more places to look deeper into ourselves, to step up further in our actions and behaviours and reckon with deeper and deeper layers of our biases, internalised racism, and the horrors of our history. In this writing, it also feels important to honour the four primary colours of alchemy, black, white, yellow, and red, and the quaternity they represent. And so, we have a brief reminder of the transitional yellowing to take us into the next phase of alchemical reddening, the *rubedo*.

Concrete Action

Are there places in you where you feel you may be leaping ahead, you have bypassed hard work, you feel superior to others because of the racial enlightenments and realisations you feel you have achieved? If so, go back to the start. Keep looking. Keep working. There is never an end to the work, and humility—not arrogance—is the sign that we are doing the work with integrity. Read Coulthard's (2014) *Red skin, white masks: Rejecting the colonial politics of recognition* for a more thorough investigation of the harmful politics of Canadian reconciliation.

Part II. Rubedo

Helms's Sixth Stage of White Racial Identity Development: Autonomy

Helms (1993) named the final stage of white racial identity development: autonomy. In this stage, there is an "internalising," "nurturing," and application of all that one has learned in the previous stages of one's life (p. 66). This stage involves an integration of learning and the new, positive white identity begins to be embodied. Here, individuals learn to become autonomous in not buying into cultural racist ideas and to instead investigate and interrogate for themselves racist values and beliefs within themselves and the world around them (p. 66). Someone in this stage has individuated in their positive racial identity development and now takes responsibility, accountability, and a personal sense of ownership for their racial identity and their actions in the world. "In this stage, the person no longer feels a need to oppress, idealise, or denigrate people on the basis of group membership characteristics such as race because race no longer symbolises threat to him or her" (p. 66). The autonomous person confronts cultural and institutional racism and actively seeks out opportunities for more learning to continually investigate their own ingrained racism and racial identities (p. 66). In this stage, there is an acknowledgement that the work is ongoing and never has an end point: it is a lifelong commitment. The autonomous person also becomes more and more aware of intersections of power, privilege, and oppression and dedicates themselves to taking a stand against all injustices (p. 66). This stage is not an achievement of perfection, but rather a lifelong commitment to the work, to accountability, humility, and integrity in racialized learning and reparations.

Rubedo

The tending of the *prima materia* is often a long, arduous, and painful process. In alchemy, the confrontation with it is known as the *nigredo* (§ 41). The *nigredo*, although difficult, is seen as the most vital step in the alchemical opus and a necessity to undergo before the *albedo*, which is seen as a young, immature equanimity or whiteness before the stage of *rubedo*, the reddening. "The *albedo* is, so to speak, the daybreak, but not till the *rubedo* is it sunrise" (Jung, 1937/1968, § 333). The *rubedo* is the goal of alchemical work and is the embodiment of the aliveness of body and soul (§ 334).

The *rubedo* is the final stage for the alchemists; it is the culmination of all other alchemical stages and operation. The *rubedo, reddening,* can be understood as a return to life, and its pulsing vitality. In the whiteness of the *albedo*, Jung (1997) believed that one was not fully living, but instead was in some sort of falsely idealised state (p. 228). He thought that it was not until the *rubedo* was achieved that one came fully alive into the "redness" of life: "Only the total experience of being can transform this ideal state of the *albedo* into a fully human mode of existence. Blood alone can reanimate a glorious state of consciousness" (p. 228). Some associations with *rubedo* are red, blood, life, pulsing, vitality, embodiment, individuation, gold, the sun, and the red phoenix rising from the ashes of the fire. The philosopher's stone can be synonymous with the *rubedo* and is the achievement alchemists work towards their whole life. Within the *rubedo* is the psychological and spiritual wholeness, the gold within, that the alchemists pointed towards. In this stage, there is a feeling of wholeness, completeness, connection to life, meaning, embodiment, fulfilment, and contentedness. The "rubedo, the reddening, [is the] libidinal activity of the soul as it resurrects and revivifies matter, crowning it in beauty and pleasure" (Marlan, 2008, Location 1889).

The *rubedo* contains all the stages within itself: "The *rubedo,* at this red juncture signifies a final dissolution of sunlit consciousness and all distinctions – all the stages, phases, operations, and colours" (Hillman, 2015, Location 4709). Like Helms's autonomous stage, the *rubedo* does not mean that there has been an arrival at a final static destination. Instead, it is an active, ongoing process of finding the right relationship to life within and outside of oneself. In terms of *rubedo* in a settler decolonising process, we can think of this as being in right relationship with ourselves, people, culture and the world around us, being in integrity with our beliefs, behaviours, and actions, and being accountable for our positionality and place in the world and with all life around us.

Alchemists thought of the *rubedo* in part as the union of opposites (Jarrett, & Jung, 1988, p. 235). *Rubedo* seen in this way is reconciling contrasting and conflicting points of view within ourselves, and further, reconciling with the conflict around us as well. The inner gold that the alchemists were working towards necessitated a "total union of opposites in symbolic form, and this they regarded as the indispensable condition for the healing of all ills" (Jung, 1955–56/1970, § 676). This gold was the addressing of struggle and finding places of commonality to help in the reparations and healing of conflict in the outer and inner worlds.

Hillman (2015) wrote that the psychological reconciliation of opposites "takes place in soul, as a recognition, an insight, an astonishment" (p. 167). He also advocated for the power of story and metaphor and their ability to lead us to this place of healing, of the meeting of opposites and dissolving of tension (p. 167).

Jung (1963) wrote about how much tension our shadow material causes within us in opposing our conscious attitudes and wreaking havoc in our ability to feel a sense of integrity, to feel calm, whole in our sense of self, and in alignment with our feelings, thoughts, behaviours, and actions in the world (p. 296). Jung valued the reconciliation of psychic opposites—what we could call today cognitive dissonance—as one of the most important parts of psychological tending, calling it the "reconciliation of opposites" (p. 296). He explained how often inner conflict paralleled conflict happening in the outside world as well. He emphasised how much the outer world affects our psyche, and conversely, how we and our psychic health affect the world at large: "what happens in the macrocosm likewise happens in the infinitesimal and most subjective reaches of the psyche" (p. 296). He described the process of *rubedo* as the alchemical lapis which we all desire and move towards, and the process of inner reconciliation and the reconciliation of the inner with the outer.

Racial **Rubedo: Where We Go from Here**

As a white settler, I do not feel that I can directly speak about where, societally, we go from here; this direction needs to come from Black, Indigenous and People of Colour and their communities. Up until this point, this book has been looking at the accountability and healing work settlers need to do on themselves so that when they work towards reparations and healing with BIPOC and Indigenous communities and people, they do so in the most responsible way possible. The following section looks primarily at historical understandings of right relationship as well as what BIPOC are saying about what these reparations could look like and what they are calling for from white people today.

In 1613, the Two Row Wampum Treaty was agreed upon by the Dutch and the Haudenosaunee, whose territory spreads throughout what is now called Ontario, Quebec, and New York (Mackey, 2016, p. 157). The wampum belt represented the agreement made and is a belt made of tiny white shells with two bands of purple shells running parallel on either side of the white (p. 157). One of the purple rows of beads represented the Haudenosaunee people, the other the Dutch. The communities are represented on the belt as parallel, separate, independent, and sovereign (p. 157). However, the row of white beads between them represents their mutual respect, understanding, and the agreements which connect them (p. 157). In this way, the understanding was that these communities would remain separate but connected (p. 157). This treaty was understood by the Haudenesaunee and many others as a model understanding between settlers and Indigenous people and as "the basis on which all subsequent treaties were made" (p. 157). The belt represented the understanding in the treaty that "while alliances and understanding (between the rows in the wampum belt) are important, we are not the same and do not know or understand in the same way." At the same time, this understanding emphasised that "these differences (the two separate rows) are important and should not be sacrificed in the name of a false unity or equality" (p. 201). The emphasis in these understandings of the wampum belt is that it "brings Indigenous and settler people together as distinct but interconnected treaty peoples, who must find new ways of interpreting the past and present in order to create more just futures together" (p. 214). Many people still think of the wampum belt treaty as a model representing what could have been if settlers had upheld their end of the agreements in these relationships and as an inspiration in envisioning what a right relationship could look like in the future (though many Nations do not have treaties, and many treaties that were created are highly unjust).

In their works, Williams, Owens, and Syedullah (2016) emphasised the fundamental need to "reclaim and repair the human spirit" for any deep change, societal healing, and justice to be possible (p. 97). They advocated that thinking any societal change can happen without the tending of collective and individual psyches akin to having "our head buried deeply in the sand of hundreds of years of a culture of domination, colonisation" (p. 97). If colonialism has brought us away from psychological health, then tending it is a part of remedying it today. The authors advocated that true reconciliation, healing, and decolonising must have, as a constant part of the work, the tending and healing of the human psyche (p. 97).

Maracle (2015) emphasised that for unsettling, decolonisation, and reparations to truly occur, settlers must let go of their tight grip on control, privilege, and power (p. 77). She also emphasised the need for settlers to want to work towards the building of "a shared common society" and in that vision to respect both the differences and "common spirit" between settlers and Indigenous Nations (p. 77). What is being called for here is a respect of autonomous separateness and, at the same time, shared humanity and mutual respect, as was called forth in the wampum belt treaty. Maracle wrote that this process "requires a new language map, shaped so that it is free of insult and the unequal power attached to authorship and authority. This is a new story" (p. 77). She advocated for the "re-languaging" in Canadian dialogue surrounding these issues and for Canadians' respect and perception of First Nations as "fellow travellers" on the path towards healing (p. 77). Maracle was clear that one of the fundamental things that needs to happen for this re-languaging to happen is to acknowledge clearly that the history of North America has been "a white male Anglo-Saxon dominated colonial settler state that is chronically engineering the re-invasion of the land" (p. 77). She wrote that once this is clearly and honestly acknowledged and accepted and we have made a clear commitment to "travel in a different direction" from this colonial history, only then will we be able to "discuss the social and physical maps—internal and external—that we will need to draw to get us moving away from this history" (p. 78).

Maracle (2015) also wrote of the importance of re-membering the past as we move forward into the future. "Humans give breath to life, give voice to their perception of life, this is a sacred act. They are taking an event that has already been committed and they are re-membering or reconstructing it in their minds. Memory serves" (p. 2). She emphasised the importance of memory, honouring the past and its truth through stories. "In a society governed first and foremost by spirit to spirit relationships to all beings, [where] memory serves much differently than in a society in which property possession determines importance" (p. 2). She also emphasised the directionality of memory, how telling stories can point us in the direction we want to go: "Indigenous people commit to memory those events and the aspects of those events that suit the direction we are moving in or the direction we want to move in if a shift is occurring" (p. 2). In our re-membering of stories, even the painful ones, we can gain grounding and honesty and can be inspired by them to move into the creation and weaving of a new narrative. Maracle also believed that by sharing that journey and the new story together, we also "mark the path travelled so that others may find the path easier to follow. Our memories serve the foregoing" (p. 3).

Ahenakew (2016) wrote about the importance of challenging colonialism within our writing and academies as well (p. 333). A part of this process, he wrote, was challenging the colonial upholding of "certainty, totality, and instrumentalization" at the expense of all other ways of knowing. An important part of unsettling these parts of colonial academia "is to make what is absent present, by using devices that redirect reading from a prosaic to a poetic orientation or from the rational to the metaphorical mind" (p. 333). Ahenakew continued, writing that valuing only linear thinking and rationality is colonial gatekeeping of the academic world: "in a mono rational logic lodged in a mind separated from the body" (p. 333). He wrote that instead "the task of poetic and metaphoric writing is to invite other senses to take part in the reading process" (p. 333).

Maybe for now we do not know the particulars of what a racial *rubedo* looks like. As Resmaa Menakem (2017) says, the work being called for now is to sit in the discomfort, figure it out, take accountability, and repair when we mess up (p. 296). For now, building a culture of accountability, humility, and repair is our first step as we shed our old colonial culture, and from there, something can be birthed anew (p. 289). This process will also involve learning from Indigenous ways of knowing, without appropriating them, while also maintaining or restoring connections to ways of knowing in our heritages. This means learning from Indigenous wisdom when we are offered it and given permission to learn it.

This process of a racial *rubedo* is one that will probably never come to a close, but rather will be about continually asking what a collective restorative justice process looks like here, and what we as individuals can do to support it. As bell hooks said, "It is only as we work for change that we see clearly that change can happen, that our lives can be transformed, that we can always renew our spirits and rekindle our hope" (hooks, 2013, p. 174).

The immensity of the actual cost of reparations and what we are talking about here also needs to be emphasised. All of this psychological processing is well and good in fixing settlers, but if it ends there it continues as settler moves to innocence, and more window-dressing of "reconciliation". True reparations will be painful, take a huge amount of work, and will change the world as we know it, and settler positions of privilege within it drastically.

In 2014, Nishnaabeg author, poet and professor, Leanne Betasamosake Simpson told me that the most important way that I as a settler can be of service and support Indigenous resurgence today is by addressing the madness of settler-colonialism: the madness of my own people. She directed me to look for the healing of this madness within settler-colonials past and lineage. She said that at one point in history before they came to Turtle Island, settler-colonials were connected to themselves and the land: she said to go find those places in our past that can help us reconnect and bring us back to our sanity. A similar concept to this remembering that Leanne suggests is called 'the deeply personal' in depth psychology: 'the deeply personal is connecting back through history, it's connecting to all that's been left out and forgotten. ... The process is one of connection or restoration or remembrance" (Jung, 1943/1969, § 944). This book has attempted to be a response to this direction from Simpson in its turning to the study of alchemy in the ancestral heritage of settler-colonialism for settlers' healing. I hope I have done it justice.

Rubedo Concrete Actions and Reflection Questions

In addition to the concrete steps outlined at the end of each previous chapter, at the minimum, I believe all Canadians should read the *United Nations Declaration of the Rights of Indigenous People* UNDRIP (32 pages long), the Truth and Reconciliation Commission's *What we have learned* report (199 pages), and the National Enquiry into Missing and Murdered Indigenous Women and Girls' *Executive summary of the final report* (121 pages). Go through all the actional steps from the previous chapters. Circle back to them time and time again. This process never ends, only deepens. And continue reading, listening to, and supporting BIPOC and Indigenous authors through their fiction and non-fiction, talks, podcasts, and events.

Oluo (2018) detailed other steps to take as a white person working on dismantling systems of white supremacy: "vote local," "bear witness," "speak up in your unions," "support POC-owned business," "boycott banks that prey on people of colour," "give money to organisations working to fight racial oppression and support communities of colour," "boycott businesses that exploit workers of colour," "support music, film, television, art and books created by people of colour," "support increases in the minimum wage," "push your mayor and city council for police reform," "demand college diversity," and "vote for diverse government representatives" (p. 230). Oluo also outlines some of the internal practices that white people wanting to work towards social justice and being an ally need to remember: "Be aware of the limits of your empathy," "don't distract or deflect," "remember your goal," "drop the prerequisites," "walk away if you must but don't give up," "build a tolerance for discomfort," and "you are not doing any favours, you are doing what is right" (p. 209).

Soeur Mystica

The final alchemical concept we will review is *soeur mystica* or mystical sisters. *Soeur mystica* was when alchemists worked alongside each other in their journeys, supporting, challenging, and holding one another accountable in their work and findings. The alchemical journey involves effort that only an individual can undertake for themselves (*Jung,* 1955–56, § 790). And yet, the whole work also revolves around reconciliation—internal reconciliation and reconciliation with an individual and their relationship to the world (*Jung,* 1955–56, § 790). Though both alchemical and unsettling work includes individual work that needs to be done, and self-accountability must always remain, both of these endeavours also have to happen in community, in connection to others involved in the same questionings, processing, and investigations.

We all need our own version of *soeur mystica,* whether that is one person, a group, a community, a therapist, or a friend. We need to have accountability and support in this work and allow it to also spread and inspire those around us as well. This may look like having a couple of people we routinely talk to about this work or joining or starting groups discussing racism, unsettling, and decolonising near you or online. Part of settler decolonising work is confronting colonial concepts of hyper individuality, tending to community, and inviting knowledge of interdependencies back into our hearts, minds, and lives. This is also true of our unsettling and alchemical work. If nothing else, our nervous systems need others for our sense of safety, wellbeing, and regulation. We cannot go about this alone; our hearts need companionship and learning to be truly accountable and responsible, and the honouring of others in our lives is a part of our healing work as well. From this healing, the lessons and care learned can expand to greater and greater spheres of our life.

Gold

Forbes (2008) discussed different Indigenous ideas of how to lead a good life, including the Navajo idea of the pollen path which follows the golden examples of the bees, asserting that "the pollen path and the red road lead to living life in a sacred manner with continual awareness of the inter-relationships of all forms of life" (p. 22). Forbes goes on to describe these different Indigenous ideas around being a "wisdom-seeker" and leading a good life. He wrote that these paths encourage one to live life knowing that it is not eternal, that everyone will eventually die, to "live a life that is worthwhile, one that is filled with precise acts, beautiful acts, meaningful acts, that help to take one along the pollen path, the path that only a wisdom-seeker can travel" (p. 187). He explained in more detail that wisdom-seekers travel the golden road of the pollen path, a path dedicated to the prospering of life around oneself, like the bees in their pollination of the world, asking and then answering, "What is a wisdom-seeker? A man or a woman who fearlessly seeks to be truly authentic as he or she travels onward in beauty and humility seeking knowledge" (Forbes, 2008, p. 187).

As should be clear by this point in the research, the appropriation of Indigenous ideas without permission, is colonial, inappropriate, and harmful. I am not advocating here that settlers start saying we are on the red road, or the golden road of the pollen path. Referencing these ideas is only to show the cross-cultural similarities between these Indigenous ways of knowing and the alchemical one. We can stay rooted in the alchemical expression of the gold and reddening of the *rubedo*, all the while knowing that it may be an expression that also resonates with and is recognised in some way by the land on which we now reside. We can perhaps feel into the archetypal breadth of these ideas and the pieces of our humanity and hearts that are shared and common among us all. This commonality is found in the inspiration the bees have woven through all our hearts and stories throughout the world and time with their pollination, their bringing life, and the abundance of food and flowers around us. Shared also is the experience of the warmth of the golden sun, sunflowers, daffodils, and the red of blood that comes with fertility, life, and vitality.

One of the last snippets of story I would like to share here is the story of the golden spruce, or *K'iid K'iyaas,* on Haida Gwaii, an island in the north of so-called British Columbia. *K'iid K'iyaas* (Elder Spruce Tree) was a very sacred tree to the Haida community, the only tree ever known to have been given a name by the Haida (Vaillant, 2006, p. 18). Unlike all other Sitka spruces, *K'iid K'iyaas* was fully golden and radiant. It had been standing as a part of the community's life, stories, and ceremonies since the early 1700s and its golden needles invoked a mythic sacredness (p. 16–18). Almost a century before white man would see or touch those shores, this golden tree grew and was a part of the Haida community. The first Europeans to see and set foot on the shores of Haida Gwaii were Juan Pérez and his crew in 1774 (p. 64) and next, in 1778, was Captain Cook (p. 66). Centuries later, a white settler named Grant Hadwin decided to chop *K'iid K'iyaas* down in "protest" of logging companies. Hadwin's family was fundamentalist Christian and he lived most of his life in a place called Gold Bridge in the interior of so-called British Columbia (p. 48). In 1997, Hadwin travelled seven hundred kilometres northwest of Gold Bridge to Haida Gwaii, the home of the golden spruce (p. 49). Hadwin cutting down the golden spruce was an act of eco-terrorism that he said he did to protest logging companies by exemplifying the pain one tree cut could cause (p. 138). This is perhaps an example of the white man's search for gold, meaning, and sanity gone terribly wrong. The grief and horror this inflicted on the Haida community continues to be felt. The golden spruce was a profound and sacred being and a part of myth and culture in that community. *K'iid K'iyaas* was with them in its golden strength before, and in support through, all the horror of first contact, colonialism, and residential schools. The devastation of having it killed out of another act of white man's insanity, violent white environmentalism and destruction was profound.

In this chapter, we could talk about the devastation the gold rushes on so-called North America wreaked on its landscape and inhabitants, and this would be accurate and relevant. But something about this white man cutting down this sacred golden tree feels so symbolic of this distorted settler alchemical search for physical gold and the squandering of spiritual gold. The golden spruce did not represent physical riches, physical gold in the ground able to be traded in for currency. Instead, it held incredible spiritual and cultural significance. In white man's *wétiko* insanity, he cut it down.

Before this incident, a cutting of *K'iid K'iyaas* had been grafted onto an ordinary Sitka spruce and this cutting has slowly grown over the years and survives today. Slowly, perhaps we settlers can start righting our colonial relationship to land and Indigenous people, no longer expressing our longing for gold by tearing up the ground in search of it and cutting down sacred trees and instead taking a good, hard look into all the shame, disconnect, and trauma within us that keeps us feeling so separate from the gold. Perhaps we can find the gold already buried somewhere deep within:

> All Trees of noblest kind for sight, smell, taste;
> And all amid them stood the Tree of Life,
> High eminent, blooming Ambrosial Fruit
> Of vegetable Gold; and next to Life
> Our Death the Tree of Knowledge grew fast by,
> Knowledge of good bought dear by knowing ill.
> —John Milton, Paradise Lost
> (Vaillant, 2006, Location 31)

Kweèt'ı̨ı̀: *Rock Diggers*

Five hundred years ago, colonisers set out across the seas. Their motivations were varied, though many of them likely shared common interests—the desire for a new world, a rebirth, the desire for gold and riches. Maybe for quite a few of these early colonial explorers, their longings were actually internal and could not, as they expected, be fulfilled by their external searchings. Alchemists believed that in some way, everyone is engaged in alchemical journeys and that the human longing for inner riches, self knowledge and healing is universal. They also believed that if the alchemical journey was not undertaken consciously, carefully, and with integrity, then disaster could ensue. This book has imagined the colonising of what is now called North America as this distorted alchemical journey gone horribly astray. It has imagined the colonisers as longing for inner gold, an inner new world, and instead seeking those things out externally and committing the world's largest genocide and bringing about potentially irreversible and apocalyptic environmental harm. And so, if I have suggested that this history was related to alchemy, why go back to alchemy now? Perhaps in the narrative's origins, there lie the keys for its healing. Perhaps ethically and intentionally following the path alchemy lays out for us—tending our *prima materia*, inner shadow, and the shame, greed, and destructive tendencies and trauma within it—is actually what will lead us to our inner gold and inner new world of wholeness, integrity, and accountability today.

This investigation of what this internal gold will look like is a process we each have to carry out for ourselves: finding our own resources, nourishment and accountability within. We can each undertake our own alchemical journey into our hearts and souls and in doing so enter into a transformative relationship engaging in unsettling and settler decolonial action today.

Captain Cook and George Vancouver

George Vancouver sailed on Captain Cook's ships as a young man then went out to chart and map what we know today as British Columbia's coastlines. Vancouver was only 14-years old when he embarked on his first voyage with Captain Cook (Cook, 2003, p. 221). Though Captain Cook did much to locate and map out a lot of so-called North America, it was Captain Vancouver who established with complete certainty that no other sea existed connecting the Pacific and Atlantic oceans (Vancouver, 2017, Location 49). And so, in our tale of a colonial alchemical journey gone devastatingly wrong, we have the captain after which this land on which I live is named, Vancouver, and his mentor and teacher, Captain Cook, who was responsible for much of the early colonial mapping, "discovering," and beginning devastating genocides with the spreading of diseases around the world.

Etymologically, alchemy is thought to come from the Arabic word *khem* for black earth or *khymatos*: to pour, to cast or mix together: to cook (Harper, 2021, § 2). And so, alchemists can be thought of as the cooks of the soul. Hillman wrote that as alchemists, "we are the cook and the cooked, unable to feel the difference" (Hillman, 2015, Location 663). Alchemist: one who bends over cauldrons, vats, and fires up the cooking tools to meld substances together. Alchemical processes are what unsettle the old and transmute, like cooking, the fixed aspects of our natures and transforms them into different states.

In its positive potential, alchemical cooking is trying to transform something that is stuck from one state to another. In its negative potential, alchemical cooking burns and ignites fires that can take over everything in their wake, causing death and destruction. In some way, Cook embodies this distorted and devastatingly destructive colonial alchemical journey. Captain Vancouver apprenticed under Cook and went on to chart out and prepare so-called British Columbia, what we now call Vancouver, and Vancouver Island (from which I write today) for colonial attack. Cook and Vancouver did find what he called "new" worlds on this earth, but probably not the new world within they might have craved. Cook's death and dismemberment were a result of his greed, arrogance, and blasphemous disrespect of the Hawaiian religion and people. Cook died February 14th, 1779, (Cook, 2003, p. 609). After Cook's death, Vancouver completed many more trips around the world, including more to what we now call Vancouver and Vancouver Island.

In 1790, Vancouver took over command of Cook's former ship, the Discovery (Bown, 2008, p. 3), and the following year, on April 1st, 1791, he and his crew set sail to eventually make their way to *Yuquot*, Friendly Sound, which he had been to with Captain Cook when he had "discovered" it years earlier in 1778 (p. 125). At the time, the Nootka Sound Crisis was underway, which was a dispute over land claims between the Spanish Empire, the United States of America, and the Kingdom of Great Britain (note how the Nuu-chah-nulth are not historically cited as even a part of these conversations around land claims on their land) (p. 3). In 1791, Vancouver was tasked to negotiate with Spanish representatives and resolve the crisis, as well as chart the land surrounding it as best he could so that the

British Empire could make appropriate plans for its settlement (p. 3). Vancouver left Britain on April Fools' Day, a bit of morbid irony perhaps, on his last sail to map out what we now know of as British Columbia, Vancouver, and Vancouver Island, for the beginning of what no one could have imagined was to come. With his foolish attempt to find fulfilment with violence, the effects of the colonialism on these shores continue today with this authors presence on these lands.

Today, we must descend into this narrative and embody it anew, working to transform it by engaging in the positive aspects of the alchemical journey and potential for settler decolonising efforts today. "You are the laboratory; you are the vessel and the stuff going through the cooking" (Hillman, 2015, Location 274). We are being cooked; we must allow ourselves to be so and descend into the discomfort of our racial histories. Only through facing it can we begin to heal it and begin to make reparations. In this healing may we find ourselves, our place in community and in integrity, and our inner, precious gold, of wholeness, accountability, and integrity, within ourselves and the world at large and in our concrete right action today.

Conclusion

Half a millennium ago, Vancouver and Cook landed on the shores of this continent. They arrived in their rowboats from their anchored ships searching perhaps for gold, the new world, or just plain adventure. They and their cultural descendants may have found what they thought they were searching for, and in the process committed the largest genocide the world has ever seen. Today, their cultural descendants in so-called North America have the second highest rates of depression in the world (World Health Organisation, 2017). The lens through which these early colonial explorers perceived the hosts who welcomed them to their coastal ecosystems continues on in the way modern settlers relate to this stolen land, viewing it as a resource to be extracted as theirs, to be done with as they will. These descendants' common daily ailments look more like bad posture from too much Snapchatting rather than the high rates of death from scurvy from lack of vitamin C, tuberculosis, and syphilis that Cook and Vancouver's crews spread around the world. However, one malady is shared between them all: the malady of the settler colonial psyche. Today, we squabble about the pros and cons of Apple vs Google Maps for our directional guidance and celestial navigation has mostly gone out of style other than by avid old-school scientists or hipsters wanting content for their Instagram feed. Though many old-age navigation techniques are antiquated and no longer useful, one forgotten tool for navigational guidance may still have some value for us.

This work has looked at how alchemical ways of imagining has the potential to steer us towards integrity, reconnection with lost parts of our soul, and healthy parts of our ancestry, which may be redemptive and healing for us and our distorted colonial culture today. Alchemy certainly is not the only useful long-forgotten navigational tool which could be helpful on this path, and it alone is certainly not enough to navigate us towards integrity, accountability, and reparations. But if you were interested enough to have immersed yourself in its depths, I hope some of its directions were, and will continue to be, useful in navigating through the waters of racial accountability and settler decolonial right action today.

If you had been able to enter into the laboratories of alchemists of old, you may have seen through flickering candlelight, and through their smoke-filled chambers, makeshift shelves holding vials and alembics of faeces. Some of these alchemists may have told you that they were trying to transmute this faeces into gold. If you could have looked past the disgusting and obviously foolish goal of this venture, you may have realised the cookstove, fire, water, earth, and air the alchemist was showing you were all metaphors for the psychological work being asked of you. The faeces the alchemist was trying to turn to gold was the metaphorical, emotional, cultural, historical shit of your own psyche. Through esoteric and often incomprehensible metaphors and allegories, the alchemist might have tried to guide you to the realisation that investigating and tending to that psychic dung was the most valuable work in the world, as only through that work could gold be created, and the inner dung be transformed to inner riches. Today, if we are willing to face with integrity, commitment, and honesty the rotten, putrid parts of ourselves and histories, like the alchemists with their vials, we have the chance to transmute our colonial shit and reclaim the inner gold of accountability, integrity, honesty, and antiracist direct action.

Eventually, may we all find what Cook, Vancouver, and these early settlers were obsessed with digging from the ground, may we *kweèt'ḭ,* rock diggers, find what we have always searched for and never collectively found: the golden vitality of integrity in the depths of our own hearts and souls. May we also unsettle and disrupt all the loose colonial rocks we find in the shadows along our way.

References

Adams, H. (1997). *A tortured people: The politics of colonization.* Penticton, BC: Theytus Books.

Ahenakew, C. (2016). Grafting Indigenous ways of knowing onto Non-Indigenous ways of being. *International Review of Qualitative Research, 9*(3), 323–340.

Alfred, T. & Corntassel, J. (2005). Being Indigenous: Resurgences against contemporary colonialism. *Government and Opposition, 40*(4), 597–614.

Allen, P. (1992). *The sacred hoop: Recovering the feminine in American Indian traditions.* Boston, MA: Beacon Press.

American Psychological Association. (2013). Stress and eating. Retrieved from https://www.apa.org/news/press/releases/stress/2013/eating

Arima, E. (2018). Nuu-chah-nulth (Nootka). Retrieved from https://www.thecanadianencyclopedia.ca/en/article/nootka-nuu-chah-nulth

Armstrong, J. (1990). The disempowerment of first North American Native peoples and empowerment through their writings. *Gatherings: The En'owkin Journal of First North American Peoples, 1*(1), 143–144.

Berman, S. (2020). Winnipeg police killed three indigenous people in 10 days. Retrieved from https://www.vice.com/en_ca/article/n7jazx/winnipeg-police-killed-three-indigenous-people-in-10-days

Blackie, S. (2018). *The enchanted life: Unlocking the magic of the everyday.* Toronto, ON: House of Anansi.

Boileau, J. (2016). Historical paper no. 1: Edward Cornwallis: Halifax Military Heritage Preservation Society. Retrieved from https://hmhps.ca/pdf/HMHPS-historical-paper-no-1-edward-cornwallis.pdf

Bown, S. (2008). *Betrayal and the lash: The epic voyage of Captain George Vancouver* [Kindle Edition]. Retrieved from www.amazon.ca

Boyd, R. (1999). *Indians, fire, and the land in the Pacific Northwest.* Corvallis, OR: Oregon State University Press.

Bragg, E. (1996). Towards ecological self: Deep ecology meets constructionist self-theory. *Journal of Environmental Psychology, 16*, 93–108.

Bransford, J. D., Brown, A. L., & Cocking, R. R. (2000). *How people learn: Brain, mind, experience, and school.* Washington DC: National Academy Press.

Bryce, P. (1922). The story of a national crime being a record of the health conditions of the Indians of Canada from 1904 to 1921. Retrieved from http://nctr.ca/reports.php

Burrows, J. (1999). Sovereignty's alchemy: An analysis of Delgamuukw v. British Columbia. *Osgoode Hall Law Journal, 37*(3), 538–596.

Camara, J. (2020). Convention speech: Jeremiah Camara—White biblical imagery is still with us. Retrieved from https://www.freethoughttoday.com/vol-37-no-03-april-2020/convention-speech-jeremiah-camara-white-biblical-imagery-is-still-with-us

Cambray, J. (2012). *Synchronicity: Nature and psyche in an interconnected universe (Reprint ed.)*. College Station: Texas A & M University Press.

Cavalli, T. F. (2002). *Alchemical psychology: Old recipes for living in a new world*. New York: Jeremy P.

CBC. (2000). Two hundred year-old scalp law still on books in Nova Scotia. Retrieved from https://www.cbc.ca/news/canada/two-hundred-year-old-scalp-law-still-on-books-in-nova-scotia-1.230906

CBC. (2008). Prime minister Stephen Harper's statement of apology. Retrieved from http://www.cbc.ca/news/canada/prime-minister-stephen-harper-s-statement-of-apology-1.73425

Clayton, S. (2008). Attending to identity: Ideology, group membership, and perceptions of justice. In K. Hegtvedt, & J. Clay-Warner (Ed.), *Advances in group processes: Justice* (pp. 241–266). Bingley, UK: Emerald.

Clayton, S. & Myers, G. (2015). *Conservation psychology: Understanding and promoting human care for nature*. West Sussex: UK: Wiley Blackwell.

Coates, T. (2015). *Between the world and me*. New York, NY: Spiegel & Grau.

Collison, J., Bee, S. & Neel, L. (2019). *Indigenous repatriation handbook*. Victoria, BC: Royal BC Museum and the Haida Gwaii Museum at Kay Llnagaay.

Conn, H. (2018). Waneek Horn-Miller. Retrieved from https://www.thecanadianencyclopedia.ca/en/article/waneek-horn-miller

Conn, H. (2019). Tina Fontaine. Retrieved from https://www.thecanadianencyclopedia.ca/en/article/tina-fontaine

Cook, J. (2003). *The journals of Captain Cook*. Retrieved from www.amazon.ca

Corntassel, J. & Chaw-win-is, T. (2009). Indigenous storytelling, truth-telling, and community approaches to reconciliation. *ESC: English Studies in Canada, 35*(1), 137–159.

Cornwell, H. (2017). *Pax and the politics of peace: Republic to principate* [Kindle edition]. Retrieved from www.amazon.ca

Coulthard, G. (2014). *Red skin, white masks: Rejecting the colonial politics of recognition*. Minneapolis: MN: University of Minnesota Press.

Crosby, A. (2015). *Ecological imperialism: The biological expansion of Europe, 900–1900 Second Edition*. New York: NY: Cambridge University Press.

Cull, I., Hancock, R., McKeown, S., Pidgeon, M., & Vedan, A. (2018). *Pulling together: A guide for front-line staff, student services, and advisors*. Victoria, BC: BCcampus.

Dana, D. (2018). *The polyvagal theory in therapy: Engaging the rhythm of regulation* [Kindle Edition]. Retrieved from www.amazon.ca

Darwin, C. (1839/1989). *Voyage of the beagle*. London, UK: Penguin Books Ltd.

DiAngelo, R. (2018). *White fragility*. Boston, MA: Beacon Press.

Donald, M. (1991). *Origins of the modern mind: Three stages in the evolution of culture and cognition*. Harvard University Press.

Edinger, E. (1991). *Anatomy of the psyche: Alchemical symbolism in psychotherapy.* Chicago, IL: Open Court.

Edinger, E. (1992). *Ego and archetype* [Kindle Edition]. Retrieved from www.amazon.ca

Eliade, M. (1979). *The forge and the crucible: The origins and structures of alchemy* (2nd ed.). Chicago, IL: University of Chicago Press.

Elliott, A. (2019). *A mind spread out on the ground* [Kindle Edition]. Retrieved from www.amazon.ca

Esgalhado, B. D. (2003). The ancestor syndrome. *Qualitative Inquiry, 9*(3), 481–494.

Fanon, F. (1961). *The wretched of the Earth* [Kindle Edition]. Retrieved from www.amazon.ca

Fenn, E. (2000). Biological warfare in eighteenth-century North America: Beyond Jeffery Amherst. *The Journal of American History*, March, 1552–1580.

Fernandez, M. & Burch, A. (2020). George Floyd, from 'I want to touch the world' to 'I can't breathe'. Retrieved from https://www.nytimes.com/article/george-floyd-who-is.html

Forbes, J. (2008). *Columbus and other cannibals: The Wetiko disease of exploitation, imperialism, and terrorism.* New York: NY: Seven Stories Press.

Fromm, E. (1976). *To have or to be?* New York: NY: Harper & Row.

Gallant, D. (2019). Sixties scoop. Retrieved from https://www.thecanadianencyclopedia.ca/en/article/sixties-scoop

Gardner, G. & Stern, P. (2002). *Environmental problems and human behavior.* Boston, MA: Allyn & Bacon.

Glaisher, J. (1871). *Travels in the air.* London, UK: Richard Bentley & Son.

Glover, F. & Cooper, C. (2020). Black enslavement in Canada. Retrieved from https://thecanadianencyclopedia.ca/en/article/black-enslavement-in-canada-plain-language-summary

Goldsworthy, A. (2016). *Pax Romana: War, peace and conquest in the Roman world* [Kindle edition]. Retrieved from www.amazon.ca

Goodchild, V. (2006). Psychoid, psychophysical, P-subtle! Alchemy and a new worldview. *Spring Journal, Alchemy 76*, 63–89.

Government of Canada. (2008). Statement of apology to former students of Indian residential schools. Retrieved from https://www.aadncaandc.gc.ca/eng/1100100015644/1100100015649

Gowriluk, C. & Grabish, A. (2020). Man killed by police on Saturday was young father with 'a smile to remember,'. Retrieved from https://www.cbc.ca/news/canada/manitoba/jason-collins-shot-dead-by-winnipeg-police-anderson-avenue-1.5530108

Gwyn, R. (2012). *Nation maker: Sir John A. Macdonald: His life, our times* [Kindle Edition]. Retrieved from www.amazon.ca

Hackett, C. & McClendon, D. (2017). Christians remain world's largest religious group, but they are declining in Europe. Retrieved from https://www.pewresearch.org/fact-tank/2017/04/05/christians-remain-worlds-largest-religious-group-but-they-are-declining-in-europe/

Haga, K. (2020). *Healing resistance: A radically different response to harm.* Berkeley, CA: Parallax Press.

Hardy v. Canada. (2018). Ann Cecile Hardy v. The Attorney General of Canada.

Harper, D. (2020). *Online etymology dictionary*. Retrieved from https://www.etymonline.com/search?q=integrity

Harper, D. (2021). *Alchemy (n.)*. Retrieved from https://www.etymonline.com/search?q=alchemy

Hawthorn, A. (2021). *Why have Indigenous communities been hit harder by the pandemic than the population at large?* Retrieved from https://www.cbc.ca/news/canada/newfoundland-labrador/apocalypse-then-indigenous-covid-1.5997774

Heidenreich, P. & Boynton, S. (2020). *Police watchdog to investigate fatal RCMP shooting of Indigenous man in New Brunswick*. Retrieved from https://globalnews.ca/news/7062499/police-watchdog-to-investigate-deadly-rcmp-shooting-in-new-brunswick/

Helms, J. (1993). *Black and white racial identity: Theory, research, and practice*. New York: NY: Greenwood Press.

Henry, N. (2015). Slavery Abolition Act, United Kingdom. Retrieved from https://www.britannica.com/topic/Slavery-Abolition-Act

Hillman, J. (1975). *Re-visioning psychology*. San Francisco, CA: Harper.

Hillman, J. (1981). The imagination of air and the collapse of alchemy. In *Eranos yearbook 50* (pp. 273–333). Ascona: Eranos Foundation.

Hillman, J. (1985). James Hillman on animals: A correspondence. *Between the Species, 1*(2), 4–8.

Hillman, J. (1986). *Notes on white supremacy: Essaying an archetypal account of historical events. Spring 1986* (pp. 29–58). Dallas, TX: Spring Publications.

Hillman, J. (1994). Man is by nature a political animal or: Patient as citizen. In S. M. Shamdasani (Ed.), *Speculations after Freud: Psychoanalysis, philsophy and culture* (pp. 27–40). London and New York: Routledge.

Hillman, J. (1997). Culture and the animal soul. *Spring: A Journal of Archetype and Culture, 62*, 11(7), 10–37.

Hillman, J. (1997). *The souls code: In search of character and calling*. London: Bantam.

Hillman, J. (2004). *A terrible love of war* [Kindle edition]. Retrieved from www.amazon.ca

Hillman, J. (2005). Peaks and vales. In G. Slater (Ed.), *Senex and puer, uniform edition Vol. 3* (pp. 71–95). Thompson, CT: Spring Publications.

Hillman, J. (2007). *Mythic figures* [Kindle version]. Retrieved from www.amazon.ca

Hillman, J. (2015). *Alchemical psychology* [Kindle version]. Retrieved from: www.amazon.ca

Holy Bible. (2003). *New revised standard version, Catholic Edition Bible* [Kindle edition]. Retrieved from www.amazon.ca

Hooks, B. (2013). *Writing beyond race: Living theory and practice* [Kindle Edition]. www.amazon.ca

Ibrahim, H. (2020). *Killing of Indigenous woman raises questions about who should be doing wellness checks*. Retrieved from https://www.cbc.ca/news/canada/new-brunswick/chantel-moore-indigenous-woman-shot-by-police-edmundston-1.560109

Ignace, M. & Ignace, R. (2017). *Secwépemc people, land, and laws: Yerí7 re Stsq'ey's-kucw*. Montreal, QC: McGill-Queen's University Press.

Jacobs, S., Thomas, W., & Lang, S. (Eds.). (1997). *Two-spirit people: Native American gender identity, sexuality, and spirituality*. Urbana, IL: University of Illinois Press.

Jacobson, M. (2005). *Whiteness of a different color: European immigrants and the alchemy of race.* New York: ACLS History E-Book Project.

Jarrett, J. & Jung, C. G. (1988). *Nietzsche's Zarathustra: Notes of the seminar given in 1934–1939*, Vol. 1. Princeton, NJ: Princeton University Press.

Jenkinson, S. (2015). *Die wise: A manifesto for sanity and soul.* Berkeley, CA: North Atlantic Books.

Jenkinson, S. (2021). Orphan wisdom. Retrieved from https://orphanwisdom.com/about/

Joseph, B. (2018). *21 things you may not know about the Indian Act: Helping Canadians make reconciliation with Indigenous peoples a reality.* Port Coquitlam, BC: Indigenous Relations Press.

Jung, C. G. (2012). *The psychology of Kundalini Yoga: Notes of the seminar given in 1932 (Jung extracts book 99).* Princeton University Press.

Jung, C. G. (2009). *The red book liber novus.* New York, NY: W. W. Norton & Co. (Original work published 1915.)

Jung, C. G. (1997a). *Jung on active imagination* (J. Chodorow, Ed.). Princeton, NJ: Princeton University Press.

Jung, C. G. (1997b). *Visions: Notes of the seminar given in 1930–1934*, Vol. I (C. Douglas, Ed.). Princeton, NJ: Princeton University Press.

Jung, C. G. (1984). *Dream analysis: Notes of the seminar given in 1928–1930.* New York, NY: Princeton University Press.

Jung, C. G. (1977). *C. G. Jung speaking: Interviews and encounters* (W. McGuire & R. F. Hull, Eds.). Princeton, NJ: Princeton University Press.

Jung, C. G. (1976a). *Letters of C. G. Jung: Volume 2, 1951–1961.* UK: Routledge.

Jung, C. G. (1976b). The Tavistock lectures: On the theory and practice of analytical psychology (R. F. C. Hull, Trans.). In H. Read et al. (Eds.), *The collected works of C. G. Jung* (Vol. 18, pp. 1–182). Princeton, NJ: Princeton University Press. (Original work published 1935.)

Jung, C. G. (1970a). Mysterium coniunctionis (R. F. C. Hull, Trans.). In H. Read et al. (Eds.), *The collected works of C. G. Jung* (Vol. 14, 2nd ed.). Princeton, NJ: Princeton University Press. (Original work published 1955–56.)

Jung, C. G. (1970b). Mind and earth (R. F. C. Hull, Trans.). In H. Read et al. (Eds.), *The collected works of C. G. Jung* (Vol. 10, 2nd ed., pp. 29–49). Princeton, NJ: Princeton University Press. (Original work published 1931.)

Jung, C. G. (1970c). The spiritual problem of modern man (R. F. C. Hull, Trans.). In H. Read et al. (Eds.), *The collected works of C. G. Jung* (Vol. 10, 2nd ed., pp. 74–94). Princeton, NJ: Princeton University Press. (Original work published 1931.)

Jung, C. G. (1970d). The role of the unconscious (R. F. C. Hull, Trans.). In H. Read et al. (Eds.), *The collected works of C. G. Jung* (Vol. 10, 2nd ed., pp. 3–28). Princeton, NJ: Princeton University Press. (Original work published 1918.)

Jung, C. G. (1969a). A review of the complex theory (R. F. C. Hull, Trans.). In H. Read et al. (Eds.), *The collected works of C. G. Jung: Vol. 8. Structure and dynamics of the psyche* (2nd ed., pp. 92–104). Princeton University Press. (Original work published 1948.)

Jung, C. G. (1969b). The psychology of Eastern meditation (R. F. C. Hull, Trans.). In H. Read et al. (Eds.), *The collected works of C. G. Jung: Vol. 11. Psychology and religion* (2nd ed., pp. 558–575). Princeton University Press. (Original work published 1943)

Jung, C. G. (1968a). Aion: Researches into the phenomenology of the self (R. F. C. Hull, Trans.). In H. Read et al. (Eds.), *The collected works of C. G. Jung* (Vol. 09ii, 2nd ed.). Princeton, NJ: Princeton University Press. (Original work published 1951.)

Jung, C. G. (1968b). The psychology of the child archetype (R. F. C. Hull, Trans.). In H. Read et al. (Eds.), *The collected works of C. G. Jung: Vol. 9 pt. 1. Archetypes and the collective unconscious* (2nd ed., pp. 151–181). Princeton University Press. (Original work published 1951.)

Jung, C. G. (1968c). Introduction to the religious and psychological problems of alchemy (R. F. C. Hull, Trans.). In H. Read et al. (Eds.), *The collected works of C. G. Jung: Vol. 12. Psychology and alchemy* (2nd ed., pp. 1–37). Princeton University Press. (Original work published 1943.)

Jung, C. G. (1968d). Religious ideas in alchemy (R. F. C. Hull, Trans.). In H. Read et al. (Eds.), *The collected works of C. G. Jung* (Vol. 12, 2nd ed., pp. 225–483). Princeton, NJ: Princeton University Press. (Original work published 1937.)

Jung, C. G. (1967a). Symbols of transformation (R. F. C. Hull, Trans.). In H. Read et al. (Eds.), *The collected works of C. G. Jung* (Vol. 5, 2nd ed.). Princeton, NJ: Princeton University Press. (Original work published 1952.)

Jung, C. G. (1967b). Paracelsus as a spiritual phenomenon (R. F. C. Hull, Trans.). In H. Read et al. (Eds.), *The collected works of C. G. Jung* (Vol. 13, pp. 109–189). Princeton, NJ: Princeton University Press. (Original work published 1942.)

Jung, C. G. (1967c). Commentary on "The secret of the golden flower" (R. F. C. Hull, Trans.). In H. Read et al. (Eds.), *The collected works of C. G. Jung: Vol. 13. Alchemical studies* (pp. 1–56). Princeton University Press. (Original work published 1929.)

Jung, C. G. (1954). The development of personality (R. F. C. Hull, Trans.). In H. Read et al. (Eds.), *The collected works of C. G. Jung: Vol. 17. Development of personality* (pp. 165–186). Princeton University Press. (Original work published 1934.)

Jurgens, W. (1970). *The faith of the early fathers: Volume 1*. Collegeville, MN: The Liturgical Press.

Keen, S. (1996). *Fire in the belly: On being a man*. London, UK: Piatkus.

Kelly, M. (2019). A Timeline of North American Exploration: 1492–1585. ThoughtCo, Feb. 16, 2021, https://www.thoughtco.com/timeline-of-exploration-1492-1585-104281

Kendi, I. (2019). *How to Be an Antiracist*. New York, NY: Random House.

Kerr, J. (2014). Greenpeace apology to Inuit for impacts of seal campaign. Retrieved from https://www.greenpeace.org/canada/en/story/5473/greenpeace-apology-to-inuit-for-impacts-of-seal-campaign/

Kimbles, S. (2000). *The cultural complex and the myth of invisibility. In the vision thing: Myth, politics and psyche in the world* (pp. 155–169). London, UK: Routledge.

Kimmerer, R. (2015). *Braiding sweetgrass* [Kindle Edition]. Retrieved from www.amazon.ca

King, R. (2018). *Mindful of race*. Louisville, CO: Sounds True.

King, T. (2013). *The inconvenient Indian: A curious account of native people in North America* [Kindle edition]. Retrieved from: www.amazon.ca

Kino-nda-niimi Collective. (2014). *The winter we danced: Voices from the past, the future, and the Idle No More movement*. Winnipeg, Manitoba: Arbeiter Ring Publishing.

Klingerman, K. (2006). *Binding femininity: An examination of the effects on tightlacing on the female pelvis.* Baton Rouge, LA: Louisiana State University.
Koester, C. (2009). Revelation's visionary challenge to ordinary empire. *Faculty Publications, 10,* 5–18.
Kruszewski, C. (1940). International affairs: Germany's Lebensraum. *The American Political Science Review, 34*(5), 964–975.
Larsen, K. (2021). Fairy Creek protest on Vancouver Island now considered largest act of civil disobedience in Canadian history. *CBC.* Retrieved from https://www.cbc.ca/news/canada/british-columbia/fairy-creek-protest-largest-act-of-civil-disobedience-1.6168210
Laski, M. (1961). *Ecstasy.* Bloomington, IN: Indiana University Press.
LHF (Legacy of Hope Foundation) (2014). Reclaiming history: The residential school system in Canada. Retrieved from http://wherearethechildren.ca/en/timeline/research/
LoCicero, A., Marlin, R. P., Jull-Patterson, D., Sweeney, N. M., Gray, B. L., & Boyd, J. W. (2016). Enabling torture: APA, clinical psychology training and the failure to disobey. *Peace and Conflict: Journal of Peace Psychology, 22*(4), 345–355.
Lebeuf, M. (2011). The role of the Royal Canadian Mounted Police during the Indian Residential School System. Royal Canadian Mounted Police, Government of Canada.
Mackey, E. (2016). *Unsettled expectations: Uncertainty, land and settler decolonization.* Halifax: Fernwood Publishing.
Macy, J. (2014). *Coming back to life: The updated guide to the work that reconnects.* [Kindle Edition]. Retrieved from www.amazon.ca
Manuel, A. & Derrickson, R. M. (2017). *The reconciliation manifesto: Recovering the land, rebuilding the economy* [Kindle Edition]. Retrieved from www.amazon.ca
Maracle, L. (1996). *I am woman: A native perspective on sociology and feminism.* Vancouver, BC: Press Gang Publishers.
Maracle, L. (2015). *Memory serves and other essays* [Kindle Edition]. Retrieved from www.amazon.ca
Maracle, L. (2017). *My conversations with Canadians.* Toronto, ON: BookThug Press.
Marlan, S. (2008). *The black sun: The alchemy and art of darkness* [Kindle Edtion]. Retrieved from www.amazon.ca
Mashford-Pringle, A., Skura, C., Stutz, S., & Yohathasan, T. (2021). What we heard: Indigenous peoples and COVID-19: Public Health Agency of Canada's companion report. *Waakebiness-Bryce Institute for Indigenous Health, Government of Canada.*
Marshall, T. (2019). Idle no more. (The Canadian encyclopedia). Retrieved from https://www.thecanadianencyclopedia.ca/en/article/idle-no-more
McCallum, I. (2008). *Ecological intelligence, rediscovering ourselves in nature.* Golden, CO: Fulcrum.
McCallum, J. (2020). Senate of Canada: Oppression, privilege and the myth of the rule of law: Senator McCallum 2020. Retrieved from https://sencanada.ca/en/sencaplus/opinion/oppression-privilege-and-the-myth-of-the-rule-of-law-senator-mccallum/

McNett, G. (2016). Using stories to facilitate learning. *College Teaching, 64*(4), 184–193.

Menakem, R. (2017). *My grandmother's hands: Racialized trauma and the pathway to mending our hearts and bodies* [Kindle Edition]. Retrieved from www.amazon.ca

Miles, S. (2005). *The hippocratic oath and the ethics of medicine.* New York: Oxford University Press.

Mitchell, S. (2018). *Sacred instructions: Indigenous wisdom for living spirit-based change* [Kindle Edition]. Retrieved from www.amazon.ca

Moore, P. A. (2013). *Confessions of a Greenpeace dropout: The making of a sensible environmentalist* [Kindle version]. Retrieved from www.amazon.ca

Moran, P. (2020). Video of RCMP hitting Inuk man with truck shows police choosing violence over protection, says lawyer. Retrieved from https://www.cbc.ca/radio/thecurrent/the-current-for-june-5-2020-1.5599723/video-of-rcmp-hitting-inuk-man-with-truck-shows-police-choosing-violence-over-protection-says-lawyer-1.5599847

Morris, B., Chrysochou, P., Christensen, J., Orquin, J., Brraza, J., Zak, P., & Mitkidis, P. (2019). Stories vs. facts: Triggering emotion and action-taking on climate change. *Climatic Change, 154*, 19–36.

Morris, J. (2020). *Recessions in higher education: A study of faculty sensitivities to changes in funding vis-à-vis periods of recession.* Economics Honors Thesis. Santa Barbara, CA: University of California Santa Barbara.

Mosby, I. (2013). Administering colonial science: Nutrition research and human biomedical experimentation in aboriginal communities and residential schools, 1942–1952. *Histoire Sociale/Social History, 46*(91), 145–172.

Nahanee, T. (2020). *Decolonize First, a liberating guide & workbook.* Nahanee Creatives Inc. Retrieved from www.nahaneecreative.com

NASA. (2021a). Climate change: How do we know? Retrieved from https://climate.nasa.gov/evidence/

NASA. (2021b). Global temperature. Retrieved from https://climate.nasa.gov/vital-signs/global-temperature/

National Geographic. (2019). Climate milestone: Earth's CO2 level passes 400 ppm. Retrieved from https://www.nationalgeographic.org/article/climate-milestone-earths-co2-level-passes-400-ppm/

Nelson, K. (2003). Narratives and the emergence of a consciousness of self. In G.D.M. Fireman, E. Ted, & O.J. Flanagan (Eds.), *Narrative and consciousness: literature, psychology and the brain.* (pp. 17–36). New York, NY: Oxford University Press.

Nichols, R. (1986). *The American Indian: Past and present.* Tucson, AZ: Newbery Award Records Inc.

Niessen, S. (2017). *Shattering the silence: The hidden history of Indian residential schools in Saskatchewan.* Regina, SA: University of Regina.

NIMMIWG. (2019). *Reclaiming power and place: The final report of the national inquiry into missing and murdered Indigenous women and girls.*

Oluo, I. (2018). *So you want to talk about race.* New York, NY: Seal Press.

Oppel, R. & Taylor, D. (2020). Here's what you need to know about Breonna Taylor's death. Retrieved from https://www.nytimes.com/article/breonna-taylor-police.html

Palmater, P. (2014). Genocide, Indian policy, and legislated elimination of Indians in Canada. *Department of Politics and Public Administration, Ryerson University*, 3(3), 27–54.

Papadopoulos, R. (2006). *The handbook of Jungian psychology: Theory, Practice and Applications.* New York: NY: Routledge.

Pawson, C. (2021). First Nation's council and chief ask '3rd-party' activists to stand down in B.C. logging dispute. *CBC News.* Retrieved from https://www.cbc.ca/news/canada/british-columbia/bc-fairy-creek-pacheedaht-first-nation-1.5986420

Pelikan, J. (2005). Christianity: Christianity in Western Europe. *Encyclopedia of Religion*, 3(2), 1687–1694.

Pellatt, M., McCoy, M., & Mathewes, R. (2015). Paleoecology and fire history of Garry oak ecosystems in Canada: Implications for conservation and environmental management. *Biodivers Conserv*, 24, 1621–1639.

Pilling, R. (2020). Money Talks about Racism in Canada. Retrieved from https://wow.nyc3.digitaloceanspaces.com/shared/money-talks-about-racism-in-canada.pdf

Pinker, S. (2003). *The language instinct: How the mind creates language.* UK: Penguin.

Plotkin, H.C. (1982). *Learning, development, and culture: Essays in evolutionary epistemology.* John Wiley & Son.

Province of British Columbia. (2020). Working on the land base. Retrieved from https://www2.gov.bc.ca/gov/content/industry/natural-resource-use

RCMP, Government of Canada. (2011). The role of the Royal Canadian Mounted Police during the Indian residential school system. *Royal Canadian Mounted Police, Government of Canada.*

RCMP, Government of Canada. (2019). Royal Canadian Mounted Police. Retrieved from https://www.rcmp-grc.gc.ca/en/cadet-training

RCMP, Government of Canada. (2020). History of the RCMP. Retrieved from https://www.rcmp-grc.gc.ca/en/history-rcmp

Regan, P. (2010). *Unsettling the settler within: Indian residential schools, truth telling, and reconciliation in Canada.* Vancouver, Canada: UBC Press.

Ridder, M. (2020). *Revenue of the cosmetic & beauty industry in the U.S. 2002–2020.* Retrieved from https://www.statista.com/statistics/243742/revenue-of-the-cosmetic-industry-in-the-us/

Roach, K. (2020). Gerald Stanley and Colten Boushie case. Retrieved from https://thecanadianencyclopedia.ca/en/article/gerald-stanley-and-colten-boushie-case

Robinson, A. (2019). Manifest destiny. Retrieved from https://www.thecanadianencyclopedia.ca/en/article/manifest-destiny

Rossi, S. (2017). Cosmologies of soul: Astrology and alchemy. In J. Stroud (Ed.), *Conversing with James Hillman: Alchemical psychology* (Vol. 3, pp. 41–46). Dallas, USA: Dallas Institute of the Humanities and Culture.

Rubenfeld, S. (2011). Medical ethics after Auschwitz. *Journal of Ecumenical Studies*, 46(4), 515–519.

Rusnell, C. & Russell, J. (2020). RCMP dashcam video shows officer tackling, punching Chief Allan Adam during arrest. Retrieved from https://www.cbc.ca/news/canada/edmonton/rcmp-chief-allan-adam-1.5608472

Russell, R. (2018). Crowdfunding as a political weapon platforms like GoFundMe allow people to voice their support—or outrage—via their wallets. Retrieved from https://thewalrus.ca/crowdfunding-as-a-political-weapon

Saad, L. (2020). *Me and white supremacy*. Naperville, IL: Sourcebooks.
Sandlos, J. (2007). *Hunters at the margin: Native people and wildlife conservation in the Northwest Territories*. Vancouver: UBC Press.
Schaefer, R. (2008). *Encyclopedia of race, ethnicity, and society, Vol. 1*. Thousand Oaks: CA: Sage Publications.
Schenk, R. (2012). *American soul: A cultural narrative*. New Orleans, LA: Spring Journal Books.
Schultz, M. (2018). 2 in 3 Americans say shopping is the most stressful part of the holiday season. Retrieved from https://www.comparecards.com/blog/2-in-3-americans-say-shopping-most-stressful-part-of-holidays/
Schultz, P. W., Zelezny, L., & Dalrymple, N. J. (2000). A multinational perspective on the relation between Judeo-Christian religious beliefs and attitudes of environmental concern. *Environment and Behavior, 41*(6), 806–820.
Schwartz-Salant, N. & Jung, C. G. (1996). *Jung on alchemy paperback*. Princeton, NJ: Princeton University Press.
Scott, D. (2004). *Conscripts of modernity: The tragedy of colonial enlightenment*. London: UK: Duke University Press.
Shimo, A. (2018). While Nestlé extracts millions of litres from their land, residents have no drinking water. Retrieved from https://www.theguardian.com/global/2018/oct/04/ontario-six-nations-nestle-running-water
Sieff, D. (2015). *Understanding and healing emotional trauma conversations with pioneering clinicians and researchers* [Kindle Edition]. Retrieved from www.amazon.ca.
Simpson, L. (2011). *Dancing on our turtle's back: Stories of Nishnaabeg re-creation, resurgence, and a new emergence*. Winnipeg, MB: Arbeiter Ring Publishing.
Simpson, L. (2013). *Islands of decolonial love* [Kindle Editions]. Retrieved from www.amazon.ca
Singer, T. (2006). The cultural complex: A statement of the theory and its application. *Psychotherapy and Politics International, 4*(3), 197–212.
Smart, A. (2018). Trudeau apologizes to Tsilhqot'in community members for 1864 hanging of chiefs. Retrieved from https://www.cbc.ca/news/canada/british-columbia/trudeau-apologizes-to-tsilhqot-in-community-members-for-1864-hanging-of-chiefs-1.4890486
Smith, L. (1949/1994). *Killers of the dream*. New York, NY: WW Norton.
Some, M. (1994). *Of water and spirit*. New York, NY: Penguin Compass.
Stannard, D. (1993). *American holocaust: The conquest of the new world*. New York, NY: Oxford University Press.
Stote, K. (2015). *An act of genocide: Colonialism and the sterilization of Aboriginal women* [Kindle Edition]. Retrieved from www.amazon.ca
Suchet, M. (2007). Unraveling whiteness. *Psychoanalytic dialogues, 17*(6), 867–886.
Tait, C. (2021). B.C. First Nation at odds with anti-logging protesters. *The Globe and Mail*. Retrieved from https://www.theglobeandmail.com/canada/british-columbia/article-first-nation-in-bc-at-odds-with-anti-logging-protesters/#:~:text=%E2%80%9CIn%20the%20past%20150%20years,manager%2C%20said%20in%20a%20statement
Talaga, T. (2017). *Seven fallen feathers: Racism, death, and hard truths in a northern city*. Toronto: Anansi.

Tarnas, R. (2006). *Cosmos and psyche: Intimations of a new world view* [Kindle Edition]. Retrieved from: www.amazon.ca.

Tarnas, R. (2013). Is the modern psyche undergoing a rite of passage? Retrieved from http://www.cosmosandpsyche.com/pages/essays

The World Counts. (2021). Hectares of forests cut down or burned. Retrieved from https://www.theworldcounts.com/challenges/planet-earth/forests-and-deserts/rate-of-deforestation/story

Thomson, H. (2021). First Nations take back decision-making responsibilities over ḥahahuułi. Retrieved from https://huuayaht.org/2021/06/07/huu-ay-aht-pacheedaht-\ditidaht-first-nations-take-back-decision-making-responsibilities-over-ḥahahuuli/

Tk̓emlúps te Secwépemc. (2021). Kamloops Indian band news release. Retrieved from https://tkemlups.ca/wp-content/uploads/05-May-27-2021-TteS-MEDIA-RELEASE.pdf

TRC. (2015a). Canada's residential schools: The history, part 1 origins to 1939, the final report of the Truth and Reconciliation Commission of Canada. *McGill-Queen's University Press, 1*.

TRC. (2015b). Canada's residential schools: Reconciliation. The final report of the Truth and Reconciliation Commission of Canada. *McGill-Queen's University Press, 6*.

TRC. (2015c). The survivors speak. *McGill-Queen's University Press, 1*.

Truelove, H. (2009). Understanding the relationship between Christian orthodoxy and environmentalism: The mediating role of perceived environmental consequences. *Environment and Behavior, 41*(6), 806–820.

Truelove, H. & Joireman, J. (2009). Understanding the relationship between Christian orthodoxy and environmentalism: The mediating role of perceived environmental consequences. *Environment and Behavior, 41*(6), 806–820.

Tuck, E. & Yang, W. (2012). Decolonization is not a metaphor. *Decolonization: Indigeneity, Education & Society, 1*(1), 1–40.

United Nations. (2008). United Nations declaration on the rights of Indigenous peoples.

United Nations. (2019). UN report: Nature's dangerous decline 'unprecedented'; Species extinction rates 'accelerating'. Retrieved from https://www.un.org/sustainabledevelopment/blog/2019/05/nature-decline-unprecedented-report/

United Nations. (2020). United Nations decade for deserts and the fight against desertification. Retrieved from https://www.un.org/en/events/desertification_decade/whynow.shtml

Vaillant, J. (2006). *The Golden Spruce: A true story of myth, madness, and greed*. [Kindle Edition]. Retrieved from www.amazon.ca

Vancouver, G. (2017). *A voyage of discovery to the North Pacific Ocean, and round the world* [Kindle Edition]. Retrieved from www.amazon.ca

Veracini, L. (2010). *Settler colonialism a theoretical overview* [Kindle Edition]. Retrieved from www.amazon.ca.

Villanueva, E. (2018). *Decolonizing wealth: Indigenous wisdom to heal divides and restore balance*. Oakland, CA: Berrett-Koehler Publishers, Inc.

von Franz, M. (1980). *Alchemy: An introduction to the symbolism and the psychology (studies in Jungian psychology)*. Toronto, ON: Inner City Books.

von Franz, M. (2003). *Psyche and matter* [Kindle version]. Retrieved from www.amazon.ca

von Franz, M. (2014). *Psychotherapy*. Boston, MA: Shambala.

Williams, A., Owens, L., & Syedullah, J. (2016). *Radical dharma: Talking race, love, and liberation*. Berkeley, CA: North Atlantic Books.

Wilson, K. (2018). *Pulling together: Foundations guide appendix B: Indian Act Timeline*. Victoria, BC: BCcampus. Retrieved from https://opentextbc.ca/indigenizationfoundations/.

Winter, J. (2021). Pacheedaht First Nation chiefs in Canada tell anti-logging protesters to leave their lands. *The Guardian*. Retrieved from https://www.theguardian.com/environment/2021/apr/14/canada-logging-blockade-first-nations-pacheedaht

Wolf, N. (2012). *Vagina* [Kindle Edition]. Retrieved from www.amazon.ca

World Health Organization. (2017). Depression and other common mental disorders. Retrieved from https://www.who.int/publications/i/item/depression-global-health-estimates

Ziegler, A. (2015). *Archetypal medicine* [Kindle Edition]. Retrieved from www.amazon.ca

Index

abuse 14, 46, 48, 51, 54, 57, 84, 91–92, 109–13, 119, 127, 129, 131, 166
accountability 2–3, 8–9, 11–13, 23–24, 59–60, 75, 159, 168, 170–72, 175–76, 179, 181–82
alchemist 7, 9–10, 13–14, 17, 61, 63–66, 71, 79, 82, 84, 98, 100, 109, 118–19, 124, 142, 144–46, 150–52, 160, 171–72, 176, 179–80, 182
ancient 2, 13, 15, 16, 17, 62–63, 70, 74, 88, 116–17
appropriation 17–19, 22–23, 177
assimilation 15, 22, 33, 55, 148, 160, 164, 166, 169

balance 8, 28, 42, 64, 81, 85, 87–89, 91, 94–95, 137, 156–57

capitalism 20, 117, 120, 132–33, 164
ceremony 3, 18, 49, 54, 69, 75, 122, 156
Christianity 3, 8, 18, 29–31, 34, 41, 46, 62, 64, 67, 69, 82, 84, 124, 138; Christian 8, 29, 30–38, 40–41, 46, 48, 51, 54, 62, 64, 66–68, 81–82, 98, 106–09, 113–14, 117, 124, 126, 144, 154, 166, 167, 178; Christian myth 8, 40, 62, 64
collective 11, 13, 16, 28, 39, 41–42, 45, 64, 65, 67–68, 130, 140, 145, 175, 182
colonial complex 27–44, 78, 85–86, 92, 94, 101, 102–03, 118–19, 121, 126, 137, 140, 148, 150, 157; colonial consciousness 2, 4, 5, 7, 8, 11, 15–16, 21–22, 28, 29, 31, 35, 39, 42, 45, 63, 87, 144; colonial disease/illness 13, 20; colonial psychology 3, 5, 12; colonizer 4, 5, 23, 67, 102, 107, 125, 128, 130, 133, 147, 149, 165, 179

control 36, 48, 54, 76, 109–10, 117, 130, 135, 149–50, 152, 162, 173
Coulthard, G. 2, 20–22, 56, 73, 127, 163–64, 166, 170

decolonizing 4, 21–23, 62, 69, 75, 101, 108, 112, 118, 129, 132, 134, 155, 164, 165, 169, 171, 173, 176, 181
delusion of white supremacy 65, 77, 143, 160–61
Depth Psychology 2, 7, 9, 18, 65, 101, 118, 175
direct action 14, 95, 121, 139, 140, 182
disconnection 25, 28, 31, 34–35, 37–39, 41, 43, 46, 131
domination 20, 28, 31, 38–39, 46, 110, 127, 130, 162–65, 168, 173
dysregulation 12–13, 152, 154

Edinger, E. 65, 82, 84–85, 87, 92–93, 100–01, 116–18, 120, 126, 146–47, 150
embodiment 8, 35, 42–43, 64, 85, 91, 96, 117–18, 121, 126, 137, 144, 154, 157, 171
environment 11, 35, 37–38, 42, 56, 97, 130, 132–37, 140, 149, 152, 154, 157, 179
explorers 1, 9, 99, 105, 179, 181

Fanon, F. 24
First Nations 1, 11, 18–19, 48–49, 51–54, 58, 102, 115–16, 122, 133, 135–36, 149–50, 163, 166, 174

imagination 7, 9, 16, 40, 63, 66, 71, 83, 90, 137, 147
imperialism 10, 24–25, 106

Index

Indigenous: Indigenous children 33, 46, 54–55, 58, 91–92, 105; Indigenous communities 19, 53, 58, 91–92, 105, 106, 111, 113–15, 129, 147, 172; Indigenous cultures 8, 39, 114; Indigenous governance 19, 50; Indigenous land 10, 21–23, 48, 56, 126–27, 141, 164; Indigenous nations 25, 127, 149, 163, 173; Indigenous peoples 4, 9, 11, 18, 23, 56, 76, 133, 163, 169; Indigenous resurgence 2, 13, 165, 175; Indigenous sovereignty 22, 126–27; Indigenous women 13, 46, 56, 57, 105, 107, 165–66, 176
individuation 17, 62, 68, 171
integrity 2, 11, 13–14, 22–24, 69, 75, 124, 136–37, 152, 159–61, 168–72, 179, 181–82

Jung, C. G. 6–7, 17–18, 27–28, 34–37, 39–42, 59, 62–68, 79, 85, 87–88, 90, 92–93, 98, 100–01, 107, 116, 118, 128–30, 146, 148, 150, 169, 171–72, 175–76; Jungian 6–7, 18, 65

lineage 2, 5, 16–18, 59, 62, 65, 69, 74, 76, 95, 109, 122, 131, 138, 141, 158, 162, 175

madness 42, 60, 72, 165, 175
Manuel, A. 10, 20, 126, 141
Maracle, L. 4, 5, 11, 19, 104–05, 109, 127, 141, 165–69, 173–74
Martin Luther King 29, 89
medical experimentation 46, 53–54
Menakem, R. 5, 12, 59, 86, 103, 111, 118–19, 121, 151–52, 175
morality 13–14, 45, 46, 131
moves to innocence 23–24, 175
myth 2, 5–8, 13, 16–17, 24, 29, 30–31, 39–40, 59, 62, 64, 66, 72, 93, 101, 122, 128, 138, 159, 165, 178; mythic 6, 9, 16–17, 28, 46, 63, 116, 128, 148, 178

new-age 17
New World 9, 35, 46, 68, 71–73, 82, 86, 98, 103–04, 120, 125, 132, 144, 179, 181

oppression 4, 8, 9, 11, 13, 16, 19, 23, 25, 42–43, 51, 71, 76–78, 86, 89, 90, 92, 103, 114, 119–20, 156, 159, 171, 176; oppressed 8, 17, 21, 67, 69, 73, 120; oppressive 71, 85, 92, 120, 127, 131, 166; oppressor 69, 153, 166

passion 16, 28, 34, 36, 39, 43, 55, 75, 81, 85, 93, 131, 133, 143–44, 147, 150–52, 154, 156–58
People of Colour (POC) 3, 11–13, 15, 17, 22, 25–26, 34, 47, 76–78, 83, 87, 103, 105, 111, 114, 129, 143, 159–60, 172, 176, 179; BIPOC 3, 11–13, 17, 25–26, 77–78, 83, 129, 160, 172, 176
power 4, 11, 16, 18, 20, 25, 29–31, 37–41, 46, 49, 56, 69, 77–78, 83, 85, 95, 101, 107–10, 113, 116–19, 126–27, 133, 136, 146–47, 155–56, 158, 161–64, 166, 168, 171–74
privilege 11, 13, 16, 18–19, 25, 58, 68, 78, 81, 86–89, 101, 108, 124, 130, 132–33, 136–37, 149, 159, 164, 171, 173, 175
purity 34, 68, 81, 161, 167

racialized discomfort 12–13
racism 1, 3–4, 10–14, 18–20, 29, 32, 66, 80–81, 89–90, 93–97, 108, 121, 124, 126, 132, 139, 143, 145, 151–53, 155–56, 158–59, 170, 176
reconciliation 4, 21–22, 56–57, 60, 75–76, 112, 137, 141, 160–68, 170, 172, 175, 176; reconciling 11, 21, 60, 67, 118, 172
redemption 28, 60, 67, 71, 75
repair 20, 94, 121, 137, 167, 173, 175
reparations 9, 60, 78, 93–94, 109, 137, 162–68, 171–72, 175, 181–82
repression 33–34, 42, 43, 68, 108, 110–11, 113, 150, 161
residential schools 15, 33, 46, 51, 53–58, 84, 87, 91, 105, 111–12, 156, 166, 178
responsibility 5, 11–13, 20–22, 50, 59, 67–69, 111, 114, 139, 159, 170

Saad, L. 89, 95, 140
separation 13, 28, 34, 36, 38–40, 64, 74, 80, 124, 140–41, 144
Simpson, L. 2, 5, 21–22, 73, 141, 158, 175
stolen 2, 8, 17–19; stolen land 10, 94, 127, 132, 139, 181

transcendence 28, 31, 34, 38, 42, 46, 81, 87, 94, 138, 162
transformation 3, 5–7, 9, 18, 61, 63, 65–66, 68–69, 74, 85, 93–94, 118, 122, 124, 131, 133, 139–40, 147, 151, 168

trauma 5, 12–14, 20, 25, 36, 55–56, 59, 86, 94, 103–04, 110–11, 113, 118–19, 121, 131–32, 140, 147, 151–52, 154, 178–79

Truth and Reconciliation Commission 56–57, 112, 176; TRC 15, 18, 33, 46–47, 48–53, 55–57, 84, 91–92, 112

Tuck E. 22–24, 85, 111, 119, 147, 153, 163, 180

unsettling 2, 20–24, 79–80, 94–96, 98, 111, 119, 121, 127, 129, 132, 137, 140, 152, 155–56, 160, 164–65, 168, 173–74, 176–77, 179

von Franz, M. 7, 8, 38, 63, 64, 80, 88, 118

Wétiko 25, 178

whiteness 2, 3, 11, 22, 59, 62, 67–69, 79, 97, 143, 159–60, 167, 169, 171; white saviour 4, 5, 78, 140, 143; white settler 2–5, 8, 11–13, 19–20, 22, 25, 28, 30, 58, 65, 129, 172, 178; white supremacy 5, 6, 10, 29, 65, 77–78, 89, 95, 108, 122, 126, 130, 139–40, 143, 158, 160–61, 176

wholeness 2, 11, 17–18, 24, 27–28, 33, 36, 40, 60, 63, 64